Delivering the
Customer-Centric
Organization

Real-World Business Process Management

Published in association with the
Workflow Management Coalition

Workflow Management Coalition

WfM
C

Edited by
LAYNA FISCHER

Excellence in Practice Series

Future Strategies Inc.
Lighthouse Point, Florida, USA

Delivering the Customer-Centric Organization:
Real-World Business Process Management

Copyright © 2012 by Future Strategies Inc.

ISBN13: 978-0984976430

Published by Future Strategies Inc., Book Division
3640-B3 North Federal Highway, #421, Lighthouse Point FL 33064 USA
954.782.3376 / 954.719.3746 fax
www.FutStrat.com
email: books@FutStrat.com

Bulk orders, academic orders and extracts: please contact the publisher.

Delivering the Customer-Centric Organization: Real-World Business Process Management

/Layna Fischer (Editor)

p. cm.

Includes bibliographical references and appendices.

1. Business Process Management. 2. Customer-Centricity. 3. Technological Innovation. 4. Information Technology. 5. Total Quality Management. 6. Management Information Systems. 7. Office Practice-Automation. 8. Knowledge Management. 9. Workflow. 10. Process Analysis

Fischer, Layna. (ed)

Delivering the Customer-Centric Organization

Table of Contents and Overview

Customer-centric organizations are concerned about shrinking volumes of business, stiffer competition and ever more demanding consumer expectations which have increased pressure on the bottom line.

The ability to successfully manage the customer value chain across the life cycle of a customer is the key to the survival of any company today. Business processes must react to changing and diverse customer needs and interactions to ensure efficient and effective outcomes.

This important book looks at the shifting nature of consumers and the workplace, and how BPM and associated emergent technologies will play a part in shaping the companies of the future.

BPM's promises are real, but the path to success is littered with pitfalls and shortcuts to failure. Best practices can help you avoid them. If you are just embarking on using its methods and tools, these authors have a wealth of experience to learn from and build on.

Whether you are a business manager or an Information Technology practitioner, this special focus on Customer-Centricity will provide valuable information about what BPM can do for you—and how to apply it.

Table of Contents

FOREWORD: TRANSFORM BUSINESS PROCESSES THROUGH BUSINESS ANALYTICS   11

Clay Richardson, Forrester Research, USA

If you're reading this, odds are you're either knee-deep implementing an enterprise-wide BPM program, or you're exploring the potential impact and value of standing up a BPM program for your organization. If neither of these apply, then maybe you're just bored and figured, why not learn about a new and exciting topic. Regardless which bucket you fall into, at some point you'll come face-to-face with BPM's multiple-personality disorder. Although "analytics" is the new term du jour in the business technology world, it really has become the glue that ties the different BPM perspectives together.

Section 1: White Papers:
Customer-Centricity and Innovation

STAYING AHEAD OF THE CURVE WITH DECISION-CENTRIC BUSINESS INTELLIGENCE   17

Sheila Donohue

Customer-related decision points which impact a financial services firm's performance are spread across the customer lifecycle, from acquisition through portfolio management and collections. These decision points which involve risk taking have traditionally been focused on credit risk management, while, as more recently seen from the financial crisis, are taking a more holistic view considering also operational risk requirements which emphasize the importance of more control and to quickly respond to market events and compliance demands. Having more information easily at your fingertips to monitor, measure and analyze performance in business processes which manage these points of risk taking decisions is essential to responding quickly and deftly to competitive and regulatory pressures.

BPM, SOCIAL TECHNOLOGY, COLLABORATION AND THE WORKPLACE OF THE FUTURE   24

John Flynn

For many customer-centric organizations, the last three years have been tough. Shrinking volumes of business, stiffer competition and ever more demanding consumer expectations have increased pressure on the bottom line. Companies have responded by reducing headcount, cutting back on unnecessary spending and 'making do' with existing IT systems and infrastructure. While these reactions have stabilized corporate finances and brought sighs of relief from shareholders, a siege mentality in the long term will not allow organizations to take advantage of the predicted 'better times ahead.'

EVIDENCE-BASED SERVICE; LISTENING TO CUSTOMERS TO IMPROVE CUSTOMER-SERVICE
PROCESSES   33

Vikas Nehru and Ajay Khanna

Every customer interaction, including sales and service, must reflect a company's brand. However, it is quite a challenge to measure the effect which customer service has on a company's brand. It is required that the customer service processes are aligned with the brand to ensure that the customers receive service which meets the expectations generated by the brand.

The company must possess the ability to measure the effect of each service interaction on brand perception and customer service KPIs. Some of these KPIs are easy to identify as they are based on interactions within the organization's self-service or agent assisted service processes. But the interactions that are happening out in the social media world can also tell a lot about the company and how it is perceived by the consumer. Companies today need to be able to establish KPIs related to social media or social-assisted service in order to remain a competitive brand in today's economy.

PREDICTIVE BPM   41

Dr. Setrag Khoshafian

Most businesses today engage in "predictions." Will a customer agree to upgrade a purchase based on an array of offers? What is the likelihood that a customer within a cluster of similar customers will default on a loan? How much more effective will a targeted marketing campaign be, compared to a random sampling? How can the churn rate of subscribers be improved? What is the likelihood that a particular financial transaction is fraudulent? These are some questions that could utilize prediction with concrete and tangible business benefits.

A "business" is a collection of policies and procedures. Almost every business policy or procedure has some aspect of prediction in it. Most of the time, policy and procedure requirements are based on intuition, best guesses, or business experience. Too frequently, no one in the organization can remember why certain policies were ever created in the first place.

CUSTOMER EXPERIENCE TRANSFORMATION—A FRAMEWORK TO ACHIEVE
MEASURABLE RESULTS   51

Vinaykumar S Mummigatti

The era of extreme competition is creating immense importance for customer experience and how companies manage their customers' expectations. The ability to successfully manage the customer value chain across the life cycle of a customer is the key to the survival of any company today. Most companies realize this but are struggling to measure and influence the customer experience. This paper is an attempt to look at various facets of customer experience and how to transform customer experience to achieve measurable business goals. Business Process Management and the convergence of technologies *(such as Portals, web 2.0, BI, Content Management)* are two key elements of this transformation and hence we will focus on how the convergence of various technologies led by BPM will help achieve the business goals around Customer Experience Transformation (CET).

FINANCIAL CRISIS FRONT LINE: SNS BANK   61

Eric D. Schabell and Stijn Hoppenbrouwers

SNS Bank, Netherlands, has made a strategic decision to empower its customers on-line by fully automating its business processes. The ability to automate these service channels is achieved by applying Business Process Management (BPM) techniques to existing selling channels. Both the publicly available and internal processes are being revamped into full scale Straight Through Processing (STP) services. This extreme use of online STP is the trigger in a shift that is of crucial importance to cost-effective banking in an ever turbulent and changing financial world. The key elements used in implementing these goals continue to be Free Open Source Software (FOSS), Service oriented architecture (SOA), and BPM. In this paper we will present an industrial application describing the efforts of the SNS Bank to make the change from traditional banking services to a full scale STP and BPM driven bank that can survive on the Financial Crisis front lines.

INTELLIGENT, AUTOMATED PROCESSES: EMBEDDING ANALYTICS IN DECISIONS   73

James Taylor

The challenge of putting BI to work in business processes is that reports and dashboards only work in manual processes. If the process is automated, if straight through processing is called for, then the analytics required are different. Embedding these analytics in rules-based decisions is the ideal way to analytically enhance these processes and build intelligent, automated processes. Building intelligent, automated processes requires that we understand the decisions in our processes. These decisions give us the points of control that we need and the places where insight might make a difference.

Section 2: Case Studies
Delivering the Customer-Centric Organization

ACHIEVEMENT AWARDS GROUP (PTY) LTD.   83

Adaptive Case Management (ACM) is imperative in enterprises where the exception to process becomes the process! ACM, a topic widely discussed and analyzed by academics, professionals and IT specialists, is what is needed whenever processes must react to changing and diverse customer or client needs and interactions to ensure efficient and effective outcomes. This means that defined, rigid processes become responsive to circumstances that require fluid processes in order to address specific requirements.

ABU DHABI COMMERCIAL BANK   101

Newgen provided the bank with a BPM-enabled workflow platform, which not only helped bank to automate its processes, but also allowed seamless integration of the BPM solution with its existing applications.

Abu Dhabi Commercial Bank (ADCB), with a strong presence in Consumer and Corporate is a leading provider of technology-enabled services. In its objective towards complete automation of processes, the bank was in urgent need for a solution that would enable end-to-end automation of their key business processes and also provide integration with its existing applications. Newgen provided the bank with a BPM-enabled workflow platform, which not only helped bank to automate its processes, but also allowed seamless integration of the BPM solution with its existing applications.

UNITED PARCEL SERVICE (UPS)   105

Founded in 1907 as a messenger company in the United States, UPS has grown into a multi-billion-dollar corporation by clearly focusing on the goal of enabling commerce around the globe. Today, UPS is a global company with one of the most recognized and admired brands in the world, managing the flow of goods, funds, and information in more than 200 countries and territories worldwide. As the global leader in its industry, UPS continues to develop the frontiers of logistics, supply chain management, and e-Commerce.

To support efforts to improve operational efficiencies and drive customer service excellence, the UPS Shared Services group identified that a pervasive BPM platform for rapid application development and deployment would solve a laundry list of challenges. Utilizing BPM, UPS has improved workload management and resource planning, improved IT's ability to measure and manage SLA attainment, and optimized the cost-to-serve model, ultimately decreasing operating costs while increasing employee and customer satisfaction.

BAA HEATHROW   111

At London's Heathrow airport, a new case is created by a system feed, every time an incoming plane is registered by air-traffic control, and closes when the plane is en route to its next destination. This event enabled case-management approach to aircraft turn-around has dramatically improved the overall efficiency of operations at Heathrow, including:

- An increase in on-time departures from 68 percent to 83 percent,
- A savings of 90 litres of fuel per flight, due to decreased time spent on the runway, yielding cost savings for airlines, and a positive environmental impact,
- A projected increase in retail revenues, by allowing passengers on faster-boarding flights to spend more time in the terminal rather than seated in airplanes awaiting take off.

LOS ANGELES COUNTY DEPARTMENT OF PUBLIC SOCIAL SERVICES (DPSS) 117

With over 10 million people, Los Angeles County is the largest county in the United States. The Los Angeles County Department of Public Social Services (DPSS) currently serves over two million participants each day and a caseload of over 1.6 million across its various public assistance programs—more than any other jurisdiction except the states of California and New York. Even though the County has developed standardized processes and workflow, the unpredictability of people and the sheer volume of cases in Los Angeles create an often overwhelmed situation. It is the goal of the Call Center personnel, who are classified as Eligibility Workers, to determine individual benefits eligibility.

LINCOLN TRUST COMPANY 120

This paper describes the experiences of implementing an enterprise wide BPM program at Lincoln Trust Company. The program was constituted in early 2007 with an initial goal of managing core processes related to physical paperwork and an ultimate goal of using BPM technology to manage all strategic processes of the organization. When the program began the company was receiving over 100,000 client documents each month with limited to no control over these instructions. Initial, overwhelming success with an enterprise wide implementation of BPM technology to workflow-enable document centric processes led to the strong desire of company management to move quickly to our next goals of understanding, improving, and automating other strategic processes. By doing so we've been able to open our back office process for collaboration with a strategic outsourcing partner, drive processes to the web, reduce costs and risks, improve customer satisfaction, and completely turn around a damaged relationship between IT and the business.

NOKIA SIEMENS NETWORKS 132

Nokia Siemens Networks was created in 2007 through the merger of the former Networks Business Group of Nokia and the carrier-related businesses of Siemens. Today, NSN is one of the world's largest network communications companies – with 60,000 employees, a leading position in all key markets across the world, and total sales of more than €15 billion a year. The Consulting and Systems Integration (CSI) unit within NSN is an organization of 4,000 staff, with sales of over €500 million a year.

CSI's particular business is an unusual mixture of high-volume/low-revenue engagements (i.e., consulting projects) and low-volume/high-revenue projects (i.e., major value-added service rollouts within large network implementations). The "mish-mash" tools landscape resulting from the NSN merger fundamentally did not meet the needs of CSI's dynamic business requirements. In addition, NSN's formation from two companies with, in many respects, polar opposite corporate environments created friction in operational execution. CSI desperately needed to get an established set of processes in place very quickly because without end-to-end visibility, fast and effective decision-making to drive the business was hampered, if not impossible. CSI looked to BPM technology to drive quick, highly-configurable, higher-value/lower cost process solutions to meet its business goals.

SWISSCARD AECS 139

The liberalization of the credit card market in Switzerland in 1997 paved the way for American Express and Credit Suisse AG to establish the joint venture company Swisscard AECS AG and to merge their credit card activities. Swisscard ideally combines the complementary strengths of the founding companies, with American Express being the global leader in card management and Credit Suisse providing strong national sales channels. On behalf of Credit Suisse, Swisscard offers the world-famous American Express card within Switzerland. It is thus the sole issuer in Switzerland with all three major brands (American Express, MasterCard and Visa) in its product portfolio.

UVIT–FINANCIAL SERVICES 161

The Univé-VGZ-IZA-Trias group (UVIT) is a Netherlands-based insurance company. During recent years, the people of UVIT have been facing increased challenges from Internet insurance competitors. Because of this, a main objective was to automate outdated processes that were primarily paper-based. To do this, UVIT chose EMC Documentum xCP for the creation of a case management application to process claims. The xCP platform is seamlessly integrated with the UVIT capture platform to digitize all incoming mail, especially the vast quantity of doctor and hospital bills customers forward for payment. The system is used by UVIT service, field, and insurance agents, while in the office, at home, and on the road.

With the new xCP system, UVIT staff now has instant access to customer documentation, which has helped improve customer response rates as well as overall processing efficiency. The amount of case documents they are now able to process is also huge– about three million in 2010, and they expect that figure to reach 50 million in the near future.

Section 3
Appendices

WFMC STRUCTURE AND MEMBERSHIP 168

FURTHER READING 172

ABOUT THE GLOBAL AWARDS FOR EXCELLENCE IN BPM AND WORKFLOW

Many of the case studies profiled in this book are winners in the prestigious annual **Global Awards for Excellence in BPM and Workflow.** These winners are companies that successfully used BPM in gaining competitive advantage within their industries.

The awards are highly coveted by organizations that seek recognition for their achievements. Now evolved into their 19th year, originally starting with, and moving through, imaging, documentation, knowledge management and more, as our industry moved forward, these awards not only provide a spotlight for companies that truly deserve recognition, but also provide tremendous insights for organizations wishing to emulate the winners' successes.

CRITERIA

The criteria for submitting an entry are fairly simple: the project should have been operational for six months prior to nomination, and have been installed within the past two years. The submission guidelines, however, are more detailed. To be recognized as winners, companies must address three critical areas: excellence in *innovation*, excellence in *implementation* and excellence in strategic *impact* to the organization. Details at www.bpmf.org.

Innovation

Innovation encompasses the innovative use of technology for strategic business objectives; the complexity of the underlying business process and IT architecture; the creative and successful deployment of advanced workflow and imaging concepts; and process innovations through business process reengineering and/or continuous improvements.

- Innovative use of BPM technology to solve unique problems
- Creative and successful implementation of advanced BPM concepts
- Level of integration with other technologies and legacy systems
- Degree of complexity in the business process and underlying IT architecture

Implementation

Hallmarks of a successful *implementation* include extensive user and line management involvement in the project while successfully managing change during the implementation process. Factors impacting the level of difficulty in achieving a successful implementation include the system complexity; integration with other advanced technologies; and the scope and scale of the implementation (e.g. size, geography, inter-company processes).

- Successful BPM and/or workflow implementation methodology
- Size, scope and quality of change management process
- Scope and scale of the implementation (e.g. size, geography, inter-and intra-company processes)

Impact

Impact is the bottom line, answering the question, "What benefit does BPM deliver to my business? Why should I care?"

- Extent and quantifiable impact of productivity improvements
- Significance of cost savings

- Level of increased revenues, product enhancements, customer service or quality improvements
- Impact of the system on competitive positioning in the marketplace
- Proven strategic importance to the organization's mission
- Degree to which the system enabled a culture change within the organization and methodology for achieving that change

Using BPM for Competitive Advantage

Examples of potential benefits include: productivity improvements; cost savings; increased revenues; product enhancements; improved customer service; improved quality; strategic impact to the organization's mission; enabling culture change; and—most importantly—changing the company's competitive position in the market. The visionary focus is now toward strategic benefits, in contrast to marginal cost savings and productivity enhancements.

While successes in these categories are prerequisites for winning a Global Excellence Award, it would reward all companies to focus on excelling in *innovation, implementation* and *impact* when installing BPM and workflow technologies. Companies must recognize that implementing innovative technology is useless unless the organization has a successful approach that delivers—and even surpasses—the anticipated benefits.

Transform Business Processes Through Business Analytics

Clay Richardson, Forrester Research, USA

If you're reading this, odds are you're either knee deep implementing an enterprise-wide BPM program, or you're exploring the potential impact and value of standing up a BPM program for your organization. If neither of these apply, then maybe you're just bored and figured, why not learn about a new and exciting topic. Regardless which bucket you fall into, at some point you'll come face-to-face with BPM's multiple-personality disorder.

This is a conversation I've been having more and more with business process professionals. Some define "business process management" as a management discipline, while others define BPM as a technology. And still, others define BPM as a capability for transforming the culture of an organization. Most BPM experts— including yours truly—agree that BPM is broad enough to house all three of these paradigms. However, I'm always amazed to see the knock-down, drag-out fights that take place over three simple words: "What is BPM?"

Before proceeding any further, it's probably a good idea to share Forrester's official definition of BPM:

> "Business process management (BPM) is a discipline that focuses on continuous improvement of end-to-end, cross-functional mission critical business processes."

Ultimately, it's safe to say, BPM means different things to different people. It all depends on your perspective and the internal business issues you're trying to tackle. The one thing that all process professionals—novice and expert alike— agree on is the "improvement" imperative that forms the foundation of BPM. When I'm refereeing—or more often when I'm teeing up—a heated debate on "What Is BPM", I always see heads shake in agreement that "improvement" is an essential ingredient for BPM, no matter which process approach is being followed. And once agreement is reached on "improvement", these conversations then focus on the role "analytics" plays in driving process improvement activities.

Although "analytics" is the new term du jour in the business technology world, it really has become the glue that ties the different BPM perspectives together. And for good reason: analytics support better analysis and also form the basis of insight on how best to improve business processes. It's fair to say that without analytics, it would be time consuming and painful to identify and carry out process improvement.

In 2008, Forrester published a report highlighting the pivotal role analytics plays in driving optimization efforts. In this visionary report, authored by Forrester analysts Boris Evelson, Colin Teubner, and John Rymer, we outlined how the convergence of business rules, business process management, and business intelligence disciplines would help companies respond quickly to rapidly changing business conditions[i]. This convergence, coined as the "Three B's", painted a future where:

- BPM automates flows of work and information –
- Analytics help drive business processes –
- Business rules automate key process decisions –

- Business intelligence powers optimization—

I can already see you shaking your head saying "What's so visionary about this? Businesses have been doing this for a while now." The key here is that these activities have typically been done separately in silos—where one group may emphasize business rules and process automation, and another group might emphasize process automation and business intelligence. Here, we're saying to truly reap the benefits of optimization it really requires all three of these disciplines—business process management, business rules management, and business intelligence—to come together and work seamlessly.

However, when the "Three B's" report was published, business process professionals faced many hurdles in leveraging analytics across these three areas to drive process improvement. The most obvious hurdle was that many teams still buried their processes, policies, and business rules in custom application code—making it almost impossible to mine for process analytics.

Another barrier for the "Three B's" at the time was the lack of standards for defining analytics across BPM, BI, and BRE environments. I recall one process professional's experience meeting with his company's BI team for the first time and commenting "I have no idea how we're going to bring these two worlds together!" While this process professional saw the need and mandate for business process and business intelligence to co-exist, he wrestled with defining metrics and standards for bridging the gaps between his firms BI, BPM, and BRE environments.

In addition to the hurdles mentioned above, technology vendors offered little in the way of a combined framework for tying analytics to process improvement, business intelligence, and business rules initiatives. So most teams, if they tried to blaze a trail towards the "Three B's", were left stuck developing custom integration across these three environments—which was costly, time consuming, and risky.

Recently, another Forrester analyst, James Kobielus, and I joined forces to revisit what's changed since the "Three B's" report was published. Our primary focus was to identify whether many of the hurdles to the "Three B's" had been removed and we also explored how teams are applying the "Three B's" as part of their standard methodology for process optimization.

At Forrester's Spring 2010 Information Technology Forum, James and I joined two additional Forrester analysts, Craig Le Clair and Boris Evelson (one of the original authors of the "Three B's" research) in panel discussion to highlight what's changed since the report was published in 2008. We highlighted key trends and themes that make the "Three B's" more accessible to business process professionals, including:

- **Never let a good recession go to waste.** The recession highlighted the need for organizations to develop more dynamic environments that could sense and respond to rapid change. While most organizations knew they needed more agile business environments, the recession accelerated the shift to embrace analytics as a foundation to drive process improvement, business intelligence, and business rules activities.
- **Steady consolidation and convergence of key technologies.** Over the last two years, we've seen significant consolidation and convergence across business process management, business rules, and business intelligence market. Now, leading stack vendors, such as IBM and Oracle offer comprehensive suites that cover BPM, BI, and BRE environments. And,

they're working hard to deliver unified offerings that leverage the same analytics and standards across all three areas—in the end, this will appear seamless to business process professionals and business stakeholders.

- **Increased focus on process quality and data quality.** Before teams can trust the insights offered up by analytics, they first must trust the underlying data and business processes. Forrester highlighted this as a major challenge for business process professionals in a 2009 report that focused on the connection between process quality and data quality[ii]. Teams are beginning to understand the important link between BPM and MDM, which is essential to improve the quality of automated decisions executed by business rules and manual decisions based on business intelligence.

Additionally, during the panel discussion, we highlighted specific patterns we see-ing for customers adopting the "Three B's" within their environments. Based on conversations with process professionals, we've identified three dominant patterns for using analytics to transform business processes.

The first pattern we identified is "predictive process analytics." In this pattern, we're seeing teams leverage a unified "Three B's" environment to detect specific process-related patterns and to automatically implement business rules changes that impact how the process executes. This is a common scenario we're seeing used in the insurance space. While insurers already used analytics for fraud detection, some insurers are taking this one step further to flag potentially fraudulent claims in real-time while the agent is on the phone gathering information from the person filing the claim. This connects BPM, BRE, and BI to highlight the probability that the claim is fraudulent as the information is being gathered.

The second "Three B's" scenario we're seeing teams adopt is around "automated process discovery." This involves mining existing application data for process metrics to better understand business processes that are buried across multiple applications and legacy environments. Using this approach, teams are able to glean key process analytics without conducting lengthy process modeling and analysis exercises. In some ways, this approach short-circuits the traditional approach to "AS-IS" modeling, since the model is literally generated based on existing application data. One team we spoke with uncovered hidden insights into their real process challenges by showing team members how the actual process was executing through different underlying legacy applications.

And finally, we're seeing business process professionals leverage analytics to deal with unstructured and ad-hoc business processes. For most business process professionals these types of processes are very difficult to get their hands around—literally. Unstructured processes are impossible to model and are often exceptions that must be handled at run-time. But process professionals also realize that allowing these unstructured processes to be handled at run-time introduces the possibility of losing valuable insight into how the overall process is executing. Leading BPM teams are using analytics to keep tabs on execution of unstructured business processes and provide management with insight on how these processes are executing. Analytics are also used to alert users when SLA's or KPI's are not being met for unstructured activities.

While we're seeing more teams leverage analytics and the "Three B's" still more work needs to be done. At the conclusion of our panel presentation, I walked away asking myself what's still missing to take this—the convergence of BPM, BRE, BI—to the next level. The key ingredients are there: The technology is now in place, some standards are coming into play, and the enterprise has the proper motivation to embrace analytics and the "Three B's". In order to take full advantage of the "Three B's" process professionals will need methodologies that support best practice for bringing together analytics with BPM, BRE, and BI activities.

This is the next phase of the "Three B's" that we're focused on at Forrester. We've already identified some early key best practices, including:

- **Develop shared glossary of performance metrics.** Often, BI and BPM teams work together to identify key metrics and performance measure that both are tracking. However, very few of these teams turn this into a shared glossary that can be used by both teams to establish performance reporting standards for both initiatives. In leading teams, we're seeing an emphasis on developing a common vocabulary for performance metrics that is shared across BI and BPM environments.

- **Empower business users with self-service analytics.** For the most part, analytics has remained the domain of data architects, report writers, and business intelligence experts. However, some organizations are delivering self-service analytics to front-line workers. These self-service environments allow front-line workers to do deep analysis and generate sophisticated reports based on exposed analytics, allowing them to make better informed and higher-quality decisions.

- **Synchronize BPM and MDM activities.** As previously mentioned, poor data quality leads to poor process quality and poor decisions. To effectively leverage process analytics, business process professionals must first link their BPM and MDM efforts. This keeps upstream and downstream data clean and allows teams to trust process-related and business-related analytics.

No matter how you decide to approach transforming your business processes, you will find analytics and the "Three B's" essential ingredient to success. If you're just starting to explore analytics as part of your BPM program, we recommend starting small by identifying street-level opportunities—for example, maybe a small group of users are interested in robust self-service analytics. Once you have success with the street level opportunity, and then look to expand process analytics to encompass additional teams and other scenarios.

---

i If your enterprise wants to move beyond mere efficiency and productivity improvements for back-office processes and seeks instead to optimize (and even transform) the business, look to the convergence of the "three B's" to serve as the foundation. See May 14, 2008 report "How The Convergence Of Business Rules, BPM, And, BI Will Drive Business Optimization"

ii If you are seeking to reduce complexity and move to optimization, link BPM and MDM activities to gain "one version of the truth" as a key foundation for business process transformation efforts. See September 21, 2009 report "Warning: Don't Assume Your Business Processes Use Master Data"

Section 1: Overview

The Customer-Centric Approach

Staying Ahead of the Curve with Decision-Centric Business Intelligence

Sheila Donohue

INTRODUCTION

Customer-related decision points which impact a financial services firm's performance are spread across the customer lifecycle, from acquisition through portfolio management and collections. These decision points which involve risk taking have traditionally been focused on credit risk management, while, as more recently seen from the financial crisis, are taking a more holistic view considering also operational risk requirements which emphasize the importance of more control and to quickly respond to market events and compliance demands. Having more information easily at your fingertips to monitor, measure and analyze performance in business processes which manage these points of risk taking decisions is essential to responding quickly and deftly to competitive and regulatory pressures.

Business process, rules management and analytics are tools well suited to assess and manage the risk and opportunity at these decision points. However, without fully integrated business intelligence tools, the firm is missing an opportunity to continuously improve their business and risk performance, finding themselves scrambling when an executive, compliance officer or customer demands information on-the-fly.

THE ESSENTIALS

Financial decision-making processes, such as loan approval and origination, portfolio monitoring and debt management, require a financial institution to have an organizational commitment to formalize, document and monitor risk processes.

This discipline involves:

- Following a structured and consistent process to identify and assess risks,
- Applying the optimal set of controls and track the relevant data,
- Monitoring the results, through a set of pre-configured reports plus the capability to design one's own reports, however, without having an underlying toolset which embraces these fundamentals, financial decision-making processes can become cumbersome and expensive to manage.

In order to support these principles and allow financial institutions to master the balance of achieving high performance results, control and agility in their financial decision-making processes, integrated solutions with the following components are needed:

Business Process Management software focused on financial decision-making which offers:

- A workflow engine which executes and tracks all process steps, both manual as well as automatic, including automatic document generation;

- An integrated case management web front end to handle exceptions and necessary manual tasks, tracing all activity details and allowing for electronic document filing;
- A graphical designer tool for a business analyst to define the process flow, activity details, data, organization and role authorities logic;
- Authentication and authorization to control permissions of persons and systems allowed to access the process and system components;
- Framework to allow for ease of integration with required data sources, application systems, third party organizations and systems;
- Data retrieval, validation and storage to verify and save all pertinent data that the process and underlying engine(s) collect, calculate and transform.

Integrated Business Rules Platform specialized in financial risk evaluation which has:
- a rules engine to make automatic decisions which incorporate risk strategies that include analytical model calculations to give more confidence to the decision;
- a graphical tool to define the decision process logic which will include analytical scoring ;
- means to integrate easily with the Business Process software component.

Integrated Business Intelligence comes into play when, upon having a streamlined, automated workflow process based on the above components, a financial institution realizes it is sitting on a goldmine of data which can be used to help monitor, improve and better control the underlying the business process and automated risk based policies and decisioning logic. Without a Business Intelligence component, the institution is by-passing a critical opportunity to leverage their decision making solution investments to stay one step ahead of their market, customer and compliance demands.

An integrated Business Intelligence solution provides the following:
- A graphical tool to easily extract data from the Business Process Management software, not only when having just implemented a new business process, but also to introduce new or different data as the business process evolves; this tool should also allow a business user to define the underlying reporting data repositories which are relational and multidimensional data layers. With such capability, a business user without technical skills can define and modify the data to report on without needing to involve IT thus empowering them to respond to business demands as they arise;
- A turn-key extraction, transform and load (ETL) procedures which start from the extraction logic that the business person defined and automatically load the reporting database;
- Front end, preferably web based, to view pre-defined reports and to easily create new and modify existing reports.

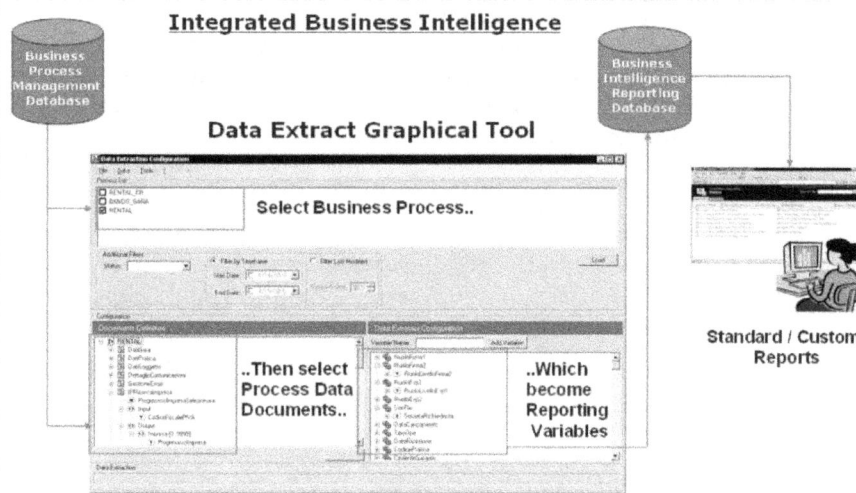

Integrated Business Intelligence

Figure 1: Business Intelligence Integrated with Business Process Management

In summary, Integrated Business Intelligence provides business users with the tools they need to extract and report on the process and performance information they need in a manner which is fully integrated with the Business Process Management and Business Rules components.

What follows are real examples of financial services institutions which were driven by competition, compliance and control to choose a business intelligence solution fully integrated with their financial decision making processes so to achieve improved process, business and risk performance.

CASE STUDY: FIAT AUTO FINANCIAL SERVICES

FIAT Auto Financial Services (FGA Capital) is the financial services arm of the Fiat group operating in 15 countries throughout Europe through various separate companies which manage all the financing activities to support automobile sales of major manufacturers by providing financing via manufacturers' networks and private channels, leasing services as well as small and medium sized business and fleet rentals.

The FIAT financial unit, having already utilized a business rules platform, for automatic scoring and decisioning of their Auto Retail loans and leases and being satisfied with its effectiveness and robustness, realized that they needed a more complete solution to fulfil the needs of their small business and corporate clientele. With non-standardized, stand-alone processes and decision making between the group companies, they realized a strong need to unify and streamline the rental application process between business units. As part of this, their priorities were to minimize manual processing, have a quick time-to-market solution implementation and have operations and risk measurements readily available for business, shareholder and regulatory reporting purposes.

To move forward, FGA Capital chose an integrated Business Process, Business Rules and Business Intelligence platform and proceeded to standardize the lending processes between the Group's companies which specialize in financing and long term rental services by re-engineering the underlying organizational model, and therefore the whole production chain, to obtain the most efficient coordination of the processes between the various group companies. The FGA Capital rental management process, implemented as illustrated in figure 2, performs automatic retrieval and validation of applicant and application information via both internal and external data sources, advanced scoring model and decision rule automation, notification to decision makers and presenting all results, to arrive at a final financing decision.

Once having defined the process, FGA Capital identified the key elements to measure performance, such as turn around times, automatic decisions and scores, types of applicants, geographic areas, types of rentals and channels, which were then extracted into the Business Intelligence tool that creates reports showing Key Performance Indicators (KPIs) and other critical process and risk information for distribution throughout the Group.

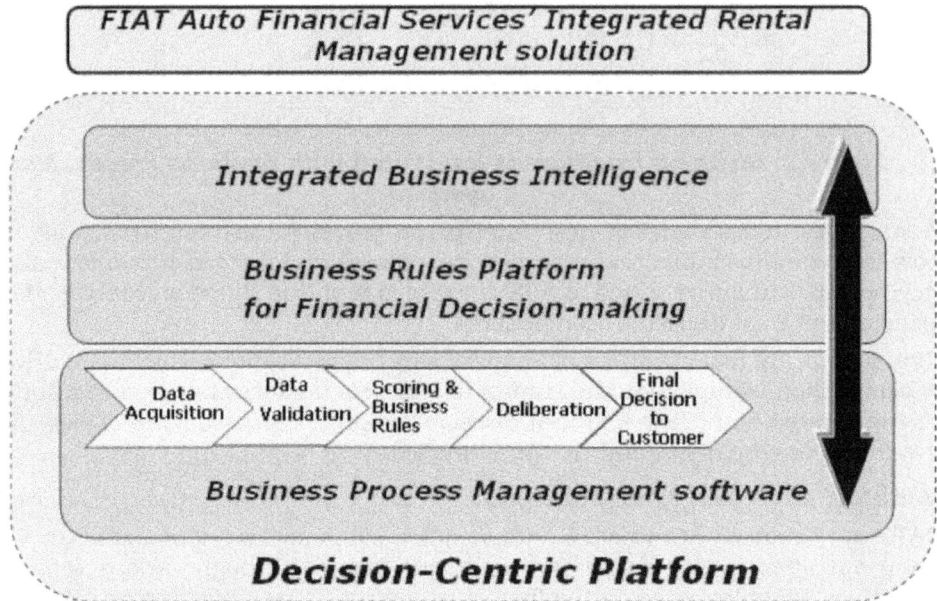

Figure 2: FIAT Auto Financial Services' integrated Rental Management solution components

Having an end-to-end solution in only four months, FGA Capital immediately began to reap the benefits of an integrated decision making process platform:

- With an automated business process, manual effort has been greatly reduced, resulting in lower costs and quicker end-to-end response;
- Processing more applications in a consistent and efficient manner between the business units;
- Credit granting policy and methodology is easily modifiable by the business user to keep in line with credit compliance requirements and credit performance evolutions;
- Easy access to information about processes helps to integrate the entire Group and allows for better communication with the customer;
- Compliance with shareholder and regulatory reporting requirements by providing timely visibility of key operating and risk measurements.

Using the platform's integrated Business Intelligence features, FGA Capital has the tools to continually monitor the process and risk performance, to identify *early* the areas of improvement by having quick, online access to information, such as the turn around times for critical process activities as shown in this report:

Activity (duration format dd hh:mm:ss)	Instances	Average	Minimum	Maximum	Applications	Rate
Application Summary	24	00 03:42:58	00 04:14:30	00 04:16:23	24	1
Checklist	14	00 03:20:19	00 04:14:32	00 04:18:31	14	1
Credit Analyst Outcome	11	00 03:29:27	00 04:14:42	00 04:19:29	7	1.57
Disbursement	10	00 04:14:42	00 04:14:32	00 04:15:06	10	1
Documents	19	00 03:21:54	00 04:14:29	00 04:18:41	19	1
Insert Main Applicant	46	00 02:29:32	00 04:14:28	00 04:17:16	18	2.56
Internal verification outcome	15	00 03:31:16	00 04:14:29	00 06:06:46	15	1
Product Data	28	00 03:11:01	00 04:14:28	00 04:15:16	15	1.87
Sociological	14	00 03:20:35	00 04:14:46	00 04:17:48	14	1
Total	181	00 03:13:38	00 04:14:28	00 06:06:46	136	1.33

Figure 3: Sample Activity Duration report

CASE STUDY: THE FINANCIAL INTERMEDIARY OF A LARGE ENERGY GROUP

Responsible for managing payment systems (electronic banking, clearing and settlement, transactional services, e-business services, cards) for its entire group, this financial intermediary of large energy group needed a platform to issue and monitor purchasing cards which allow cardholders to pay for fuel and related products and services for its clients performing professional and commercial transportation throughout Europe.

Besides needing a paperless loan origination and monitoring processes integrated with the group's internal systems as well as external data sources and to make the organization more efficient, such as by removing redundant operations and having tools to help identify process bottlenecks and setbacks, the firm was driven by the central bank's compliance requirements regarding credit and control policy rules.

Having first chosen Business Process Management and Business Rules Platform products to perform the issuing and portfolio monitoring of its purchasing cards for its Small and Medium Business and Corporate segments, this firm realized the need for credit risk and business operations business intelligence tools, taking advantage of the historical archive of application and credit data already available in the existing platform. Selecting Business Intelligence tools already integrated with the Business Process Management and Business Rules components, this firm now has improved process and risk operation through the introduction of tracking, monitoring and performance measurement tools.

For example, this Risk Class Distribution report is displaying the risk class as calculated by the Business Rules Platform showing trends of how the risk groupings change from month to month. Reports parameters can be easily changed so to analyze different aspects of the portfolio and drill down to necessary details:

Risk Class

(#clients/Risk Class)

RiskClass / Month	2008-01		2008-02		2008-03	
	# Clients	%	# Clients	%	# Clients	%
High		0 %		0 %	4	5 %
Low	6	8 %	12	16 %	18	24 %
Medium-High	2	3 %	4	5 %	4	5 %
Medium-Low	6	8 %	6	8 %	4	5 %
TOTAL	14	19 %	22	30 %	30	41 %

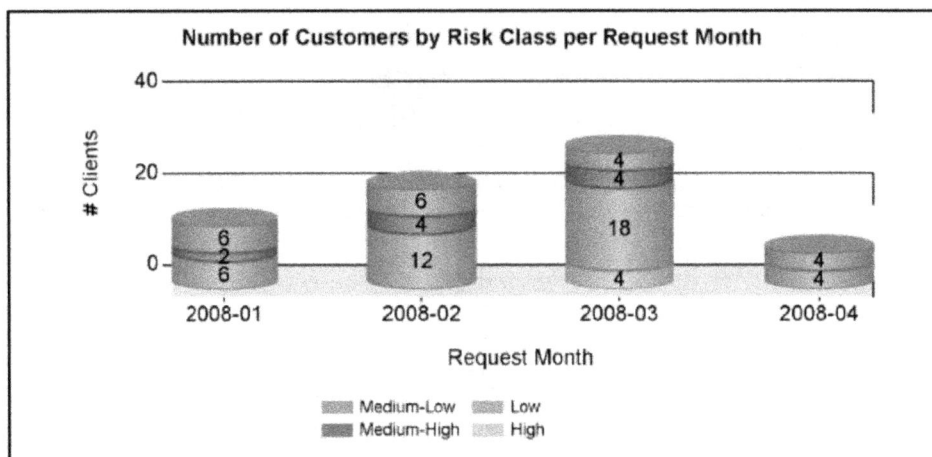

Figure 4: Example of a Risk Class Distribution Report

CASE STUDY: MEDIUM – LARGE ITALIAN BANK

This bank, with more than 250 branches across Italy, is seeking to improve the quality of its consumer and small business credit portfolio at a time when the financial crisis is putting pressure on margins and the Central Bank is requiring increased monitoring and control of portfolio credit quality and effectiveness of the bank's policies.

With non-standardized credit policy enforcement and unstructured monitoring due to lack of sufficient tools, this bank decided to proceed with an implementation using a Business Rules Platform and integrated Business Intelligence component, so to reduce underwriting and financial offer response times, while reducing risk and subsequently increasing the quality of its credit portfolio. Besides improving credit granting during the loan origination phase, this bank is focused on its existing customer portfolio, so to proactive identify the risks and opportunities within.

Using the Business Intelligence solution, the bank's portfolio is being monitored to identify deviations and analyze the cause(s) in order to define the necessary corrective measures to be taken such as to adjust scoring models, policy rules and credit decisioning methodology.

This sample report is comparing the decision made at application time to the current customer payment performance to see if the decisioning methodology is aligned with expectations or in need of adjustment:

Current Performance of Installment applications

Strategy / Sys Decision Grp /Risk Class			Delinquency Class			
			Bad		Good	Indeterminate
			Serious delinquency	Write off	No delinquency	Mild delinquency
Personal_Loans	AP-Approve	Low	1636	90	34064	1117
	RFP-Policy Reject	?	255	2	1102	32
		High	1			12
		Low	13		26	
		Medium	27		38	
	RF-Reject	High	1073	98	46115	1256
	RV-Refer	Medium	93		1345	18
	Total		3098	190	82690	2435

Comparison Delinquency Class

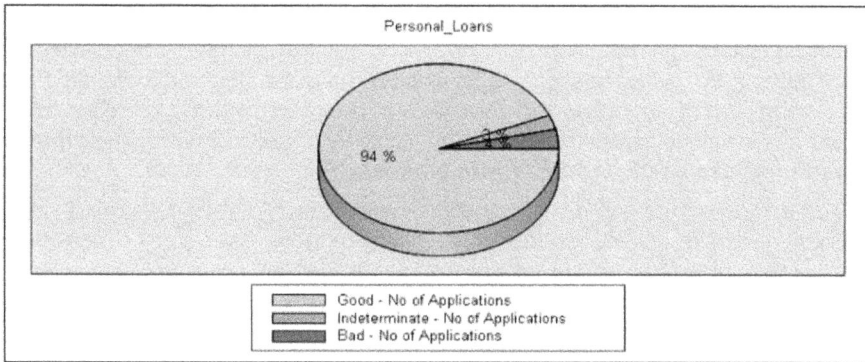

Personal_Loans

94 %

Good - No of Applications
Indeterminate - No of Applications
Bad - No of Applications

Figure 5: Application Performance Report

CONCLUSIONS

Business Intelligence tools that are integrated with the financial decision-making applications already used by the firm help to empower the business users to focus on their knowledge worker core competency and respond timely and effectively to ever evolving business and compliance demands. With these tools, whether in a risk, operations or business management role, leveraging your existing data assets to make better decisions and respond to business and compliance demands is a worthwhile investment to stay ahead of the curve.

ABOUT CRIF DECISION SOLUTIONS

CRIF Decision Solutions, part of the CRIF Group (www.crif.com), provides consulting, analytics and solutions which help financial institutions to be more efficient and innovative in their procedures and processes, from customer targeting and acquisition to portfolio management, debt collection and fraud management.

BPM, Social Technology, Collaboration and the Workplace of the Future

John Flynn

INTRODUCTION

For many customer-centric organizations, the last three years have been tough. Shrinking volumes of business, stiffer competition and ever more demanding consumer expectations have increased pressure on the bottom line. Companies have responded by reducing headcount, cutting back on unnecessary spending and 'making do' with existing IT systems and infrastructure. While these reactions have stabilized corporate finances and brought sighs of relief from shareholders, a siege mentality in the long term will not allow organizations to take advantage of the predicted 'better times ahead.'

Taking into account the shifting power base from West to East and the genuine emergence of the Global Economy, the future now looks very different from the past. Companies that would traditionally ride out an economic downturn by battening down the hatches until the storm blows over, may find that when they emerge from their entrenchment, they are ill-equipped to capitalize on the changing world around them. This chapter takes a look at the changing nature of consumers and the workplace, and how BPM and associated emergent technologies will play a part in shaping the companies of the future.

THE DEMAND FOR FLEXIBILITY

What we are witnessing today is a drive toward flexibility. Industry analysts are telling us that companies must have flexible processes. We live in a world of mass customization, where customers want to tailor the products and services they consume, and the workforce of today is starting to expect flexibility in how it delivers its skills to the companies that employ them.

Alongside this, there is an ongoing technology race to deliver the coolest, fastest and most functionally-rich technology to today's consumer generation. This is starting to result in a blurring of the lines between the concept of social and business technology. It has been fascinating to witness the change in the approach to developing technology over the last thirty years, and how the high R&D costs of producing new technology, originally meant that new products were generally developed for commercial use, and then subsequently adapted for domestic and entertainment purposes. An example of that of course, is the desktop computer, which was originally developed to run word processing, accountancy and other specialist commercial applications.

The 'infamous' 1977 quote by the then-chairman of the DEC corporation Ken Olsen: 'I can see no reason why any individual would have a computer in their home' reflected the mood of the times. Today, however, virtually every home has a computer which is in regular use, predominantly to connect to the Internet, and mainly for social and recreational purposes. In many ways it is difficult for those living in the developed world to imagine the home without a computer.

Whilst Olsen's quote was very much taken out of context as he was referring to a computer running a home, he probably didn't foresee the somewhat ironic acquisition of the once-mighty DEC Corporation by the PC manufacturer Compaq in 1998.

Currently, developments that either leverage existing technologies or break new ground are often aimed at the mass consumer market. Mobile telecoms are an illustration of that phenomenon, although it is true to say that the current generation of hand-held and portable devices offers providers of goods and services a whole new set of opportunities to not only market, sell and distribute their offers, but also to find new, easier, faster and cheaper ways of processing their work. In fact, it is these mass-market technologies that will deliver the flexibility that organizations will need to survive and flourish when the global economy is buoyant again.

This whole topic however, presents challenges in its own right.

The Challenges

So far we haven't mentioned BPM, and with good reason. As companies contemplate implementing processes that go way beyond their traditional organizational boundaries, additional aspects also need to be considered way before technology becomes the part of the answer. There are many challenges that consumer-focused organizations will face now and in the future

Corporate Structure

Traditional companies cannot stay with or revert to the status quo. There are many other more nimble organizations out there ready to 'eat their lunch.' By maintaining or returning to established resource cost models, they will not be able to respond to the flexibility and speed-to-market demands of tomorrow's consumer at a cost that is sustainable. A flexible corporate structure and ongoing operation will need to be established, not only to address consumer demand, but to leverage the aspirations of an increasingly convenience-driven labor force.

In order to process work effectively in the future, companies will need to take advantage of the increasing number of approaches available and keep in mind an observation recently quoted by Schoeman Rudman of the South African BPM consultants Value Consulting, 'Work is not where people go, it is what people do'.

Regulation

Regulation is relentless, but following on from a number of high profile malpractice incidents, often with catastrophic financial consequences, regulation is here to stay. For some industries however, the regulators wield a double-edged sword by dictating procedure, while actually compromising the possibility of compliance. An example of this can be found in the UK water utility industry, which is regulated by OFWAT—the Water Services Regulation Authority. All regulated regional water companies are assessed on number performance measurements, predominantly around customer service and satisfaction. The results of these rankings are used to govern the rates that they can set for the services they provide. This means that the poorer performers have an incentive to improve, but cannot necessarily raise the funds to implement the required improvements. For those at the wrong end of the rankings, the aim is to improve service standards without adding more human resource costs to the bottom line. The challenge is in achieving that aim.

Skills

With many valuable skills displaced by the economic downturn, current operation is challenging, and future expansion looks almost impossible without hiring in the necessary capability. Companies are nervous about increasing headcount without the guarantee of additional revenue streams to fund it. This feeds the herd mentality of some industries and prolongs blockages to economic activity.

Technology

There is a pattern emerging from companies' attitudes to IT spend. Projects that have long lifecycles, i.e. greater than 12 months, and are not backed by a cast-iron business case which demonstrates in-year payback, rarely see the light of day. Project sponsors are looking to invest where the CFO can see the best return for the money in terms of increased revenue or reduced costs. Furthermore, companies are looking at different ways of prolonging the longevity of their legacy IT applications, as expensive upgrades or system replacement projects for technologies sake are not a consideration any more.

This probably goes some way to explain the overall year-on-year increase in spend on BPM technologies in the last five years, and the optimism shown generally amongst the analyst and supplier communities. It is these technologies that potentially offer organizations a way of addressing the issues and challenges already described. However, other behavioral changes need to be introduced at the same time to have any significant impact. The following sections will explore some of the evolving and emerging approaches to building a sustainable cost effective business operation that benefits from new advancements in technology and mindset change in the way work is processed.

COLLABORATION

This is a much-talked about topic and one which attracts much debate. In essence the subject is concerned with how a number of individuals contribute to the completion of a task and how the collaborative process is managed. It is also a topic that highlights the challenges faced by the current crop of BPM solutions when trying to manage what are essentially unstructured processes.

Firstly though, let us consider the conventional manner in which work is processed. Most conventional process maps, millions of which have been produced over the last few years, illustrate a structured sequence of events that represent the steps an item of work passes through on route to completion. Along the way, there are potential branches and wait states that cope with any variance and the events that happen during the execution of the process, but in essence, the whole activity is managed in a repeatable, predictable and chronologically ordered manner. Non-technology focused techniques, such as Lean Six Sigma, have evolved over the years to improve these structured processes and many organizations have been hugely successful in saving costs and improving customer service as a result. It is also true to say that BPM-based technology applications such as BPM Suites have been architected to support these structured processes and, indeed, have in many cases, delivered value in automating the distribution of work throughout an enterprise and reducing the number of human activities required to complete a task.

The diagram below illustrates a typical process, such as a new customer acquisition, involving both human participants and fully-automated process steps.

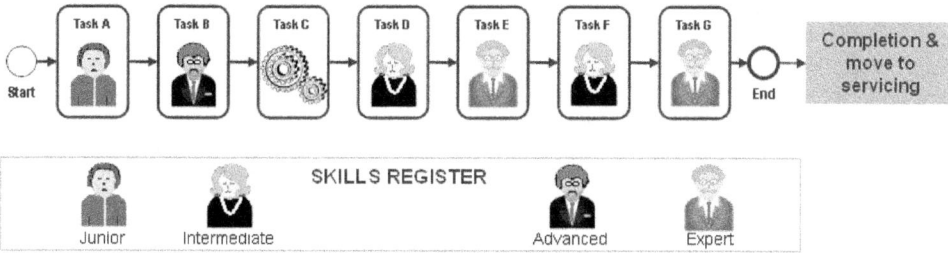

In this scenario, if the system is configured correctly, the work is delivered to the least qualified participant capable of performing that part of the process to the required standard and timeliness. This means that higher cost resources will be focused on activities where they add value, and not preoccupied with tasks that can be performed by someone less senior and subsequently lower cost. Task C has been defined as a fully-automated activity and requires no user intervention and could be performing activities such as credit checks and data evaluation. Whilst the diagram shows a linear flow, in reality it is likely that there are a number of branches, which are followed depending on the outcome of the related task.

This illustration demonstrates the activity of a typical back-office operation whether or not any technology is deployed to manage the process. The model though, does rely on a set of conditions for it to work.

One of these conditions is process knowledge, where it is assumed that the processes are defined and understood. Every eventuality that may occur has a route in the process to cater for it, even if it is a route to an exceptions area. Otherwise items of work that fall outside of the understood process can potentially be lost.

Additionally, in order to ensure the work to be processed is completed in the required time, a process must have use of guaranteed resources. This means either contracted employees who have dedicated commitments to the process, or outsourced providers who are contracted to complete whole or part processes. Staffing a process in this way however, means that expanding and contacting capacity in line with demand is difficult to achieve in an efficient manner. Capacity planning tools go some way to predict workloads, but often depend on historical knowledge and don't cater for unpredicted events such as unforeseen change in demand for a particular product. Companies operating on this way tend to err on the light side for resource planning, as they do not wish to pay for employee idle time. This can affect customer service and overall performance if volumes increase.

In addition to sufficient resources to staff a process, organizations will need the right level of expertise to support the operation. This can be either as 'resident' resources or bought in as required. In both cases, the right skill levels need to be managed and planned to ensure a consultative capacity is present to support the ongoing operation.

It is now recognized that not all processes run in this manner. In fact some organizations have a degree of unpredictability in most of their processes, which make them difficult to not only model, but also to apply traditional BPMS technology. The uncertainty aspect of a process re-introduces the one key component that BPM initiatives often seek to eliminate; *human beings*.

Below is a process definition taken from a large international insurance company, and driven by a BPMS software application.

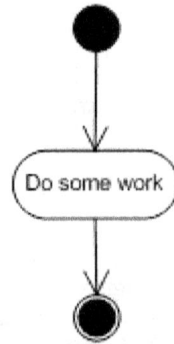

In the 'Do some work' task human participants work together to complete what is required and then hand back to the BPMS application for it to decide what happens next. There is no modeling used to define what happens in this step.

It is true to say also that in any customer-centric process, there is generally an element of collaboration between the human participants, conducted on as needed interdepartmental basis. This is often in the guise of asking for help or providing expertise to junior colleagues as required.

Modern-day collaboration tends to fall into one of three categories, formal collaboration, informal or casual collaboration and mass collaboration. The first two types have more relevance to processing work and the latter tends to be an emerging characteristic of behavior that is influencing the world around us.

Formal Collaboration

This type of activity occurs when a formal agreement is constructed between parties that are going to collaborate to process work. Types of arrangement that fall into this category include sub-contracting, outsourcing, off-shoring etc. These are scenarios that are fairly common in business operations today and indeed have existed for many years. BPM technologies have for some time been used to manage this type of collaboration by supporting the hand-off of work between the collaborating participants, while ensuring that the steps in the process are completed to the required quality and within the agreed service level timescales. The BPM engines provide the required reporting capability so that the 'collaborators' can be remunerated for the contributions to the process. In some cases, the BPM technology is extended into the external participants so that a more joined-up view of the process can be seen and the external participant can benefit from some of the functionality it provides.

With this type of collaboration however, the processes are still quite structured, and the organization commissioning the external participants may view their roles in a manner not dissimilar from the 'Do Some Work' step in the process described previously. This means that as long as the quality of the deliverables and Service Level Agreements (SLAs) are maintained satisfactorily; how the work is actually completed is largely irrelevant.

Another example of formal collaboration is self-service. Organizations have for some time allowed processes to be initiated by their customers via the web. In many cases, for straightforward requests, the subsequent fulfillment process can be completely automated. Most of us apply for products and services on line, and the suppliers of these goods and services aim to use as little manual effort as possible to fulfill the request. For a product purchase activity, the supplier will automate the validation of the request, the inventory check, the collection of the payment and the instruction to the warehouse to pack and send the goods. This last step is often the only human activity involved, which then requires formal collaboration with the courier company to initiate the collection of the products from the supplier and the subsequent delivery of them to the consumer.

This process initiation activity is not the only way in which the end customer can now collaborate with a process. More and more organizations are using email and SMS/mobile-texting technology to request data and effectively have the customer perform data entry on a company's behalf. An example of this may be the application for financial service products where only once the account application has been accepted, following the appropriate credit checks and other due diligence, the customer has to enter in additional security data. This is often achieved by sending the customer an email with a link to a secure page in which to enter the data. This last point does raise the overall issue of security, and in a formal collaboration agreement, there is a requirement for rigid security around access to both data and functionality. Who gets to see and do what, and how that impacts any data protection regulations is a big topic for organizations to consider.

Casual Collaboration and Crowdsourcing

In many ways, casual collaboration has its roots in activities such as fruit-picking and general building labor, where workers would make themselves available by queuing up at the farm or waiting for the collection bus, and would be paid for the output they produced on the day. The terms of engagement were relatively simple and informal and the payment rates offered by the company were sufficient to attract enough labor to complete the work. Fast-forward seventy years and we are starting to see a similar paradigm, but in this case supported by sophisticated technology and managed using complex analysis tools.

At the start of this chapter, the impact of the global economic downturn and the changing nature of the working populous were discussed. These two characteristics are providing the momentum behind companies' propensity to look at different ways of processing their work, and casual collaboration is starting to play a part in their thinking. One type of casual collaboration is known as 'crowdsourcing' and this involves putting tasks out in the public domain for people to complete.

An early adopter of this approach is Amazon with their 'Mechanical Turk' online workplace. The name is derived from a 19th century invention devised by Wolfgang Von Kemplen, a chess-playing mannequin that was purported to be a fully automated robot that could intelligently play chess. In reality, hidden underneath the mannequin was a small chess master operating the device to great effect, beating many notable chess players of the time. However, this was an example of combining technology and human knowledge to carry out a task and aptly captures the essence of Amazon's online workplace.

The process begins with workers with particular skills, registering themselves onto the site and looking for suitable activities (Human Intelligence Tasks or HITs) for them to perform. HITs range from providing opinions on designs to rather menial work such finding US zip codes for certain types of business. It is important to remember that what may look like a pointless activity is often part of a bigger project. The worker doesn't get to see the bigger picture and many tasks do not produce a high degree of job satisfaction. The companies that require the HITs to be performed, pay money into a Mechanical Turk account and allocate a reward to the HITs they want completing. If the work is not selected and completed, they have the option of increasing the reward until it finds a level where someone is willing to complete the HIT. More complicated and higher risk HITs require a qualification, which can be obtained by taking tests on the site.

Whilst this concept is becoming more established, nobody has become rich by performing HITs and the work is generally low level and mundane. One of the big impediments to the benefit that a crowdsourcing approach can deliver is the security of data. Individual's personal details and records cannot be put out into the public domain for anonymous workers to process. Or can they?

An interesting development, patented by DST Technologies begins to address this challenge. Know as SPiNS (Secure Processing in a Non-Secure environment), this technology allows data to be captured from hand-completed forms that are difficult to recognize electronically, in a crowdsourced fashion. It does this by extracting portions of fields from the form and then blending them with data from other forms, and presenting an anonymous version of the form for an online data entry clerk to key in. When the results are returned, the software reassembles the data into its proper form allowing it to be processed as if it was keyed in securely.

This type of collaboration is still somewhat in its infancy but is gives us a clue as to what can be achieved in the future. Whilst the crowdsourcing approach is generally associated with low value, mundane work, conceptually there is no reason why more sophisticated, professional services cannot be provided in that way.

At the start of this chapter, changing attitudes amongst the developed world's labor force were discussed. Generation Z or the 'Playstation generation' as they are sometimes known, have a different outlook to how they operate in the world than those whose first job after leaving education was in the 1980s. The rise of social technology and instant access to data and functionality provides them with more alternatives to earn money. Additionally, those with key skills that have been displaced by the global economic downturn, and those with new skills emerging from higher education, will be able to market their capabilities and perform their jobs in a different way to the conventional office based paradigm.

This is where BPM technologies will need to evolve to in order to provide the management and control of the necessary business processes, but support the flexibility required in a collaborative workplace. The next generation of social networks could potentially have an online workplace where not only the individuals declared skills are recorded, but their performance is monitored and their capability continually assessed, resulting in automated rankings and subsequent earning potential. There are many issues to consider here and it is no coincidence that the Mechanical Turk site is currently US-centric and operates in US dollars. The potential tax liability and regulatory issues around where, geographically, work is completed are just two of the considerations to be taken into account. Additionally, although the technology to support such operations is there in parts, the traditional BPMS tool sets that work well for structured internally coordinated business processes need to evolve or be supplemented by products that cope with less structured disparately-fractured processes and provide the means to ensure quality, acceptable levels of customer service and cost-effectiveness.

Mass Collaboration

This type of collaboration is less relevant to the topic of this chapter, but nevertheless an interesting take on how to use collaborative resources to achieve a goal. The excellent book—*Wikinomics* by Don Tapscott and Anthony Williams, explores this topic in great detail. Mass collaboration effectively brings together complementary skills and ideas for a specific purpose. The most prolific example of mass collaboration is open source software and specifically the Linux operating system. Major institutions that, up until recently, would not have entertained the introduction of open source software are now basing their IT strategies around it. Now that the self-policing activities of the bodies that promote the software have gained credibility, legal departments are taking a more relaxed view of bona fide open source products.

But it is not just software that benefits from mass collaboration; music, building design, the ergonomics of everyday products are benefiting from the vast amount of skill and ideas across the world.

One specific type of mass collaboration is 'Crowd Casting.' This name, as it suggests, involves the broadcasting of information to multiple potential contributors with the aim of achieving the desired result. An example of that approach was the Goldcorp Challenge.

Goldcorp is a Toronto-based gold prospecting and mining company that in the latter part of the 20th century was seriously underperforming. Their chairman, Rob McEwan, a mutual fund manager, had found himself in the job as a result of a takeover battle where he ended up as the majority owner of the Red Lake gold mine. The mine was unproductive and although adjacent competitor mines were yielding gold, it was proving difficult to locate rich sources in its 55,000 acre span. Whilst attending a summit on technology in 1999, McEwan learnt about Linus Torvalds, the Swedish software engineer, who pioneered the Linux operating system. This gave McEwan the idea that if he could tap into the best geologist skills in the world, they may succeed where his own geologists were struggling.

McEwan then decided to break a traditional mining taboo by publishing all of the company's geology surveys and mining data online and issuing a challenge to produce a plan to identify the location of the gold. The total size of the prize was $575,000. Over 1400 entrants from 50 countries started work on the challenge and a judging committee selected the top entries for subsequent investigation. The winning entry was a collaboration between a specialist simulation company, Fractal Graphics and a mineral exploration company, Taylor Wall and Associates, both Australian organizations who, despite not visiting the site, came up with a powerful three-dimensional model of the mine, illustrating the likely locations of the gold.

The result—over eight million ounces have been mined since 2002 generating over $3billion in revenue. A good return on the $575,000 prize money investment.

SOCIAL BPM

So now in the early part of the 21st century, a number of factors are coming together in a way that will drive the way the world operates in the future. Firstly we seem to assume that the current downturn will magically go away and everything will be OK once again. In reality, it is likely to take effort and inspired thinking for organizations to thrive in a more competitive future. With other areas of the globe now using the technology produced by the developed world to compete against it, the successful companies of tomorrow will be those who harness all available assets to deliver the required results. We may have to work hard at bringing back the better times and this means understanding the psyche of both the consumer and the worker and using technology to leverage the best from both.

As of January 2011 there were over 600 million Facebook subscribers. That in itself is a powerful base of skills, knowledge and opportunity. The term *Social BPM* seems to be emerging, but like the term BPM itself 10 years ago, there appears to be different interpretations of what it actually means. A valid definition may be the use of contemporary non-industrial technology such as social networks, wikis and mashups to deliver work, activities and services to consumers and process participants as required. This will extend the now-commonplace use of technologies such as email and SMS/texting to incorporate the use of these more sophisticated personal applications to blend an individual's business and social activities. By evolving the current crop of BPM tools and technologies, the opportunity for companies to take advantage of the global skills base will expand. The challenge for the BPM solutions providers is to cope with ad hoc and unstructured processes in a way they have not had to before, and legislate for the different ways that companies will want to have their work processed.

There are some exciting and potentially challenging times ahead. Organizations using the power of emerging technologies to exploit the opportunities offered by the global skills base are likely to be the pack leaders in the future. But we are reaching the point where having a shape on a process diagram labeled 'Do Some Work' will no longer be sufficient to make that happen.

References

(Tapscott and Williams 2005) Don Tapscott and Anthony D. Williams. Wikinomics—How Mass Collaboration Changes Everything: Portfolio, 2006.

Amazon's Mechanical Turk
http://en.wikipedia.org/wiki/Amazon_Mechanical_Turk

Evidence-Based Service; Listening to Customers to Improve Customer-Service Processes

Vikas Nehru and Ajay Khanna

INTRODUCTION

Every customer interaction, including sales and service, must reflect a company's brand. However, it is quite a challenge to measure the effect which customer service has on a company's brand. It is required that the customer service processes are aligned with the brand to ensure that the customers receive service which meets the expectations generated by the brand.

The company must possess the ability to measure the effect of each service interaction on brand perception and customer service KPIs. Some of these KPIs are easy to identify as they are based on interactions within the organization's self-service or agent assisted service processes. But the interactions that are happening out in the social media world can also tell a lot about the company and how it is perceived by the consumer. Companies today need to be able to establish KPIs related to social media or social-assisted service in order to remain a competitive brand in today's economy.

Evidence-based improvement utilizes experimentation and rigorous measurement, and has the potential to allow customer service organizations to determine how each type of customer interaction affects the service process and your brand. By deliberately changing and testing a service process and then re-measuring its impact, the organization can discover the optimum process to satisfy customers and reinforce brand while still meeting company KPI objectives.

This paper will discuss how process management, social monitoring, customer feedback and analytics come together to provide customers with an unprecedented service experience.

CHANGING FACE OF BRAND

A brand is a combination of the promises of the vendor, associated expectation from the customer, and actual customer experience. Once simply a manufacturer's mark, brands now play a starring role in the global economy. It is no exaggeration to say that brand power underpins the prosperity of nearly every successful organization. By creating a meaningful context for the relationship between the company and customer, the brand contributes to two of the most important questions in the purchase process: Why buy? And why buy from *you*? In the past, brand was controlled by the company and defined by sales, marketing, and advertising activities. Customer service brand management was not emphasized, and in many cases, the customer experience after the purchase of a product was very different than its pre-sale brand image. We are aware of the fact that the US economy has made a significant movement from being a manufacturing economy to becoming a services economy. This has made it critical for companies to focus on customer relationships, rather than solely on transactions. Now, every interaction between a company and customer affects the brand, and the power of the customer to shape the brand image has never been greater. In today's world the voice of the customer is heard loudly via social media outlets such as blogs, discussion boards, and rating and review sites. The brand is no longer controlled by the company. Support and service activities significantly influence a customer's perception of a brand. In fact, customer service along with social listening and understanding customer sentiments has become critically important to the bottom line of most companies.

Do not assume that if a customer has a problem they are going to come to you first. Today's customer is empowered, having access to significantly more information than was readily available 10 years ago. They will often seek out answers in the social world, finding people with experiences similar to theirs before they decide to reach out to company. Today customers have access to many forms of social media such as Twitter, Facebook, Yelp, blogs, forums, SMS and others. A company's perceptions within these media influence the buying decisions of prospective customers. Companies do not have to be silent observers to this. They can harness this raw information to their advantage to improve service offerings and processes.

IMPORTANCE OF ALIGNING CUSTOMER SERVICE PROCESSES WITH BRAND

The customer experience can only be optimized when every customer interaction aligns with the brand, which is dependent on an underlying customer service process. If this does not happen then the customer becomes frustrated and dissatisfied as the experience does not match with the brand expectation. There may also be inconsistencies in the customer experience across different channels (online, retail, call center etc.). This confusion and inconsistency leads to loss of trust, fewer referrals, less repeat business and ultimately lower revenues.

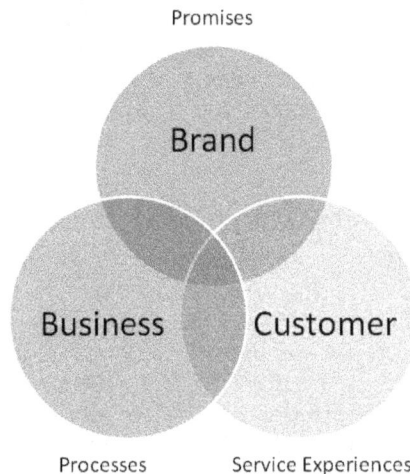

Promises

Brand

Business   Customer

Processes   Service Experiences

In this business reality, it is crucial that each customer interaction matches a company's brand. This entails:

- Delivering on the brand promise in a repeatable, dependable, and consistent manner throughout every interaction.
- Understanding the essence of your brand, and aligning your service delivery with your brand in a way that resonates with your customers. This alignment is of critical importance as companies attempt to do business in today's highly competitive business environment while maintaining low costs. Efficient customer service processes will ensure that you can deliver on company's brand while keeping the costs to a minimum.

PROBLEMS WITH ESTABLISHED PRACTICES

When companies attempt to attain their service objectives, success is often elusive. Poor service causes customer churns, high call handling times, agent turnover, and dissatisfied customers. However, this is not an indicator of overall customer service, but rather a reflection of how difficult it is to systematically measure customer service programs against a company's brand and business goals.

The following list summarizes common errors that are routinely made on the road to brand alignment.

- Service offering is not in line with brand expectation. When customer service does not match the brand, confusion and unrealistic expectations are generated. Service activities are not tied to business outcomes. There is a language disconnect between customer service managers, who talk in the language of average handle time and volume of emails, and C-level executives who care about company performance, overall customer loyalty and churn. This results in a lack of executive support for tactical customer service initiatives.
- Service Organizations blinded by the accepted truth. Applying a deeply held, but unexamined and untested ideology can lead to ineffective service.
- Relying on the past data to determine current processes. Applying processes and technologies that worked in the past can lead to productivity challenges if they are used blindly without sufficient regard for your new company's size, maturity, or management philosophy. Past lessons are relevant, but it is important to thoroughly analyze what the problems were, how the company operated, whether there were any measurable results, and whether or not the methodologies are appropriate for your organization.
- Benchmarking the factors that have no impact on your business goals. Focusing on the wrong metrics or processes can result in inaccurate conclusions which may not be fundamental to a customer service organization's success.

Customer service organizations are constantly asked to improve their customer satisfaction while reducing costs. Also, many companies have increasing pressure to become a profit center with responsibility to cross-sell and up-sell. The regulatory compliance pressures are increasing in industries like banking, healthcare, etc. And, if this was not enough, the social media has created an environment where even a slight misstep by service organizations can be made known to a huge population in a matter of seconds. The barrier to switch services is low, creating a perfect storm for the customer service managers who are juggling multiple KPIs and trying to balance the competing needs of the company and the customers. In such a socio-economic situation, the service providers cannot simply keep following old practices; there has to be a different, more agile way of managing service processes and operations.

Value of Evidence based practices

The difficulty in determining the best course of action to achieve a distant or hard-to-measure outcome is not unique to customer service. It has long been a problem in the field of healthcare and has led to an innovative approach called evidence-based medicine. Evidence-based medicine emerged in the 1980s as physicians began systematic reviews of the evidence for preventive services when writing clinical practice guidelines. Evidence-based medicine applies the best available information gleaned from a scientific method to ensure the best prediction of outcomes in medical treatment. It is becoming the gold standard for clinical practice. The medical field's evolution in thinking has led to several other evidence-based practices, including evidence-based policy and evidence-based management. Regardless of the field to which it is applied, evidence-based methodologies have a few things in common:

- **Rigor**: Making sure that your decisions are based on facts collected from interaction events and data. Proper analytics on this data drives a company's actions. However, you do not need to wait for the best evidence, but can work off of the facts at hand. If you wait to gather optimal facts, the opportunity for action may lapse.
- **Experimentation**: Treating the status quo as an unfinished prototype, and encouraging experimentation and learning by taking appropriate actions.
- **Measurability**: Avoiding decisions based on untested but strongly held beliefs, past practice, or uncritical external benchmarking.

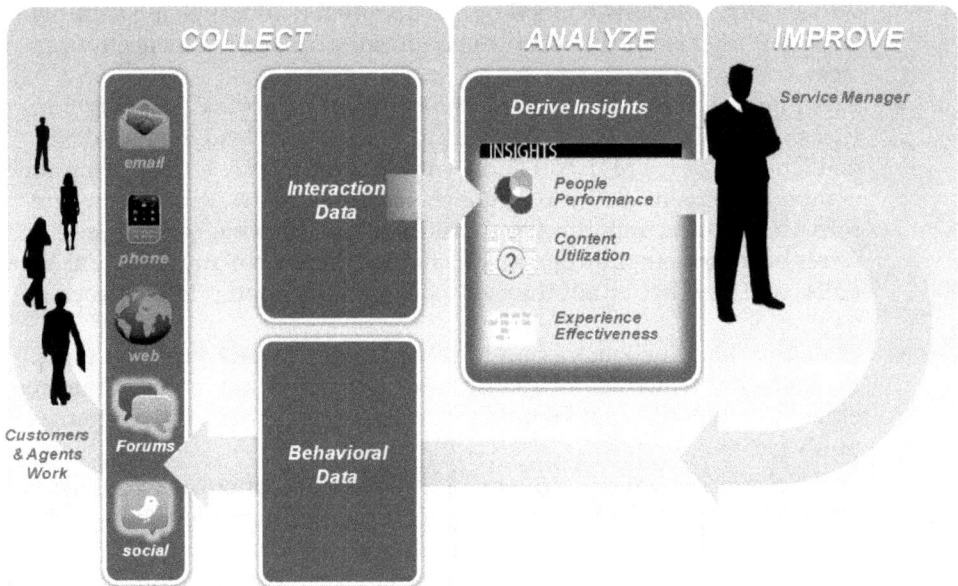

Aspects of evidence-based practice are already in use outside the medical field. In customer service processes there is no dearth of evidence. The only challenge is to identify the appropriate places to look and the best metrics to measure. Today we cannot just base our decisions on the data collected internally or via surveys. The activity happening outside the company in social media needs to be harnessed into useful and actionable information.

EVIDENCE-BASED SERVICE IMPROVEMENT

Rigorous, evidence-based practice provides the best solution for escaping the high-risk game of managing complex service functions based on instinct and emulation. With the appropriate collection and use of evidence, aligning the service experience with brand promise is now feasible. The goal is to determine—through experimentation, rigorous measurement and analytics—how each service activity affects the KPI scorecard, such as the cost of the interaction, customer satisfaction with the service experience, compliance with company or regulatory policy, and the ability to generate increased sales. By changing the process, and re-measuring the impact, you can determine the optimal process to achieve a balanced scorecard and tie discrete service activity to desired business outcomes.

First you need to collect data relevant to your particular field of customer service. The evidence required to make improvement decisions come from multiple sources. This feedback can be from interactional data generated from various interactions with the customer. These interactions can be phone conversations, email exchanges or chat sessions. You can also gauge feedback by examining products purchased, products returned and customer complaints, or any other information customers have submitted on your website.

Another form of feedback is behavioral data. This is more unstructured and may include things such as website page abandonment, time spent on searches, patterns of movement away from self-service processes, making a call, etc.

These days critical feedback is also generated by the social world. This data resides in forums, blogs, Facebook, tweets etc. Social monitoring of these forms of media provides you with significant information about customer sentiment: their peeves, issues and frustrations. This data needs to be searched and classified into topics of interest.

Once you have identified the sources of relevant data, you must determine the kind of analysis that you'll need to perform in order to extract useful information. This analysis can determine if there are any positive or negative trends in your metrics that you need to address. It will provide insights into why these trends are emerging, and which factors are affecting your KPIs. Data generated from the social media provides insights into your customer sentiments and other emerging emotional trends about your products, brands or even competing brands. This information can be categorized and used to adjust your operational tactics and strategies.

This analysis leads to actions for improvement. These actions can be immediate, triage or for long-term results. The insights from the analysis will help you adjust your service processes, business rules, and the types of knowledge being delivered to customers or agents. It will also allow you to fine tune the call flows and perform resource leveling across various channels, helping you to create highly efficient processes.

In order to deliver these improvements your customer service processes need to be agile enough to allow you to actually take action once possible improvements have been identified. In the next sections we will discuss ways to make this happen.

EVIDENCE-BASED SERVICE GUIDING PRINCIPALS

There are several guiding principles for implementing evidence-based service:

- **Choose the right starting point for your organization**. Evidence-based service is a management philosophy which can be implemented at a micro or macro level. It can be used at a granular level to fine tune a particular service process or function, like auto-response rates for email service, or it can be implemented at a global level across all the people, processes, and technologies used to support the service offering.
- **Commit to incremental improvement**. Don't assume that current business processes are too much of a mess to fix or impossible to change because of organizational resistance. Benchmark your baseline performance and then continuously drive incremental change.

- **Demand data**. All decisions must be data driven and managed within a balanced KPI scorecard. If you do not have the data, invest in the processes and systems required to obtain it. As most activities in a service organization are mediated by IT systems, these can be leveraged to obtain data for measurement.
- **Look outside your organization for data.** Look for data from the social media. Data from social platforms can be analysed and used to improve service processes helping you understand your customers, competitors and trends, and allowing you to improve service and product offerings.
- **Eliminate noise**. While collecting data, whether internal or from social interaction, find out what data is statistically and strategically significant for you. What metrics should you observe? Which will have the greatest impact on your processes and strategies?
- **Apply Analytics**. Relevant analytical techniques will allow you to gain insights into business processes and customer behaviour. These insights are then employed to improve the business processes and overall customer service experience.
- **Benchmark against best in industry**. Get real data on what has statistically worked for other companies and apply it thoughtfully to your particular situation.
- **Use a "customer's eye" view**. Start with a realistic, honest benchmark of your service experience before launching on an evidence-based service project. Your goal is to positively alter the brand and measure the impact brand has on customer perception, not just internal performance metrics.

IMPLEMENTATION

As we have noted, you can use evidence-based techniques at any point in your call center or Web self-service lifecycle. Some opportunities for utilizing these techniques are when implementing service experience management process, case management, integrating email processes with knowledge management, or when completely transforming your service operation. There are several key steps to implementing evidence-based service.

1. Asses the current service processes; define the solution and strategy.

- Start by determining the communication channels that your customers expect you to offer and which are in line with your brand.
- Look at the types of service issues you encounter and determine which problems are best supported by which channel.
- Define your goals, objectives, KPI metrics, and growth strategy.

2. Investigate the social media and channels your target demographics use.
- Examine where there is maximum buzz, not only about your product, but about your market category and competitors.
- Determine the type of data you would like to extract from this buzz. Is it customer complaints, complements, ideation or competitive analysis?
- Establish how you will respond once you identify a pattern or a critical instance of customer complaint, etc. Also consider how you will reward a customer who is your best spokesperson.

3. Define and implement your technical and business solution.
- Use your goals, objectives, and metrics to model the solution and pinpoint company-specific strategies that will govern the implementation.
- Implement using BPM-based platforms and methodologies to make sure deployments are completed on time and on budget, meet your business objectives, are agile, and achieve the projected ROI.

4. Benchmark your organization against a service experience maturity model.
- A benchmark against a maturity model will help you assess your service operation against industry best practices to identify where changes and improvements can be made. The outcomes of the benchmark will include gap analysis and recommendations for complying with best practices.
- Using evidence-based service, you can optimize your solution to implement the recommendations of the benchmark.

5. Plan to holistically improve the maturity of your service organization. With evidence-based service guiding your decisions, you can transform your total service offering by analyzing and refining each aspect of the service experience. This may include:
- Process Optimization—Assessing the maturity and performance of customer service processes.
- Segmentation Optimization—Assessing the effectiveness of service delivery for each market segment.
- Multi-Channel Optimization—Assessing each channel, including social, against the maturity model and benchmark.
- Content Audit and Transformation—Evaluating customer service content and authoring processes to effectively re-engineer content.
- Knowledge Management Tuning—Designing context driven searches to increase the presentation of relevant content infused at appropriate points in the process.

Applying evidence-based practices to customer service requires a technology solution that offers several key capabilities including the ability to:
- Easily model and deploy service processes across all of the people and technology involved in the process.
- Provide an ability to define, monitor and measure various interaction and behavioural KPIs.
- Apply evidence-based techniques by changing discrete elements in a process to measure the impact on a balanced scorecard of KPIs.

- Quickly deploy newer versions of processes.
- Monitor and measure impact of changes made to process in real-time, so that impact is immediately understood and can be instantly modified to achieve improved business outcomes.

These capabilities will allow companies to create service experience management solution to deliver an evidence-based service platform. The service experience management platform enables you to model the complete flow of any service process, from a simple customer interaction via phone or web, to a complicated investigative process for managing the discovery of information across data sources, knowledge, case tracking, and email components. Each process needs to be visually modeled by business owners and then immediately deployed for use by agents and visitors to your Web site. The platform then monitors and measures the success of the process based on your KPIs in real time. You can choose which KPIs to measure at each step in the process. The process can then be changed at any time and at any step to determine the optimal solution.

These unique capabilities enable your organization to deliver the service experience that is ideal for maintaining a balanced scorecard of KPIs and effectively supporting your company's brand. By enabling you to orchestrate all your processes, knowledge, and technology, service experience management helps you maximize the value of each service interaction with your customers.

CONCLUSION

When customer service processes and brand promise are in alignment, you can deliver experiences that will resonate with your customers, helping increase satisfaction and loyalty, while effectively managing the costs for service delivery. The organization has to listen to feedback from customers as well as from the business process to deliver the brand promise.

Evidence-based service offers a powerful new ways of thinking about customer service. Evidence-based practices, when combined with social listening and analytics, yield measurable benefits in customer service operations. These practices support the company's brand image and achieve a balance between the competitive pressures of reducing costs, satisfying customers, increasing revenue, and complying with ever-growing regulations.

REFERENCES

Evidence-based Management (EBM), http://www.evidence-basedmanagement.com/index.html (accessed March 8, 2011).

Predictive BPM

Dr. Setrag Khoshafian

Most businesses today engage in "predictions." Will a customer agree to upgrade a purchase based on an array of offers? What is the likelihood that a customer within a cluster of similar customers will default on a loan? How much more effective will a targeted marketing campaign be, compared to a random sampling? How can the churn rate of subscribers be improved? What is the likelihood that a particular financial transaction is fraudulent? These are some questions that could utilize prediction with concrete and tangible business benefits.

A "business" is a collection of policies and procedures. Almost every business policy or procedure has some aspect of prediction in it. Most of the time, policy and procedure requirements are based on intuition, best guesses, or business experience. Too frequently, no one in the organization can remember why certain policies were ever created in the first place.

There are actually several sources of policies and procedures that guide business operations. Here are some of them:

- *Policy and Procedure Manuals:* These reveal how things get done in the organization. You have manuals for handling customer interactions, for building products, for HR, for services, and more. Often, new employees are trained on these manuals; their jobs entail understanding and implementation of procedures and enforcement of policies.

- *People's Heads:* Almost invariably, there are designated "knowledge workers" who know how to get things done. They know the written, and often unwritten, policies and procedures and have these in their heads. These are the go-to people for specific tasks or procedures, and every organization has them. Equally important, they know which policies or procedures can be ignored—those little workarounds that technically break the rules but actually get things done. These people are also often the source of innovation—either of new products and services or process innovation. Their understanding of the organization puts them in a unique position to be able to identify how the organization could work better.

- *ERP and Point Solutions:* ERP solutions contain embedded business process logic. The customizations and configuration are based on an understanding of the policies and procedures at the time the system was implemented. However, because these business rules and processes are embedded within the solutions, they are not easy to extend and so become "ossified" and difficult to change.

- *Legacy or Custom Code:* Policies and procedures can also be implemented in homegrown legacy code. This code spans proprietary extensions of ERP solutions, such as ABAP, as well as programs in languages such as COBOL, Java, or C/C++/C#. In fact, the majority of legacy code is in COBOL. Sometimes millions of lines of code have been written to accommodate stakeholder requirements. This code is very difficult to maintain and change, and it is increasingly becoming a serious impediment to agility and change.

- *Automated Models:* This is the newest and most important category. Here, policies and procedures are directly captured through the business process management (BPM) suite and automated for execution in solutions that are easy to change. BPM suites can allow business stakeholders to directly capture their requirements in the tool itself.

But there is another—perhaps less obvious and often less direct—source for both policies and procedures: *data.* There are many sources of data, including the following:

- *Operational* or transactional data from legacy, point-solution, or ERP applications
- Process instance and *case data* from BPM suites
- Data from *external sources* including, but not limited to, public and census data
- *Data warehouses* and/or data marts that aggregate databases (mostly relational) from a plethora of sources, including transactional, operational, or BPM databases

The volume, variation, and sources of data are exploding. The "data" here is, by and large, raw data that is not analyzed. For reporting, analytics, or predictive discovery the raw data needs to be extracted, cleaned, and transformed. Data warehouses/data marts are populated from operational databases, external sources, and BPM case and work data. The whole notion of *data mining* is one of detecting patterns—often operational behavioral patterns—in data. These patterns could be used to forecast future behavior. The detected patterns (called "models" in predictive analytics lingo) could become "operationalized" to help determine business responses. Predictive analytics is a scientific discipline within data mining that uses measurable *predictors* to assess probable outcomes of specific events. Predictive analytics can help the organization continually monitor and adapt operations—especially those realized through BPM suites—for anticipated future behavior. Predictive models often combine historical and operational data from the business to identify the risk or opportunity associated with a specific customer or transaction.

The essence of predictive BPM is the execution of discovered models that predict future behavior, in the context of automated BPM solutions. BPM suites are the platforms that automate policies and procedures. Thus, in predictive BPM there is a close affinity between what is discovered and its execution. For instance, scoring a potential customer for credit risk could involve simple aggregation of data or information about the customer and application of a weighted formula to score the risk. The decision of what to do with a specific score, or a detected pattern in general, is the policy—the decision logic. The policy itself is executed in the context of a process or case, automated through the BPM suite (e.g., the credit application).

From any of the aforementioned data sources and even combining multiple data sources, predictive analysts aggregate and mine historic enterprise operational data (and sometimes publicly available data) in order to detect patterns (models). These patterns can then be used to make predictions about the behavior of future instances. Predictive models deliver segmentation and scoring. For example, depending upon geographical location, demographics, age group, and/or purchasing power of a customer, you can score the likelihood of a customer responding to a marketing offer. Or given the transaction history and types of activities across claims, you can determine the likelihood of fraud. The predictive models can be captured in BPM suites through declarative expressions, properties, situational rules, flows, decision tables, and decision trees.

Predictive analytics is widely used in many industries. There are also applications of predicative analytics such as customer relationship management (CRM) that could be used across many industries.

Here are some examples:

- *Insurance:* In the insurance industry, companies frequently model the risk of insurance applications based on the factors they identify as indicators of future accidents, health risks, and premature deaths. These factors include attributes such as age, body mass index, lifestyle activities, and accident record. These predictive factors are what the insurance companies use to rate insurance applicants so as to create the right balance in their risk portfolios, and help determine what premium each applicant should pay to offset that risk.
- *Financial Services:* Credit scoring in consumer finance can be used to predict the likelihood of timely payments. Predictive modeling can also be used to assess the risk of fraud.
- *Telecommunications:* Customer churn (losing customers who switch to an alternative provider) is one of the most critical challenges in some industries—especially in telecom. Customer data could be used to analyze and predict potential customer churn—through better understanding of customer preferences and behavior and emerging trends.
- *Customer Experience and Marketing:* Marketing campaigns and customer relationships is another major area of predictive analytics that has applicability across many vertical industries. For example, in many industries there is a need to predict whether a prospect will respond favorably to a specific marketing or promotional offer.

Predictive models can greatly enhance the efficiency of processes, improve the customer experience, and reduce potential risks. The following figure illustrates the taxonomy of the type of knowledge or insight we can get from data, and the corresponding business value.

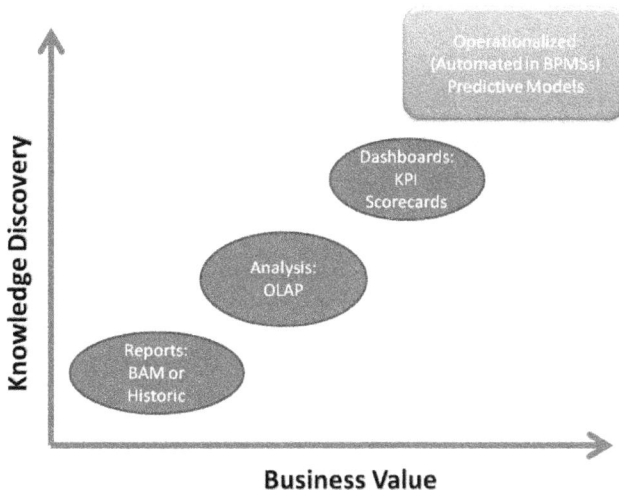

Figure 1: Knowledge Discovery vs. Business Value

Reports can be sourced from real-time business activity monitoring or data warehouses that contain historical data, potentially from multiple sources. BPM suites are increasingly becoming a key source of data for both business activity monitoring (BAM) and data warehouses. Reports are useful for understanding what happened (historic) or what is happening now (BAM).

Analysis goes further in data insight and attempts to "slice and dice" the data along different dimensions and perspectives. It attempts to discover trends and glean insight from aggregated data.

Dashboards allow business stakeholders to have a role-specific, strategic key-performance perspective on their operations. The users can drill down and potentially act on detected bottlenecks.

Predictive modeling and *automation* of decisions provides the greatest business value. Here models that are discovered from historic data are used not only to predict future behavior but to actually *enact the predictive decision in an executing process at the point of execution*. In other words, the current process instance or case provides a context in which the predictive models are operationalized.

The tools and techniques used in predictive modeling, in general, are more complex than reporting, Online Analytical Processing (OLAP), or dashboard tools. But at the same time, since the models are applied to pragmatic business questions, their recommendations have tremendous business value.

Many applications can benefit from automating predictive models. A TDWI[1] survey discovered "Cross-sell/up-sell" to be the top application of predictive analysis. Other top contenders included "Campaign management," "Customer acquisition," and "Retention." If and when these models are enacted and executed in the context of BPM-centric next-generation customer relationship management solutions, application of the predictive model will be executed at the point of interaction with the customer. For instance, if a call center receives a call from a customer following up on a complaint case (automated in the BPM suite), the customer provides additional information about his/her situation. If the enacted predictive model indicates a high likelihood that the customer will switch to another provider, an automated BPM policy could kick in and make an attractive offer to the customer—potentially avoiding the churn. The key value proposition of predictive BPM is the execution of the deepest data knowledge or insight, through BPM suite applications or solutions. The discovered decision is executed in BPM suite solutions.

THE TWO BPMS AND THE EMERGENCE OF PBPM

Predictive BPM is an emerging enterprise solution that aligns business processes with business intelligence. Two interrelated "BPM" acronyms enable predictive business processes. One designates the modeling and automation of processes (business *process* management). The other focuses on monitoring key performance indicators and managing the performance of the business (business *performance* management). BPM suites allow you to model and execute your policies and procedures or flows. They include human workflow, enterprise application integration, business to business choreographies, business rules, collaboration, and solution frameworks. Business process management suites typically support business activity monitoring and process performance capabilities. The other BPM—business performance management—includes monitoring and analysis of applications from a variety of sources: business processes, enterprise resource planning applications, customer relationship management systems, or any com-

---

[1] From www.tdwi.org, research report "Predictive Analytics Extending the Value of Your Data Warehousing Investment," by Wayne W. Eckerson, January 2007. Or see http://www.bi-bestpractices.com/view-articles/5642

mercial or homegrown applications. Business performance management supports strategic methodologies, analysis of ROI, key performance indicator measures, robust performance reporting and portals, data warehousing, OLAP, and business intelligence and data mining with predictive analysis.

We are witnessing the amalgamation of these two disciplines into Predictive BPM (PBPM): business process management and business performance management, especially business intelligence (BI). The dynamic combination of BI and BPM will enable you to monitor, report, analyze, learn, make changes, and improve your business processes in real time. The ultimate objective is to declare your desired performances (KPIs) and let the PBPM system figure out the best way to realize the objective, through predictive analytics, dynamic learning from data, and BPM case automation. This is a tall order. However, it is definitely the trend and becoming a reality.

Many technologies are involved in round-trip improvement life cycles, from strategic measures to underlying operational process applications that increasingly are becoming the main source of data for analysis and predictive modeling. We believe there are huge opportunities with enterprise architectures that clearly delineate and at the same time aggregate the functions of process and performance management. PBPM means that the event dimensions that are used to model, analyze, and extract predictive models from data warehouses are enacted in business process applications. It also means that business process management suites are the main, if not the sole, source of data for information warehouses. PBPM also implies the connection of high-level KPI measures to the execution of policies and processes. Monitored performance metrics such as KPIs in various perspectives are predictive: Stakeholders can take action *in the context of operational processes and policies.* Within PBPM frameworks, continuous improvement life cycles, with *performance* and *analytics*, are key functions in the round-trip improvement of process applications.

The following figure illustrates the continuous improvement life cycle with predictive BPM:

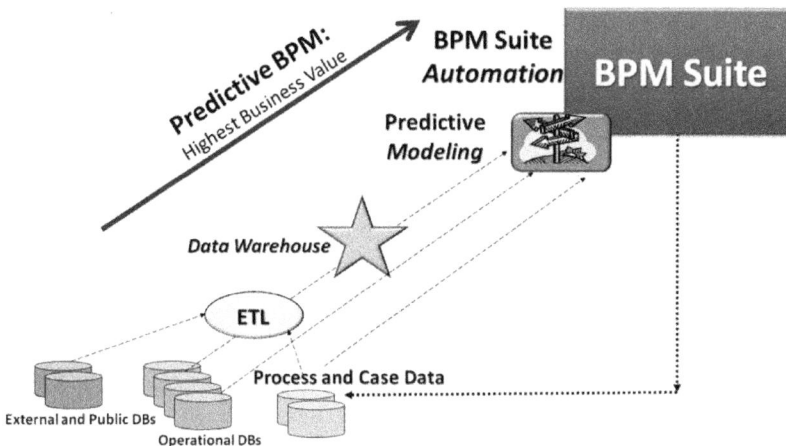

Figure 2: Continuous Improvement Cycle

Enterprise solutions typically have real-time reporting capabilities. BPM suites include BAM portals that allow business managers to run reports, analyze performance, and take action to remediate potential operational process bottlenecks.

BAM can also provide monitoring, reporting, and analysis from multiple enterprise solutions or operations.

Data warehouses can have several sources of external or operational data. These may involve mainframe applications, ERP applications, CRM tools, message queues, and most important, BPM process and case data.

The key observation here—and the focus of this paper—is that there are interesting patterns in the data. These patterns could be mined and subsequently operationalized. How? Through predictive modeling.

As discussed in the next section, there are different types of predictive models: clustering, associations, regression, trees, and more advanced models such as neural networks or Bayesian probabilistic models. All the data sources—BPM case data, operational databases, external databases, data warehouses, etc.—could be used to create predictive models. Predictive modeling could itself be part of the Predictive BPM tooling in a cohesive, unified PBPM platform.[2] Alternatively, predictive models can be imported from other analytical tools.[3] This is similar to importing business rules or process models that are defined in, say, XML or Visio. The main point is that the discovered predictive decision logic is deployed and executed in the context of automated BPM solutions. The operationalization and automation of the models is the key value proposition of PBPM.

Execution of the processes with all the business rules and decision logic continuously generates new case data. Potentially, there could be changes in the patterns or customer behaviors. Similar changes could be reflected in operational databases or external data sources. Data is never static. Thus, new patterns and behavior could be detected. The discovered predictive models can then introduce change to the PBPM. The continuous improvement cycle thus continues, with the PBPM keeping pace with newly discovered models.

BPM suites provide many advantages for business stakeholders. An understanding of the performance of operational processes and the automatic triggering of actions through changes in process states are key measurable benefits. These benefits bridge the gaps between the goals and objectives of the business stakeholders and the underlying IT systems that address these goals and objectives. Capturing and acting on business rules and business processes is the core value proposition in predictive BPM.

PREDICTIVE MODELING

Prediction is ubiquitous. Almost every business flow or business rule has some element of prediction in it. Most of the time requirements arise from intuition, history, experience, or ad hoc mechanisms to capture policies and procedures. Sometimes the original reasons for enacting these policies have long been obsolete. In contrast, predictive modeling is a scientific discipline within data mining that uses measurable *predictors* to predict the behavior of customers. These predictors can be an ordinal or numerical value that can be predicted from other variable values. Historical data is analyzed and modeled to predict future behavior.

---

[2] The discovery and deployment of models is itself a process with concrete phases and steps. This process has been standardized by an industry- and tool-neutral organization: CRISP-DM.org. CRISP stands for CRoss Industry Standard Process—Data Mining. See http://www.crisp-dm.org/.

[3] The Predictive Model Markup Language (PMML) is defined by the Data Mining Group (DMG). PMML is the Predictive Analytics XML standard to exchange predictive models between tools. See http://www.dmg.org/.

Examples of predictors include purchasing preferences, geographical location, age, income, and properties pertaining to the history of activities.

Several predictive models can be discovered from either operational or historic data. The latter is often managed through data warehouses and data marts. Here are some of the categories of predictive models:

- *Classification Models:* In classification one or more variables classify objects (e.g., customers). Then, given a new instance, the class of the instance can be determined from the classification models. *Tree models* are perhaps the most popular type of classification model. In tree models you partition the data by input variables. At each level of the tree you will typically use a different partitioning variable. Then, at the leaves of the tree, you will have the conclusions—namely the class. Through manual, semi-automated, or automated algorithms, the decision tree can be built by "predicting" the outcome of one or more predictable properties (attributes, or variables) based on other input properties. For instance, a model might predict customer buying patterns by partitioning on the customer's age, household size, geographical location (east, west, central, etc.), income, and purchase history. Each of these "features" will be used to provide the branches of the tree. Tree modeling algorithms will systematically partition the data. For new customer interactions, traversing the tree for specific values—the age, the household size, etc.—and reaching a leaf will predict the potential behavior of the customer: "will probably buy" or "will probably not buy." Thus, once the tree model is constructed and validated, it can be used as a predictor.

- *Regression Models:* There are different types of regression models (linear, nonlinear, multiple, logistic, etc.). Linear regression is probably the most popular of the regression models. Here the idea is to find the best-fit linear model $(Y = a*X)$ of a dependent variable Y. For example, a linear regression predictive model can predict *TotalSales* as a linear function of investment in *MarketingAndAdvertising*: *TotalSales = C1 + C2*MarketingAndAdvertising*. The predictive model will attempt to best fit the linear model, discovering the values for *C1* and *C2*.

- *Clustering Models:* Here you can have clusters or segments of your data or records. For instance, you might have a cluster based on the type of customer and his or her geographical location. Then the behavior of clusters could be different. For instance, you might determine that customers in cluster C1 might be quite different in their purchasing practices or their responses to, say, marketing campaigns than customers in cluster C2.

- *Advanced Models:* Predictive modeling can be very complex. The aforementioned models have many variations. Furthermore, there are more complex models—such as neural networks and Bayesian probabilistic models—that could be more appropriate in situations where there are complex or unknown relationship dependencies between variables.

The list here is by no means exhaustive. Some simple algorithms—such as binning—can provide amazingly good results in the prediction of future behavior. So the main philosophy of predictive models is to aggregate and mine historic operational data (and sometimes publicly available data) in order to make predictions about behaviors, within operations automated through BPM solutions.

REALIZING PREDICTIVE BPM

The previous section provided an overview of the relationship between predictive model discovery and BPM suites. This section further expands upon the robust requirements or capabilities in a BPM suite that are essential for predictive BPM. The three fundamental characteristics of PBPM can be summarized as follows:

- *Rich Collection of Rule Types*: Predictive models are usually captured in decision rules. The BPM suite needs to support a rich collection of rule types to handle the discovered models and operationalize them (i.e., automate or execute the predictive model in the context of an automated process application). A BPM suite cohesively integrates business rules, which can include decision-making criteria, evaluation of conformance, risk assessments, expressions, event rules (including event correlation, triggers, etc.) time constraints, task reassignment decisions, or decisions on quality. These business rules need to be captured and executed in the context of process flows. Behind every decision, service level, task assignment, calculation, constraint, integration, and user interaction, there are rules. The rules then drive the processes. The following figure illustrates business rules, including expressions, decision rules, integration rules (for just-in-time information from ERP or other legacy systems), UI rules, constraints, and event rules. The process is represented through the familiar swim-lane diagram. But what is interesting is the fact that behind every task assignment, link, decision, etc., there are business rules that are driving the processes—very similar to the way the nervous system directs the movement of the muscles.

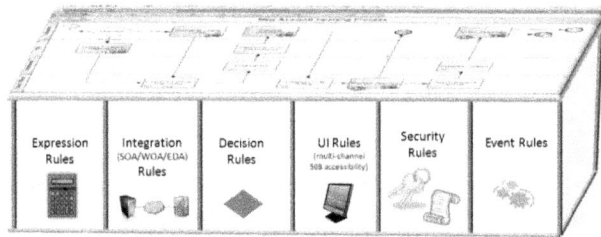

Figure 3: Business Rules Driving the Business Process

- *Circumstances and Situational Execution of Rules:* The assets here are the BPM assets for execution: processes, decision rules, constraints, event rules, UI, integration, information models, security, organization models, etc.

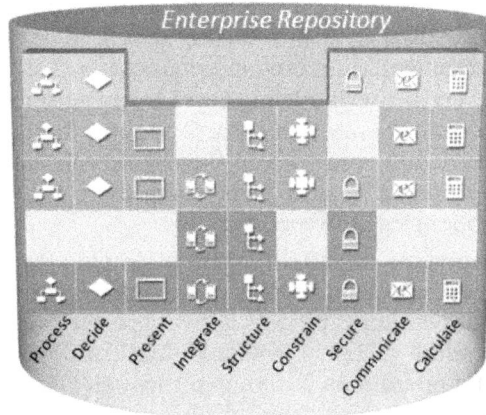

Figure 4: Dynamic Multidimensional Enterprise Repository

The BPM assets need to be organized in a dynamic multidimensional repository. Its dimensions include temporal versioning, but other dimensions are equally important. The repository will support central models and constrained customization for branches or departments, or geographical locations or offices. There can be a dimension that addresses the type of customer—the case subject. Access control/security is another dimension. This multidimensional repository provides a framework to organize, change, deploy, and execute the assets. With PBPM it offers a powerful multi-dimensional organization of the assets to reflect different segments or clusters, associating different business rules for each cluster. The PBPM engine can situationally determine which policy to apply, for a given context. The context is determined through values along the dimensions of the repository: the geographical location of the customer, time, type of service or issue, channel, type of customer, etc.

- *Ad hoc, Smart, and Dynamic Case Management:* A case is the collaboration of multiple tasks for a business objective. Case management brings together multiple related transactions to give a business person a complete picture of what is actually going on. Cases involve multiple flows, tasks, and content. Smart and dynamic case management involves ad hoc processing. This means that at case execution or processing time you can add new tasks, execute additional flow fragments, add content, or create sub-cases—all on an ad hoc basis. In smart case management, knowledge workers can discover policies and procedures (business or decision rules) and immediately automate them in the case management solution. Predictive analytics can dynamically discover models that need to be leveraged in the context of the case. Smart and dynamic case management also provides support for selection of the most appropriate UI, decision logic, flow fragment, or integration, depending upon the context, at case execution time. Dynamic situational selection can reflect the predictive behavior discovered in clusters depending upon the geographical location (where, what language), the time (when), the type of the customer (who), or the purpose (why) of the case.

Cases are event-driven: they generate and respond to events. Event management—including complex event processing—and case management are joined at the hip. A case event is an occurrence that pertains to any aspect of the case's life cycle, content, interactions, or associations. Events consist of a source, priority, time stamp, and data. Events are ubiquitous; in fact, many components of a business application deal with events. All the changes that a case undergoes throughout its life cycle are events. There are also events that pertain to the case subject: for instance, the case subject moves to another state. Then there are the external events (external to the case) that need to be processed. Events could be generated by people, devices, cases, or circumstances.

CONCLUSION

Data mining, and especially predictive modeling techniques, can be used to detect business patterns and then invoke or operationalize the discovered rules in the context of BPM solutions. This is the essence of predictive BPM. The predictive models are deployed and empower BPM solutions. For instance, consider a process that deals with transaction disputes (e.g., purchases, credit cards, etc.). After executing repeatedly and keeping track of the process data, the data mining discovers that, almost always, when the customer has made total purchases in excess of $1,000 and the disputed amount is less than $50, the decision was to write it off. Now this pattern is captured in a rule that automates the decision logic of a write-off dispute process. It could be "mined" from the process data. The rule can then be associated with a decision point within an automated process. After the customer dispute information is collected, the BPM suite can automatically decide to write off—essentially executing the rule—without human intervention. As this example illustrates, the mining of the rule also involved the aggregate history of customer transactions.

Predictive BPM is quite compelling. In BPM suites, the focus is on the operational execution of the processes and the goal-driven policies that support the business rules. In predictive analytics, the focus is on analyzing the historic data and discovering related patterns or models that incorporate the statistical relationships uncovered in the historical data. These analysis tools are not designed to execute the models in the context of business processes. Best practice in the industry involves an intense amount of rekeying, and translation of the predictive model for operational code. These translations slow the process of making the models executable and introduce the potential for error. BPM suites eliminate this manual translation and offer an exponential increase in bandwidth to accommodate new and varied predictive models. BPM suites allow you to directly capture and execute your predictive models.

With PBPM, you can mine and discover rules or processes from your process data, your data warehouse, or other operational data sources. The discovered rules or processes can then be automated. The new rules will be executed in the context of processes and generate new process data. As the behavior of various users in a process application changes (due to competition, customer behavior, or market pressures, for example), new process data will be generated. The discovery cycle continues, and the data mining will discover the new rules and redeploy them to the BPM execution environment.

It is this ability not only to discover but to automate and execute the processes that delivers the greatest business value. Before the dawn of business process management suites—with their strong support of process flows and business rules—BI applications focused on different types of reporting and analysis. Data warehouses provide some value in aggregating historical data from a variety of sources, but mining and exploring the data provides greater value. Users can run reports and better understand and employ the patterns in the data warehouse. Predictive models go a step further and discover models and patterns that are not obvious or at all evident through simple exploration and analysis of the data in the warehouse. But the ultimate business value emanates from the operational execution of the new policies discovered by predictive modeling.

Customer Experience Transformation—A Framework to Achieve Measurable Results

Vinaykumar S Mummigatti

INTRODUCTION

The era of extreme competition is creating immense importance for customer experience and how companies manage their customers' expectations. The ability to successfully manage the customer value chain across the life cycle of a customer is the key to the survival of any company today. Most companies realize this but are struggling to measure and influence the customer experience. This paper is an attempt to look at various facets of customer experience and how to transform customer experience to achieve measurable business goals. **Business Process Management** and the **convergence** of technologies *(such as Portals, web 2.0, BI, Content Management)* are two key elements of this transformation and hence we will focus on how the convergence of various technologies led by BPM will help achieve the business goals around **Customer Experience Transformation (CET)**.

Customer experience can be defined as the sum total of customer perception about a company and its offerings, based on multiple touch points that a customer faces such as branding, marketing, buying process, education, presales and post sales support, merchandising, website visits and the exposure through social media. It is measured by how customers translate this experience through buying behavior, purchase patterns, maintaining their relationship or how they voice their perceptions in larger forums.

Customer experience should be a seemingly easy topic to manage. Most large enterprises have built sophisticated CRM systems over the years, implemented ERP systems to achieve high transaction efficiencies, developed Portals that are loaded with information, and established global call centers that are supposed to handle customer service 24x7 as per SLAs (Service level agreements). Significant investments have been made in Data Warehouses and Business Intelligence systems. Large content repositories using the best of content management systems for web content and documents have been established.

However, all these investments have failed to deliver the desired outcomes in managing customer experience. There is a still a big disconnect between these investments as they are built in silos. There is no cohesive strategy binding these investments to the CEM goals.

Gartner research states "Increasingly, companies are turning to customer experience initiatives to boost the bottom line, but it's an effort that requires cooperation across the organization and extends beyond just CRM. In fact, targeting, attracting and retaining new customers remains a top priority for CIOs, a Gartner survey of 1,500 CIOs worldwide found. Yet CIOs have little involvement in customer experience initiatives," according to Ed Thompson, research vice president with Gartner.

The focus of this article is to present the different tenets of Customer Experience Management (CEM) which help in (1) acquiring customers (2) managing the sum total of experience at various touch points (3) measuring the customer experience KPIs in real time, and (4) taking initiatives based on outcomes to ensure we achieve the business goals. Let us look at how we move beyond CRM into CEM and what kind of solutions we need to develop to convert customer experience into measurable business goals through a combination of technologies related to data, content and process management.

BUSINESS AND TECHNICAL CHALLENGES IN CUSTOMER EXPERIENCE MANAGEMENT

Most large enterprises have redundant systems created by diverse departments or lines of business. Due to these silos, the structure does not permit a cohesive strategy to offer unified customer experience. As we set strategic goals and vision around delivering ultimate customer experience, we fail to execute the strategies as we have still not been able to pull together a well defined approach and framework defining roles, metrics and processes with an ability to track customer experience KPIs (Key Performance Indicators).

Sam Walton clearly articulated the importance of the customer, "There is only one boss. The customer. And he can fire everybody in the company from the chairman on down, simply by spending his money somewhere else." This simple but powerful statement states the single most important constituent in our company's performance is our customer.

According to Bernd Schmitt, CEM is the process of strategically managing a customer's entire relationship with a product or company. It moves beyond the outcome-based concepts of customer satisfaction and loyalty and focuses on the *process* a company engages to develop customer knowledge, align the organization, design the customer experience, and continuously *innovate*. CEM provides the key principles and frameworks for orchestrating the total customer experience.

In one of my previous engagements with a Fortune 500 Consumer Electronics company, the CIO posed us a challenge. In the CIO's own words *"We are rated either number one or two in product-quality research in most of the product segments in which we're present. Whereas we are rated number eleven in customer satisfaction research compared to our peers. While we stand out in product quality as the best, we are unable to leverage our engineering excellence in delivering customer value and satisfaction. We have seen declining revenues and profitability while our competition is eating into our market share. What can we do to achieve the desired improvement in customer satisfaction as it is hurting our entire business performance and we have recorded one of the lowest revenues during current year?"* From televisions and cameras to laptops and audio devices, this company has more than 50 product lines and has been rated as an innovator and known for its high-end quality. This situation brings out a common problem seen across most enterprises—why does our product or service excellence in itself does not ensure high level of customer experience?

It would be very relevant to present some of the findings from the study we conducted on the business- and technology-related challenges. Some of the business challenges that were identified in this scenario were:

- **Quality:** Inability to track defects and product failures beyond call centers all the way to product service and engineering groups.
- **Service Operations:** Turnaround time for the average customer request was much higher than industry benchmark. The processes for customer returns

and warranty claims management were in chaos. Repeat requests for parts and service were a direct reflection of existing inefficiencies.

- **Call Center Management:** Percentage of "first-call resolution" was very low with a high rate of abandoned calls. "Call waiting" and "average call" durations were much above the industry average.
- **Parts Management:** Huge back-order on parts requests. The inventory management was not aligned to the service center.

From a technology perspective the challenges identified were:

- **Redundant Data:** Diverse systems of records created silos of customer data and services data. Majority of the customer requests needed the Call center operator to access a minimum of 4 back end systems. The call center operator's ability to interpret the information and generate solutions for a customer's query or problem was very limited.
- **Disparate Systems:** Lack of integration between systems handling parts and model details, inventory status, customer details and product registration details., Sales data and service data were completely isolated. Reports were often inaccurate mostly due to legacy data integration issues.
- **Lack of Collaboration:** Multiple surveys were conducted by different teams and systems. For example, phone surveys, chat surveys, repair surveys and support surveys were not synthesized to create one single version of the truth for executive decision-makers.
- **Poor Knowledge Management:** Lack of a single Knowledge management system caused delay in accessing the right support information from manuals, bulletins or specifications.
- **No Process Management Capabilities:** Lack of event processing, workflow automation, alerts, notifications, work allocation, dynamic correspondence, BAM (Business Activity Monitoring), and tracking of KPIs. the process for tracking technician availability to schedule appointments for Fields Service was not in place. There was no system in place to measure efficiency and productivity of service teams.
- **No Portals/User Friendly Web Interface**: Corporate websites provided only the basic information about company and products but lacked any self-service capabilities for end-users around service or purchases.

This scenario might present an extreme case of inefficiency when measured against the standards of some of the companies who are on the leading edge of customer experience management. But this case presents a comprehensive set of parameters which influence the customer experience. Although this scenario is from a manufacturing segment, it is no different from a wealth management firm or a retail bank or a life insurance and annuities carrier. We can map these situations to any industry with multiple customer touch points.

James Richardson, CMO at Cisco Systems, summarizes the level of seriousness every company needs to have around CEM, "Orchestrating the total customer experience is a very realistic and worthy goal, and one we strive to achieve at Cisco. For example, we work closely with our customers through all stages of a network implementation—plan, design, implement, and operate. And customers buy our products and services both directly from us, as well as though many other routes to market. We couldn't provide the level of customer satisfaction that our customers expect if we did not orchestrate our marketing around the *total experience.*"

BUSINESS CASE FOR CUSTOMER EXPERIENCE TRANSFORMATION (CET)

Most enterprises have made significant investments in their customer service departments and activities. Hence it is very difficult to initiate a transformation as it calls for a fundamental change in the organization, processes and systems. The biggest hurdle to CET is the resistance to change. CET is about making a fundamental change to the portfolio of customer experience activities and investments in alignment with the corporate strategy.

According to 2009 Customer Experience Management Benchmark Study by the Strativity Group, 48 percent of the surveyed companies increased investments in customer experience over the past three years by 10 percent driving a 60 percent average improvement in satisfaction scores. Such statistics are easy to reference after the fact.

How do we create a business case and what areas do we need to address while calculating the ROI from a CET program? The below diagram is a high level representation of parameters which help drive customer experience programs.

Figure 1: Business Drivers for a CET Initiative

Let us start with some fundamental questions that will determine why we should make investments in CET:

- Are we able to measure KPIs such as customer retention rate, ability to up-sell/cross-sell, customer loyalty, customer satisfaction across all product lines and service lines, and new customer acquisition rate?
- Are we able to capture and convert customer feedback and responses into meaningful actions?
- What is the competition doing in terms of branding, customer acquisition, and benchmarks around key customer services? Are our competitors growing faster than us? Are we losing customers to competition?
- How efficient are our call centers in terms of various call metrics and operational efficiencies? Are they inundated with customer and product data and information? How much time is spent in accessing content and data?
- Are we using the latest Web 2.0 technologies to enhance customer experience and to collaborate internally and externally? Are we able to influence customer experience directly and indirectly?
- Do we have any metrics on customer experience across each channel and are we able to track the same kind of metrics across all channels?

- Today's customers want 24x7 access to services irrespective of time zone or geography. What levels of self service are we providing vis-à-vis our competition?
- Have we segmented our customer base and defined a strategy addressing the service levels and positioning targeted for each segment? Is this built into our systems and do we collect data which can help us drill down into each micro segment to present customers with targeted services and products? Are we able to make our customers feel that they are being treated as individuals with tailored data, content and information offered at their finger tips?
- Do we have clearly-defined processes driving all aspects of customer interaction and fulfillment? Are the processes aligned to overall strategy and are able to deliver measurable outcomes.

BUSINESS FRAMEWORK FOR CUSTOMER EXPERIENCE TRANSFORMATION

According to Forrester's "Customer Service Innovation and Assessment Report" almost 50 percent of respondents said that an obstacle to improving customer experience was the lack of defined customer experience management processes. The overall Customer Experience Transformation (CET) framework is based on our ability to tie business strategy to customer service goals, measuring outcomes and continuously optimizing to bridge the gaps. This is described in the framework below.

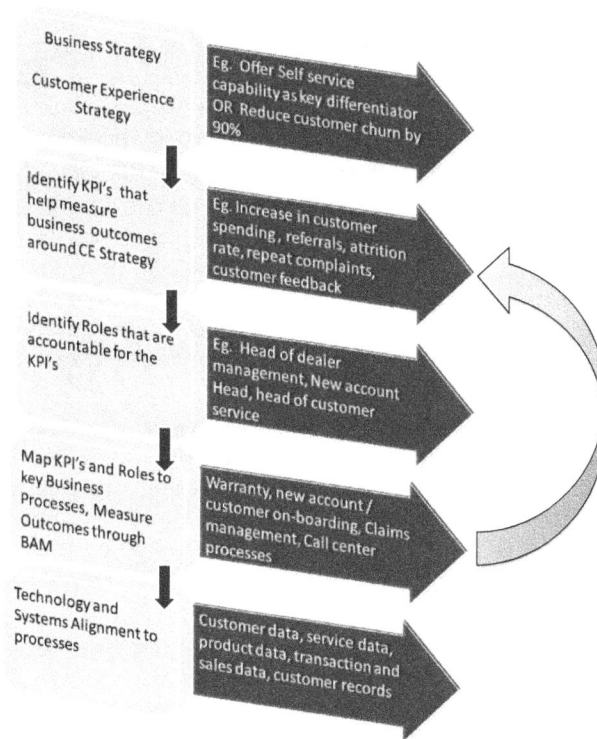

Figure 2: Business Blueprint for CET

CET stands out compared to CRM or other customer service activities in its strategic importance and long-term if not permanent impact. It is also a more holistic approach spanning different organizational elements therefore requiring a fundamental change. The key elements of such an initiative are elaborated below:

- **Define the Customer Experience Strategy:** Any CET initiative begins with the definition of the overall strategy and business goals around customer experience management. A clear articulation of the CE strategy sets the overall direction.
- **Define KPIs:** The next step is to identify the key metrics that help us track customer experience, i.e., data points related to transactions, operations and processes that are critical from a customer experience standpoint as well as their larger impact on product and service quality, branding and positioning, channel productivity, revenues, and profitability.
- **Define Roles:** We need to map roles to KPIs at points of customer interaction and larger levels of aggregation. Key roles in product development/management, distribution, pricing and promotions need to be identified and assigned KPIs. Only then we can reap the benefits from a sophisticated CEM system.
- **Define Processes:** We need to define the key processes at every level of customer touch points that will help trigger follow-on activities based on customer behavior and synthesize people and systems in a seamless flow. These processes must enable automation across all customer service activities and ensure measurement of relative performance through BAM (business activity monitoring) dashboards. Process automation also drives uniform communication across stakeholders and the integration of systems to eliminate redundant data access and entry by operators.
- **Align Technology Investments:** Investments in technology systems need to be aligned to the above parameters. One of the biggest hindrances to customer experience improvement is the rigidity of legacy systems. Also how we leverage leading edge technologies such as Web 2.0 and collaboration tools, portals, content management systems and search engines, determines our ability to deliver best-in-class customer experience.

Forrester analyst Natalie L. Petouhoff states, "Customer service drives brand perception, customer loyalty, and repurchase probability, and it's a core element in an enterprise's competitive strategy. Customer service is the last differentiating competitive factor with price and product no longer driving customer preferences." This message conveys the importance of *total customer experience* in all stages of the customer life cycle.

As we have seen in the example provided in the previous section, a company's fortunes are driven by its customers. As market dynamics change and competition evolves there is a constant threat of customer churn. Every company needs to measure customer experience, align business goals to these metrics, define roles and processes that help in optimizing the customer experience, and build systems that support the overall framework.

CET is about driving fundamental change in the way we manage customers across multiple touch points through all phases of the customer life cycle. As we continue to measure the customer experience and benchmark those metrics, we need to align the processes bringing together people, data, systems and content. Business processes are the underlying linkages between people, systems, and external entities like suppliers and customers. The best CET programs integrate strategy, organizational structure, people, processes, and technology in a holistic approach.

A conceptual representation of such a solution (applicable to multiple industries) is shown below:

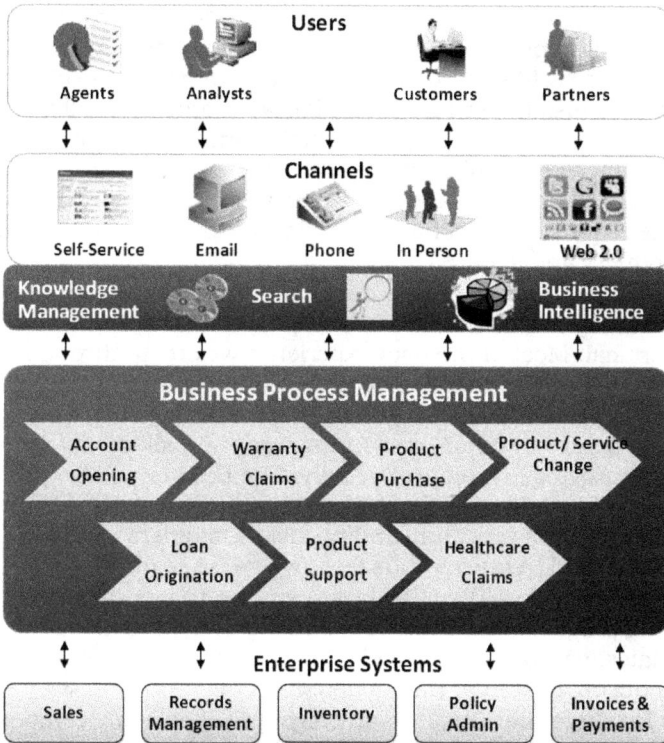

Figure 3: Conceptual Framework for a CEM solution

This diagram depicts the need for a cohesive approach where customer experience is delivered through multiple channels but the underlying data, processes and information layers are seamless and unified. Enabling unified delivery channels with a set of collaboration, knowledge management and search tools helps users with information delivered per specific context thus enabling self-service capabilities. The BPM layer orchestrates the overall dynamics between data, process, KPIs, roles and systems. Lastly we need to wrap the back-end systems with unified data entry and access layers so as to eliminate redundant data entry and insulate the users from being forced to access multiple legacy systems for each transaction.

TECHNOLOGY CONVERGENCE & ROLE OF BPM

One of the biggest challenges facing CET is that no single technology or product vendor can help achieve all customer experience functions. By its very definition, CET programs are meant to bring diverse systems, people and processes together toward the achievement of customer-related goals. Hence, we need to conceive a solution spanning multiple technology products bringing together the best of breed capabilities offered by each stack.

Let us explore the key components in an integrated CEM solution which would address the various topics we have discussed thus far:

- **Integrated Portals** for Customers and Agents/Call Center Operators: The role of a Portal is to aggregate information from multiple sources. Portals must offer an ability to personalize and bring in context sensitive information in order to make customers feel a sense of relationship with the portal. The portal must also act as a work management interface where the customer/operator will carry out all kinds of requests be it for online purchases or information request or complaints and claims. Embedding the collaboration features such as Chat and IM on portals and agent desktops can help in productivity improvements and real time resolutions of cases increasing overall "call resolution" rates. It is also important for the Portal to provide intelligent search on data and content scattered across multiple sources to improve work-completion times and achieve customer delight. Customer empowerment is the crux of satisfaction; the more we empower customers to manage their own service requests, the better perception we are creating in terms of our brand, products and services.

- **Business Process Management:** As we automate various processes around customer management and call center operations the role of the BPM layer becomes critical. Most of the user experience we create through portals and self-enablement will be based on workflow and process automation sourced in the back-end. The BPM layer provides Process and Rules automation to integrate diverse legacy systems, measuring work and allocating work dynamically thus improving overall productivity. The BPM layer also provides the ability to keep customers in the loop as the work progresses through dynamic correspondence thus providing audit trails. Customers can view the real time status of their work requests thus feeling a sense of intimacy and transparency from the provider. The BPM layer can also trigger departmental and customer facing processes addressing product quality, logistics issues, supply chain updates, campaigns, market research and surveys based on events generated during customer interactions.
- **Business Intelligence:** Business Intelligence (BI) is a key component of any CEM solution, invaluable in terms of gaining customer insight, triggering customer interactions and continuously optimizing marketing investments.

From a customer insight standpoint, BI tools provide quality customer data, predict customer behavior and profile/segment customers as outlined below:
- *Data integration* Pulls data from any source and ensures customer information is organized as a single source of truth and provides 360 degree view of customer.
- *Web behavior tracking* helps get the most out of e-business channels and improves the effectiveness of marketing campaigns.
- *Forecasting* helps in trend analysis and decision making.
- *Analytics* provides descriptive and predictive insights through response models, churn analysis, customer value and profitability analysis.
- In terms of helping manage customer interactions and optimizing investments to generate the highest ROI, BI tools help in:
- *Campaign management* helps send the right offers to the right customers across the right channels.
- *E-mail/mobile marketing* provides large-scale multimedia messaging capabilities, including e-mail and SMS within single-channel or multi-channel marketing campaigns.
- *Event trigger alerts* inform most opportune time to reach out to customers.

Here, it is relevant to mention a quote from Forrester analyst Connie Moore published in internetnews.com, "I think the BI vendors are missing the boat on process. They don't really understand process because they focus on analysis of data. Operational data, tactical data, strategic data; the data needs to be put into action. The BI vendors don't understand the whole process world. BPM vendors are increasingly realizing they need to improve their business processes, rules and event management with greater intelligence or analytics capabilities. As BPM goes beyond process, some BPM vendors are cleverly adding integration with collaboration, portals and BI."

This quote sums up the foundation of convergence solutions proposed in this section.

- **Web 2.0:** Web 2.0 is a broad set of technologies and concepts including wikis, blogs, mash-ups, and social networking sites that are dramatically changing the way we are using the Internet. Web 2.0 technologies have led to a sharp increase in community-based collaboration and a proliferation of social media activities. At an individual company level, we are no longer able to direct the customer opinion as there are much larger influences at play through social media. How companies leverage communities and blogs, participate and influence the flow of discussions, and trigger back-end processes based on information captured through social media are key to a sustained customer experience strategy. The customer-facing portals need to have Web 2.0 features in order to achieve stickiness with the viewers inducing them to buy products/services and contribute to surveys.

- **ECM, Collaboration, Search:** As we collect and store volumes of customer content and records, our ability to organize this content and make it accessible across multiple channels is very important. We also need to incorporate search engines across the channels to have seamless access to these records and content. Collaboration tools such as IM and Chat can be crucial in keeping customers engaged with contact centers.

We see five key components to any CEM solution. How well we bring these components together through a seamless business architecture and design is the key to CET. The next generation CEM solution must have all five components and provide a seamless ability to manage the customer across all channels with a single set of KPIs. A high-level solution is represented below.

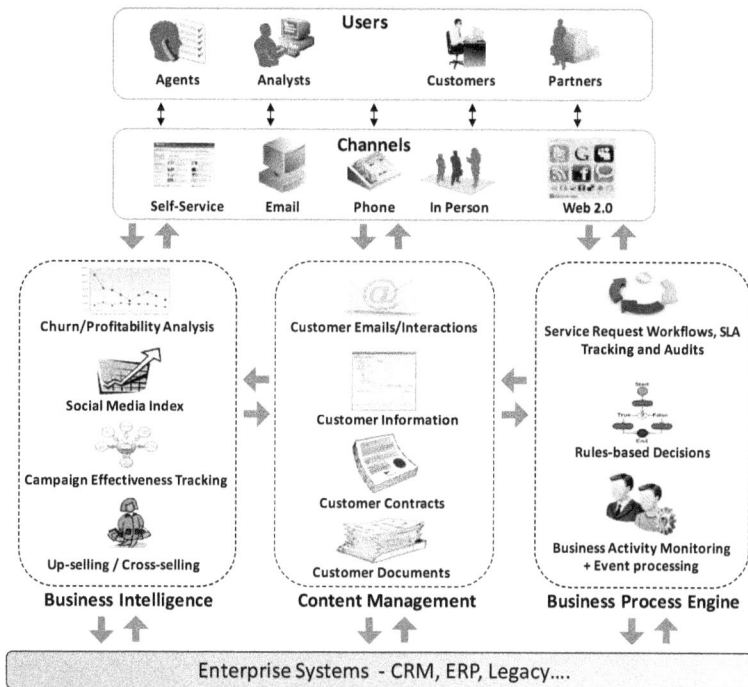

Figure 4: Technology blueprint for a CEM solution

An underlying assumption behind this solution is that we are not replacing any of the core transactional systems which have been built over the years.

SUMMARY AND KEY TAKEAWAYS

Having discussed various aspects of a typical CET initiative in detail, here is a summary of key takeaways:

- Start your CET initiative with the definition of your overarching customer strategy.
- Define and weight your metrics according to outcomes desired. Remember, if you can't measure it you can't manage it.
- Make sure that all roles and KPIs are identified and communicated to key stakeholders.
- There is no single technology that meets all CEM requirements. Assess the technology landscape and plan a solution as described in Figure 4.
- View CET as not a one-time project but an ongoing initiative. Constant measurement and alignment to goals and changing business conditions are key to sustained success.

CET is a widely applicable topic across all industries. The changing business dynamics has created so many uncertainties. Our customers are the last thing we can afford to lose sight of. Inability to manage our customers, forecast customer trends and influence broader perceptions can mean a debacle for every enterprise. Let us realize this fact and put concentrated effort to manage our most important assets; OUR CUSTOMERS!

REFERENCES

Forrester's "Customer Service Innovation Framework and Self-Assessment" by Natalie L. Petouhoff, Ph.D.

Gartner webinar on "Customer Experience Management : Raising Customer Satisfaction, Loyalty and Advocacy" By Ed Thompson & Jim Davies

http://www.sas.com : Product white papers

Business Intelligence and BPM: Merging? Article by Clint Boulton

"Customer Experience Optimization" article by David Jacques

"Customer Experience—The Marriage of Marketing and Business Process" article by Victor Howard.

Financial Crisis Front Line: SNS Bank

Eric D. Schabell and Stijn Hoppenbrouwers

ABSTRACT

SNS Bank, Netherlands, has made a strategic decision to empower its customers on-line by fully automating its business processes. The ability to automate these service channels is achieved by applying Business Process Management (BPM) techniques to existing selling channels. Both the publicly available and internal processes are being revamped into full scale Straight Through Processing (STP) services. This extreme use of online STP is the trigger in a shift that is of crucial importance to cost-effective banking in an ever turbulent and changing financial world. The key elements used in implementing these goals continue to be Free Open Source Software (FOSS), Service oriented architecture (SOA), and BPM. In this paper we will present an industrial application describing the efforts of the SNS Bank to make the change from traditional banking services to a full scale STP and BPM driven bank that can survive on the Financial Crisis front lines.

INTRODUCTION

The Dutch SNS Bank is making a strategic move to automate its support and selling channels to provide its customers with modern on-line services. Realizing that it will take more than just an on-line web shop to excel in the financial world, the bank has also moved to automate many internal processes. The key elements used in implementing these goals are full scale Straight Through Processing (STP) [1] and Business Process Management (BPM) [2].

In this paper we present the efforts made to change from traditional banking services to a full scale STP and BPM driven financial institution during the current world wide Financial Crisis. We begin in *Full Scale STP* by clarifying what the various concepts mean to us and why they are of importance to the future of SNS Bank. In the section *A case study* we take a closer look at the STP Purchasing project. We will provide some insights into the application of STP with BPM within an open source development environment, discuss the component architecture, take a look at our process modeling steps, examine how we utilized customer testing, and conclude with an overview of some general empirical data. We will present our experiences, both good and bad, in dealing with a large BPM implementation. As can be expected, there will always be challenges to be met when such an expansive shift in strategy is being implemented, and in *Observations* we start our tour of the issues encountered in the project. *The benefits* section will discuss the brighter side, outlining the positive impact that this project has had in the technical realm. This will leave the reader with a good idea of the challenges involved, hopefully helping in implementing other industry BPM applications. Finally, in *Moving ahead* we will look at applying the lessons we have learned to survival on the Financial Crisis front lines.

FULL SCALE STP

The application of STP with BPM is not a new phenomenon in the financial industry, with other banks having reported some success with relatively straight forward on-line financial solutions [3, 4]. Some are even dreaming of taking on the more challenging processes within the banking industry, such as mortgage processes [5]. The difference between these types of solutions and the one presented here concerns complexity. We offer the following definitions:

Definition 1 (Business Process Management) Business Process Management concerns aligning business processes to the customers want and needs by applying relevant methods, tools and solutions.

This is a simple and straight-forward look at how we intend to apply BPM within our organization.

Definition 2 (Straight Through Processing) Processing a business transaction automatically, without requiring people to be involved in the process. The purpose of STP is to create efficiencies, eliminate mistakes, and reduce costs by having machines instead of people process business transactions.

This definition is in line with most of the definitions we have encountered in the financial world [6, 7, 8]. It will work fine as a beginning definition of how we construct our processes, but we need to refine it a bit for real world financial business processing.

Definition 3 (Full Scale STP) A straight through process (STP) implementation that requires the solution to encompass a wide range of system integration and will include human tasks which embody the complex decision making that automation either cannot legally implement, or is precluded by technical limitations.

We exclude cost as a factor to determining if an implementation is full scale STP or not. We feel that cost, in terms of time, money, or other value risk, is a business concern that is not related to complexity, but rather to some current operational or environmental situation (i.e. budgets, deadline pressures, politics, environment, etc.).

The drive to push for full scale STP with BPM is multifaceted. The leading goals are cost reduction, manpower reduction in business processes, removing potential (human) mistakes, and channel independent processing. Users should experience such processes as transparent, quick, simple, directly usable, and should be able to complete their task in one attempt.

SNS Bank is targeting effective and efficient processing where as much human intervention as possible has been removed. The customer will be kept informed at crucial process steps, communication always being an important factor in customer experience. For the cases that are exceptions or fall out of STP processing, there will be clear and predefined processes to ensure expeditious handling. Last but not least, the entire communication process is as paperless as can be. This encapsulates the SNS Bank's idea of full scale STP processing.

As Heckl and Moormaan [9] concluded "...long term success cannot be achieved without the development of new business ideas, innovative products and services, and customer retention." We believe that such success can only be achieved if BPM techniques are fully integrated. Full scale STP with BPM will continue to be expanded on and implemented throughout the range of products, sales channels, and business processes that affect both customer and customer support. We believe that the time for full scale STP with BPM is now.

A CASE STUDY

In the beginning of 2007 the first full scale STP project at SNS was launched, with the goal of putting four new savings products on-line at the start of 2008. This project is known as *STP Purchasing* and will provide us with a case for closer examination of full scale STP with BPM. This section will present the component architecture, take a look at how the process was modeled, show how customer testing was used to verify the solution, and provide some empirical data of the results.

Overview

The goals for this project were for a customer to be asked as few questions as possible during the purchasing process, that the entire process would be completed within a maximum of five clicks in the on-line website, and that the customer would be kept informed during all crucial steps in the process with clear, directed communication relevant to a specific purchasing process. A further desire was to maximize paperless communication with the customer. It was essential to maintain as short a processing time as possible, with processes involving human action stages causing no more than one-day delay. It should be volume independent, deliver reusable processes, reusable services, be multi-label, and multi-channel. Above all, the project should provide a full scale STP solution with a maximum degree of automation.

With our definition of full scale STP [definition 3] in mind, we already assume that the process is not free from human tasks. There are several instances in which we could not avoid having human interaction as part of this process. The resulting challenges will be discussed in more detail later on in this section. The project resulted in a general end-to-end purchasing process, initially for savings products, and a new process for document scanning and storage. A purchasing request database implementing the data model for each processing request was delivered along with a BPM process flow; a web front end was created for the initial savings products and the relevant SOA services. A new department was created, called *Process Management Evaluation and Processing*. Total project IT investment was 14,000 hours.

Architecture

The SNS implementation environment for full scale STP with BPM is one of pure Java [10]. The emphasis is on building solutions within the bank's own IT department, making use of Free Open Source Software (FOSS) where possible, achieving reusability of existing applied solution components, and using best of breed components when forced to shop outside of our existing code base.

There was a shift in component strategy in 2004 from three main commercial suppliers to one where FOSS components are preferred when possible. Open source is now quite pervasive throughout the solution architecture of all SNS projects. Furthermore, the development environment and tooling used to implement the solution consists of almost only FOSS. This is outside the scope of this paper and will therefore be excluded from further discussion. The component architecture as shown in Figure 1 (UML package-style visualization) is a very generic and high-level view. We will discuss the components as shown, from left to right.

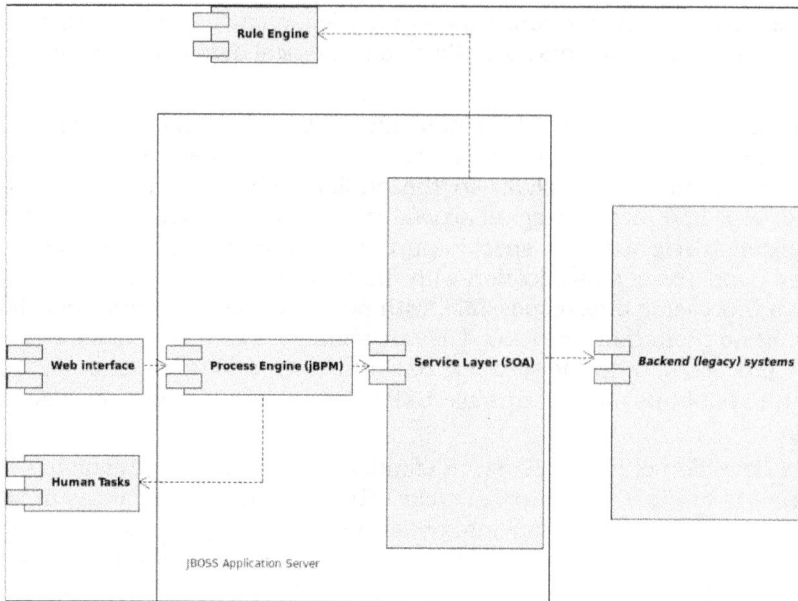

Figure 1: STP Purchasing architecture

Web interface

The entry point for any full scale STP application is the web interface as seen by the customer in the on-line banking website. This is a Java based website that makes use of a content management system. In the STP Purchasing project it provides the user with the option to apply for one of four saving products. If placed, a request is gathered together with user information, verified through various web services, and then using a web service it is deposited into the *Request Database*.

One might expect that a request is submitted directly to the jBPM process engine, but each request is put into a database to ensure that no single customer request is every lost due to the process engine begin unavailable. This is required by a banking regulation that ensures that no risks are taken with customer-submitted information. We must and will always be able to trace and audit every single step in the chain of events from customer request to product delivery. This small design step has been left out of the component diagram as it happens underwater and is of little importance to industries where intensive risk protection is not needed; we mention this in the interest of completeness.

Human tasks

A human action interface was implemented to provide functional administrators with the ability to deal with tasks as they drop out of the automated process for various reasons. Furthermore, Service Centre employees provide input to the system through another interface with the document monitoring section of the process flow. Communication with the customer can require for a human task to be performed, such as customer's reply to questions which needs to be judged on completeness, correctness, and validity. This input to the jBPM process flow causes pending processes to be triggered into their next stages, to be stopped, or to be restarted. The interfaces have been created in-house by the project development team.

Within the project process definition it is always possible to encounter problems, planned or not, that need human intervention to be solved. This intervention is called a human task, where the process is dumped into a task bucket for further action by an authorized person. We refer to the need to invoke human tasks as having the process *fall out* of the process flow. This fall out can then classified as either technical or functional. The first is often related to some error in processing a request within a process step, the latter is related to a problem in the application flow logic. When we look at full scale STP we are concerned with processes that by definition contain planned functional fall out points in their process descriptions.

STP Purchasing supplies a web-based Java interface that enables humans to manipulate the tasks that they have been authorized to view. This component makes use of web services in the SOA layer to retrieve and manipulate process data located in various locations. It is mostly concerned with the *Request Database* where we find the complete request data structure that is maintained during the process lifecycle. One example of a functional fall out is a planned review of the applying customer credit rating results. This process might legally require that more than one person must review the customer's rating results before approving them as new bank customers.

Rule engine

This is a non-FOSS component supplied by a third party which we access from STP with BPM projects for business rules. This allows the business entity to maintain their own rule set regarding their businesses unit within the financial organization. For example, within a savings product you will have various rules and regulations as to the various conditions that must be met before a customer can be allowed to purchase that specific product. These rules and regulations can change over time or due to a special offer on that product during a specific time frame. It is often a wish from the contracting business unit to be able to manipulate these rules and regulations without having to contact the software vendor (i.e. project team).

JBOSS: jBPM and Service Layer (SOA)

The application server is an open source component called JBOSS [11], from the JBOSS component family we have adopted the jBPM engine [12] and its process definition language (PDL) implemented in jPDL [13]. These are the main FOSS components in our project solution and are considered core components in the enterprise architecture.

The jBPM process engine is used for all BPM projects, so component selection was not an issue. The BPM process flows are defined by the information analyst together with the business customer for the application. It is a process involving workshops and use cases. It provides the lead developer of the project with a starting point, in the form of a process flow. This is mapped almost one-to-one into the process definition language, which delivers a jPDL file. The resulting process definition is used for matching nodes to business services. In most cases this again is a one-to-one mapping and the design of the services is the most time consuming part of the implementation. Should there be any technical details that call for adjustment to the flow, consultation ensues with the information analyst, and eventually with the business customer. Individual developers are then given technical designs based on use case realizations that allow them to integrate their implementations into the proper process steps.

The project was completed using only simple nodes that contain all business logic in plain Java. Basic service calls were combined in the Java code to achieve what later could be implemented as a more complex business service. There were no nodes implemented as actual wait states, where the process can wait for action from an external system. Our backend systems are not yet set up to trigger jBPM process instances to allow for real wait states. To facilitate wait states, a polling mechanism was used at points in the process were external systems need to be checked for completion of a task. For example, while waiting for a customer to correctly identify herself by returning a signed contract with a copy of a valid identification, the process will use a scheduler to periodically poll the backend system via a web service to determine if the identification has been completed. Once completion is detected, the scheduler triggers the process via a web service. Furthermore, there are the standard decision nodes, transitions, and human task nodes within the project's process implementation.

We have implemented a standard Service Oriented Architecture (SOA) [14], referred to in-house as our Service Oriented Architecture Layer (SOAL). Granularities of the services in this layer have been defined as basic services, business services, and some very simple composite business services (CBS) [15]. A basic service brings the existing transaction out of the backend system and makes it available through a web service. For example, to validate a postcode, the basic service *postcodeCheck* has been created to expose the backend mainframe transaction that checks if a given postcode is valid. The business services handle more complex processing that may consist of one or more basic services. One of the more complicated issues is that of allowing the existence of CBS's in our SOA layer. These are business services that can contain not only calls to basic services, but to other business services, if the business service being called is in the same classification category as the caller.

The SOA layer deploys web services with versions. If a new release of the SOA layer contains services with interface changes, then the version of the release will be increased. To support backwards compatibility, a total of three versions are maintained for production applications to use. This allows for applications to upgrade to the newer versions over time.

Backend systems

These systems can be anything in the wide variety that exists within our banking infrastructure: banking applications that provide and interface, external third party services, legacy systems, or some form of data storage like a data warehousing solution. It should be noted that these systems are always approached from our projects via the SOA layer in the form of a web service. We will provide the three most important backend systems that are used in STP Purchasing.

A *request database* was implemented for tracking each purchasing request as it migrates through the BPM process flow. This was the direct implementation of our purchasing request data model. As stated in context of the *web interface* and *human task* components, this database is filled with the initial request data, manipulated by the process as it migrates through the various steps, and directly affected when technical or functional fall out occurs. Access is arranged by a very specific service dedicated to accessing, reporting, and updating data in the database works for the web interface, the human task interface, and from inside the process itself.

Another important component in the backend is the *customer information system*, used to maintain all customer and prospect contact information. This is a marketing data pool and there is a specific service dedicated to accessing and updating the information kept here.

A central system in our backend network is a legacy COBOL mainframe. This is where the bank customers are managed and it is accessed via web services that make use of a Java communication layer. This layer bridges the gap between Java and COBOL mainframe functions which are provided when functionality is exposed from the mainframe.

Customer testing

From the very beginning of the project, customer input was sought. An initial proto-type was created for which four customers and four internal customer support personnel were invited to conduct usability testing in a controlled environment. These eight sessions were 90 minutes long, each dealing with a single respondent and a task assignment walk-through. The walk-through was done by the respondent with verbal communication accompanying all actions which were recorded by an observer sitting in a different room with a hidden view.

Even though it was a small usability test, it did provide relevant details which led to advice for the development team in the areas of information structure, interaction, navigation, content, graphical information, style, layout, and features. Our view is that any steps taken to improve customer satisfaction should be exploited to the fullest.

Another customer test took place before the project was released into production. It was a last test that the business users took to examine the entire project. The testing users were guided by a test leader during the earlier project iterations to develop functional stories. These were then set up in the databases to allow them to test actions on submitting new requests, handling functional fall out, schedulers, and other such actions as deemed necessary for project acceptance. This is a standard practice in our project release cycle and it remains a valuable feedback loop for finding functional problems before the project hits production status.

The running process

Empirical data providing results concerning running STP Purchasing in production since February 2008 is presented in Table 1. The numbers represent the total number of processes per month, with a rather large spike in the months starting in September 2008. This was the beginning of the worldwide Financial Crisis, which lead many Dutch citizens to spread their savings to different financial institutions.

Table 1: Production process overview – 2008/2009 monthly

Month	Requests
Feb	750
Mar	2750
Apr	2000
May	1200
Jun	1100
Jul	1500
Aug	850
Sep	4250
Oct	2250
Nov	1000
Dec	2340
Jan	3715
Feb	3210

Taking a look at Table 1, we can clarify some of the dips and peaks in the numbers. In February 2008 the project was released half way through the month, resulting in a low start number. It picked up steam and was pretty steady until August 2008, which we believe is due to the vacation period when most Dutch people tend to be on their holidays and away from computers. In September we see the explosion of interest due to the Financial Crisis, followed by a leveling of interest. At the end of

November 2008 the second set of five *deposito products* hit production. Logging shows us that the number gains for December 2008 to Feb 17th 2009 can indeed be attributed to the new *deposito products*, which were almost exclusively purchased. It should be noted that at the time of this publication, the numbers were climbing steadily each month. This could be attributed to the competitive interest rates being offered, by the worsening of the Financial Crisis, or a combination of both. More time will be needed to evaluate the eventual results and we plan to continue to track them during the remainder of the Financial Crisis.

Table 2: Status overview of customer processes

Status	Percentage
Completed on time	52%
Rejected for various reasons	8%
Human action (functional)	0.7%
Human action (technical)	0.3%
Currently in a fall out status	4%
In Document Monitoring	12%
Taken out of STP flow, completed by hand	23%

Another view of results is given in Table 2, which shows us percentages of the various statuses a process can be in. We must take into consideration that our metrics are limited and that we are only able to report on process totals. Even so, it is encouraging that the amount of functional and technical fallout that needs attention is both less than one percent of the total. Also encouraging is that over 50 percent of all processes are completing on time. The ones that do not complete on time and are listed in *Document Monitoring* tend to be waiting for customer response to documentation problems as previously discussed. We have a timer running that ensures a customer receives reminders several times. Should the customer not reply at all, we eventually abort the request. The category listing 23 percent of processes taken out of the engine and completed by hand needs more explanation. This feature was added to allow special cases to be handled in the original manner, by hand.

With only eight percent being rejected due to various reasons, it appears we are hitting the target audience and providing a process that is effective.

OBSERVATIONS

Not everything is as pretty as it seems and there are some technical issues remaining, at which we will take a closer look at here.

Technical challenges

There are some interesting technical challenges that need to be watched for future projects. They cover issues concerning BPM, business logic, and (business) service releases. A currently completing BPM reference implementation project [16] has taken a closer look at these challenges and has come up with a few solutions and suggested ways of dealing with them.

Starting with the BPM issues, we have spent much effort to move the business logic out of the BPM process engine and down into the architecture to the SOA layer. This keeps the BPM engine lean and mean, requiring a lot less testing during the deployment phases of a project. Once the BPM flow is working, tests are passing, handlers call the correct services, and the infrastructure to support all of this is available, then there is not really much looking back. The main focus is on searching out application problems that are contained in the SOA layer. Developers spend their time testing and maintaining the business logic in the services, where it belongs. The delivered BPM flow should be almost maintenance free.

Many of the problems that the developers encountered with BPM process definition designs as described by Brahe [3] were avoided in our process by keeping the process flow definition, creation, and modification out of the hands of the developers. Modeling took place at a higher level, with a small group containing information analysts, business representatives and the lead developer. This process led to a completed BPM process definition in the selected process definition language, but expression in that language happened only at the end of the modeling process. In future we would like to look into ways of more directly generating actual BPM process designs close to the chosen process definition language, together with the business.

Individual developers were able to concentrate more on working out the individual process steps (nodes and handlers) the given initial business service designs, test coverage, and documentation. This has worked well for us and we will continue to use this approach in the future.

Although there has been some literature on the use of SOA [17, 18], we have found that most of the issues it discussed were of little help when dealing with our own service construction. It seems that issues are often related to local conditions and infrastructure limitations. One complex issue arose in our environment: unreliable services due to all web service calls being implemented over the HTTP protocol [19]. The problem becomes even more complicated when the basic services, themselves mapping to single backend transactions, are unreliable. It is conceivable that a service call is made to some complex business service that makes use of several basic services, and that it fails somewhere in the processes of executing basic services. We have no ability to implement anything other than a functional rollback and often are not sure what state the backend systems are left in.

There are potential problems with any service releases in the SOA layer that migrate to a major version number. For example, all minor version number releases from v1.0 to v1.1 of a given service contain no interface changes. These are therefore backwards compatible and should continue to work with all previously written consumers of the service. For major version changes, such as v1.1 to v2.0, we are confronted with a service containing an interface change that might break existing consumers of that service.

Service granularity has started to become a problem with more and more projects attempting to make use of basic, business, and composite business services that they find in the SOA layer. We hope to spend more time on looking into composite business service issues and do some ground work with regard to guidelines for future projects.

A very sticky problem that has raised its ugly head is what to do with BPM process instances that are running when the new service release is planned. We are looking at our options at this time but have come up with the following strategy to provide a choice depending on the given situation:

1. Phase out older service versions as old process instances have completed
2. Build service converters that translate calls between different versions
3. Activate a new BPM process instance for each existing old process instance
4. Build a process converter that translates old processes into the new process definition (one time)
5. Human interaction to guide the process or complete the process flow

This is an integral part of our current SOA service release strategy and can be found in the internal SOA documentation.

A solution is currently being tested that provides a custom class loader for each individual jBPM process engine. This allows each deployed process definition to provide the exact service version for each service it uses. Different deployed processes can thus access any of the SOA layer deployed service versions, independent of each other. This will have a positive effect on testing phases when multiple processes can be deployed on a single jBPM process engine, thereby saving extra hardware resources. This solution will also allow older instances of a process to be run next to newer ones so that they can be phased out as mentioned above.

All contact between the process and internal systems is realized via web services. These calls are synchronous, but many of the backend systems are not. Many systems run in batch, which means that the web services provide transactions to functionality that can only report that the request has been received correctly. For example, a fictitious account is opened via a web service call, but this actually happens in a night batch run on the backend mainframe. The web service call will get the mainframe reply, *Account Opened*, but this process will not actually be completed until later. This indirectly means that web services can not be transactional or atomic in nature and a great effort is made in business service implementations to create as much of a functional roll back as can be achieved. More often than not, it means having to fall out of the process with a technical problem to be fixed by human hands.

At the time of this writing, a *state-proxy* is being implemented to allow for real wait states in the process definitions. When using a wait state, the business service call is done through our state-proxy. The process is then put into a wait state and the proxy handles the web service call, returning either an exception or the results. The state-proxy can then be expanded with extra plug-in like functions, such as dealing with service windows for known down time on backend systems running a batch, allowing for technical retires to services that can be offline for short periods of time, and dealing with standard exceptions. These plug-ins are on the drawing board for future implementation.

The scheduler discussed in above in the *Architecture* section is a point of concern. It does not scale well and in the future we will need to look into getting our backend systems to trigger on certain events. This should be possible in principle; the discussion is underway.

Another nice-to-have would be to remove the non-FOSS rule engine discussed in the *Architecture* section. We want to spend some time looking into the JBOSS rule engine in the coming year which seems to provide a solution that is integrated in our existing development tooling.

THE BENEFITS

As we have seen, the benefits of BPM are promising, based on the generic data collected in the deployed production process. A closer look at customer and development benefits will make it clear that much has been gained already.

Improving the customer experience

A key concept in the vision of this solution is that the customer must be central to the process. A customer centric business model is not new [9], but we feel that aligning the entire strategy to empower one's customers is breaking the mould. As strategic products are made available through full scale STP with BPM we are able to adjust easily to customer needs. Products and product lines can be introduced into existing business processes in a cost effective manner. The flexibility to combine extends beyond products, product lines, and selling channels to become a very effective tool to reach customer bases in a timely and personalized fashion.

Customer communication can be personalized and tailored to specific processes, products, and customers' personal needs as the data generated by their behavior within the processes is documented. There have been very positive reactions from customers with regards to the speed, quality, and the level of detail in communications.

Development process improvements

The initial STP Purchasing project has provided a starting point for the IT department to build on for future full scale STP with BPM projects. Lessons learned and best practices are being applied, resulting in some interesting improvements to the process.

To our initial surprise, BPM process definitions can be easily changed with a minimal impact on the development time. The work is not in the process definition, but in the business services and basic services in the underlying structure.

A standard way of implementing process nodes and testing has made this part of the development process much less critical. It is important to focus on what we call the *Happy Flow* during initial development. This is the backbone of the process flow which represents a positive test case that processes as expected. For example, we would focus in the STP Purchasing project on a single savings product being requested by a verified and known customer of the bank. This means that you do not have to deal with any exceptions during the initial run through your process implementation. The focus of the first iteration of development is to get this Happy Flow working. By providing a quick working Happy Flow, the business can be shown tangible progress in the project at an early stage.

With an ever growing base of BPM process definitions it is clear that the time to market for similar products is much quicker. We have projects with estimates ranging from one third to one half of the initial development hours put into STP Purchasing. This is quite a big improvement. One thing of note here would be that the development of business services should always be carefully considered, as they tend to be the focus point of complexity.

The initial process definitions as provided by the information analysts and business analysts are not in our process definition language. Much depends on the quality of this process flow model, but with some care and attention to this step it is not too much trouble to map the process flow model to our process definition language. The generated image of the flow is a very good communication tool with the business. No better way to let them see the business services and understand where the development time is spent. Bringing the business closer to the development team with regards to communication about the process flow has been a positive experience that we would like to see continued.

MOVING AHEAD

In this paper we presented the efforts of a Dutch bank at migrating from traditional banking services to a full scale STP with BPM driven financial institution during the current world-wide Financial Crisis. The components being used to realize the STP Purchasing project were described and some basic resulting empirical data were presented for evaluation. The issues and benefits were covered along with the challenges yet faced by the IT organization. The large shift in strategy has started to deliver the desired results and we expect these will continue to roll in as future full-scale STP with BPM projects are implemented.

The positive effects on customer interaction, improvements on accelerating product deployment, and more flexible product/customer support channels have energized some internal ideas about becoming a facilitator to external third party enterprises. Imagine a future where individual entrepreneurs would be able to open a banking store with complete full scale STP with BPM selling channels for products and services.

We hope that our experiences, lessons, and observations will be of value to the industry as a whole. This is a financial industry story as we experience it on the front lines, but it could be applied to many different situations to help you survive the current Financial Crisis.

REFERENCES

1. Khanna, A.: Straight Through Processing For Financial Services: The Complete Guide. Academic Press, Burlington, MA. (Nov 2007)
2. van der Aalst, W.M.P., Hofstede, and A.H.M, Weske,M: Business Process Management: A Survey. In: van der Aalst, W.M.P., Hofstede, A.H.M., and Weske, M. (eds) BPM 2003, LNCS, vol. 2678, pp. 1–12. Springer, Heidelberg (2003)
3. Brahe, S.: BPM on Top of SOA: Experiences from the Financial Industry. In: Alonso, G., Dadam, P., and M.Rosemaan (eds) BPM 2007, LNCS 4714, pp. 96–111, Springer, Heidelberg (2007)
4. Guerra, A.: Bloomberg Aims To Simplify Straight-Through Processing. On: Information-Week, On http://www.informationweek.com/817/bloomberg.htm (18 Dec 2000)
5. Strickland, R., Aach, D.: Getting to straight-through processing: in theory, there is a way to deliver faster and better service in the mortgage lending business. On: BNet Business Network, http://findarticles.com/p/articles/mi_hb5246/is_/ai_n29277448 (Feb 2006)
6. The Free Dictionary, http://encyclopedia2.thefreedictionary.com/Straight+Through+Processing (10 Feb 2009)
7. Answers.com, http://www.answers.com/topic/straight-through-processing (10 Feb 2009)
8. Investopedia, http://www.investopedia.com/terms/s/straightthroughprocessing.asp (10 Feb 2009)
9. Heckl, D., Moormann, J.: Matching Customer Process with Business Processes of Banks: The Example of Small and Medium-Sized Enterprises as Bank Customers. In: Alonso, G., Dadam, P., and M.Rosemaan (eds) BPM 2007, LNCS 4714, pp. 112–124, Springer, Heidelberg (2007)
10. Java Technology. 18 March 2008, http://java.sun.com (19 March 2008)
11. Jboss.org: Community Driven. http://labs.jboss.com (19 March 2008)
12. jBPM Overview. http://labs.jboss.com/jbossjbpm/jbpm overview (19 March 2008)
13. Welcome to jBPM jPDL. http://labs.jboss.com/jbossjbpm/jpdl (19 March 2008)
14. Erl, T.: Service Oriented Architecture: Concepts, Technology and Design. Prentice-Hall, Englewood Cliffs (2005)
15. Neuman, S.: Composite Business Services. IBM Global Business Services, http://www-935.ibm.com/services/us/index.wss/offering/gbs/a1027243 (25 October 2008)
16. Schabell, E., Benckhuizen, J.: Software Architecture Document – jBPM Reference Project. SNS Bank IT, s-Hertogenbosch (2008)
17. Mahajan, R.: SOA and the Enterprise – Lessons from the City. In: IEEE International Conference on Web Services (ICWS'06), pp. 939–944, IEEE Computer Society, Los Alamitos (2006)
18. Acharya, M., Kulkarni, A., Kuppili, R., Mani, R., More, N., Narayanan, S., Patel, P., Schuelke, K.W., Subramanian, S.N.: SOA in the Real World - Experiences. In: Benatallah, B., Casati, F., Traverso, P. (eds) ICSOC 2005, LNCS, vol. 3826, pp. 437–4449, Springer, Heidelberg (2005)
19. HTTP – Hypertext Transfer Protocol. 27 Feb 2008, http://www.w3.org/Protocols (19 March 2008)

Intelligent, Automated Processes: Embedding Analytics in Decisions

James Taylor

The challenge of putting BI to work in business processes is that reports and dashboards only work in manual processes. If the process is automated, if straight through processing is called for, then the analytics required are different. Embedding these analytics in rules-based decisions is the ideal way to analytically enhance these processes and build intelligent, automated processes.

BUSINESS INTELLIGENCE AND BUSINESS PROCESS

There is a clear and obvious synergy between Business Intelligence (BI) and Business Process Management (BPM).

BI can use BPM

BI helps us understand what is happening in our business, what our results are, how well we are doing. If we are using BPM to define and manage our business processes then clearly information about our processes should be included in this analysis. We can consider the number of times a process executes, which steps are involved in each execution and how long things take—all of these are data about how our business is operating.

BPM can use BI

BPM helps us structure and manage the work that must be performed in our business. Often the tasks we need to perform, or how those tasks are carried out, are dependent on the current state of the business. The analysis of the state of our business using BI can and should be an input to these tasks. For instance, information about past customer orders or the frequency with which a particular supplier misses deadlines drives behavior in specific tasks.

BI is particularly helpful for Decisions

BI is particularly helpful to a certain subset of the tasks within our business processes-decisions. When we must decide how to treat a customer, what the risk of a particular supplier being late or how likely a particular approach is to work for a particular transaction, BI provides insight and information to help us do that.

BI and BPM can and do complement each other and organizations that adopt both approaches and technologies and use them together can gain significantly from the synergies inherent in these two closely related areas.

THE CHALLENGES OF AUTOMATED PROCESSES

When it comes to automated processes, however, there are challenges in combining BI and BPM. In an automated process, where the objective is straight through processing, the tasks or activities in our process are handled by computers, by systems, not by people. Herein lies the challenge as BI products and approaches focus on the presentation of information to people so they can use that information effectively. A dashboard, for instance, that allows a manager to see the status of their department or a report detailing last month's sales for a sales manager. With no people involved, automated processes have no obvious home for BI. There is no-one to watch the dashboard, no-one to read the report.

Automated processes need insight too

Yet the need for applying insight about our business is real and compelling. Just as people add intelligence to a manual process by using information to make better, more intelligent, decisions so an automated process must be informed by what we know. We need to take what we know about how our business operates, by what has worked or not worked in the past and the current state of the business and apply this business insight in the context of our automated processes.

To do this we must address three critical issues:

1. We must understand exactly what decisions are being made in our process.
   Computers are much more literal than people so much greater precision in definition is essential

2. We must be able to turn our data into insight that can be consumed by a computer.
   Traditional BI representations are aimed at people so something different is required.

3. We must be able to define the actions to be taken, and the constraints on those actions, so that the computer can act not just "understand." We need the process to keep moving, it cannot wait for a person to take action, so the computer must be able to act on its own.

DECISIONS AND PROCESSES

Building intelligent, automated processes requires that we understand the decisions in our processes. These decisions give us the points of control that we need and the places where insight might make a difference.

What is a decision?

Whether made by a person or a computer, a decision is a selection, a choice, made from a range of possible options. It might be a selection from Yes/No, from a list of products or even from a numeric range. A decision also involves taking action not just adding to what is known. It is not enough to find out something new or to create new knowledge; we must act on it if what we are doing is to be considered a decision. Decisions are also typically made after some consideration, after some analysis. Making a decision is a task, an activity within our process not just a branch or gateway within it.

Different types of decisions

Decisions are embedded in every kind of process and can be strategic, tactical or operational. Strategic decisions are the responsibility of the executive suite and are typically one-off decisions that make a significant difference to the overall direction of the organization. Tactical decisions are about managerial control, setting short term and local policies within a strategic framework. It is the last group —operational decisions—that is critical when it comes to automated processes.

> ✓ *Understand the decisions that matter to your business. Consider a decision audit to see what strategic, tactical and operational decisions you have that make a difference to your business processes. A broad but shallow understanding of your decisions will help you focus your effort.*

Automated processes are operational

Automated processes are high volume, high throughput processes or those requiring very fast turnaround times. Most organizations do not automate processes otherwise. While high performance, high volume processes may be constrained by tactical decisions or re-designed due to strategic ones, it is *operational* decisions that are embedded in them.

Little decisions add up

Operational decisions are low value, high volume decisions each of which impacts a single customer, a single transaction, a single instance of the process of which they are part. Just as an operational process can be automated by defining a standard way to execute the process and then doing so repeatedly, so can an operational decision be defined in a standard way and executed repeatedly in the context of such a process. While these decisions are individually low value, their cumulative value can be significant. For instance the individual decision about how to price a particular insurance policy might have a modest value but even a small insurance company makes many such decisions, ensuring that the overall value of the way we make the underwriting decision is significant.

Insight-driven operational decisions

Not every operational decision requires insight to make correctly or effectively. Deciding if a customer is eligible for a product, for instance, or deciding what the right discount is for a particular customer are operational decisions but they may be driven by a fixed set of business rules (of which more later). Two main categories of operational decisions do, however, require insight and these can be described as risk-based and opportunity-based operational decisions.

Risk-based operational decisions

In risk-based operational decisions, insight is required as to the risk of this particular transaction, this particular customer. For instance, an assessment of how likely this transaction is to be fraudulent given the history of other fraudulent transactions. This kind of decision includes decisions about fraud, about credit or perhaps about deliveries or suppliers where there is a risk of a negative outcome. Without insight, information, as to the likelihood of that negative outcome it is hard to make a good decision.

Opportunity-based operational decisions

Opportunity based decisions do not have a bad outcome but require that a choice is made between different degrees of opportunity. For instance, in marketing decisions, the wrong offer represents a lesser opportunity than the right offer. Insight into which choice will offer the greatest opportunity is not critical but will maximize the value of the decision being made.

> ✓ *Understand the link to performance management and metrics/KPIs*
> *One of the critical success factors for effective management of decisions, and effective use of analytic insight in decision making, is the linkage of decisions to the metrics and KPIs they impact. Without this understanding it is hard to tell a good decision from a bad one and hard therefore to determine what insight will help you make a good decision.*

Decision Services

To embed decisions in business processes we must develop decision services. A decision service is a service that answers business questions for other services, a service that makes decisions. Such a service should generally be stateless and have no side-effects (such as emails sent or databases being updated) so that any process that relies on the decision can use the decision service without fear of unintended consequences. Decision services have simple interfaces, allowing data to be passed in and returning simple information about the decision made and perhaps the way in which the decision was made.

EMBEDDING ANALYTICS IN DECISIONS

Once we have identified a risk-based or opportunity-based operational decision that we plan to implement as a decision service, we must determine how analytic insight can help us and what kind of analytic insight we need. Clearly visualizations, reports and dashboards are not going to be helpful to delivering insights to a decision service in an automated process. There are, after all, no eyes to look at these things. Instead we must develop the insight we need as something executable, something our automated process can use.

Different kinds of analytic insight

Analytics, analytic insight, covers a wide range of possible meanings. One of the simplest definitions of analytics is:

> Analytics simplify data to amplify its meaning.

This clearly states the purpose of analytics—to make it easier to get value, meaning, from data—but also covers a wide range of techniques and technologies. In particular it includes a range of analytics from business intelligence to descriptive analytics, predictive analytics and even optimization. It can be helpful to consider these different techniques as points on a spectrum, as shown in Figure 1 below.

As we move from left to right—from business intelligence to optimization—we increase the sophistication of the analytics involved. Descriptive analytic techniques or data mining creates segmentation, clustering, rules based on what happened or what worked (and did not work) in the past. Predictive analytic techniques turn uncertainty about the future into usable probabilities, giving us propensities or likelihoods for future behavior on the part of customers, parts, suppliers etc. Optimization and simulation help us manage the complex tradeoffs of a business, finding the most profitable or most effective scenario.

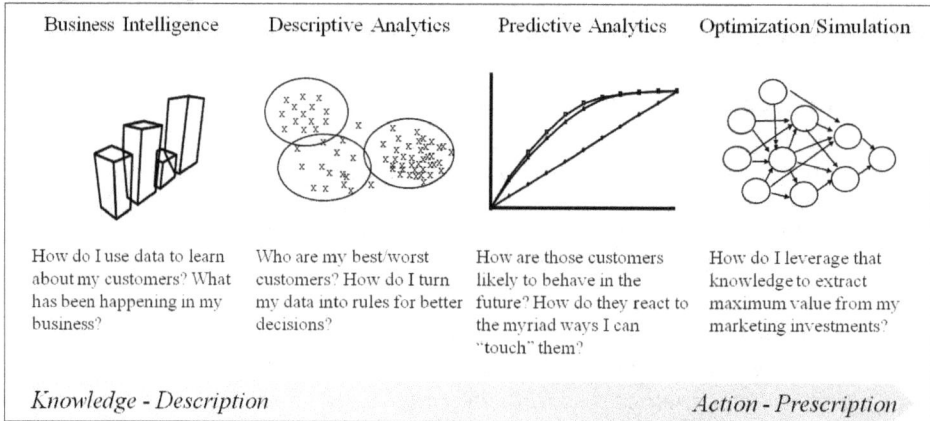

Business Intelligence	Descriptive Analytics	Predictive Analytics	Optimization/Simulation
How do I use data to learn about my customers? What has been happening in my business?	Who are my best/worst customers? How do I turn my data into rules for better decisions?	How are those customers likely to behave in the future? How do they react to the myriad ways I can "touch" them?	How do I leverage that knowledge to extract maximum value from my marketing investments?

Knowledge - Description   *Action - Prescription*

Figure 1: Increasingly sophisticated analytics

Embeddable analytics

More important for the creation of intelligent, automated processes than the increasing sophistication of these analytics techniques, is their embeddability. While business intelligence can be embedded into a process, as in-process dashboards or reports, business intelligence cannot be embedded into *automated* processes. As noted above, there is no-one to look at dashboards, no-one to interpret reports. What we need are techniques that allow someone to develop insight about our data outside a particular process instance and then embed that insight into an operational decision so that every process instance has access to it.

Instead of relying on the analytic skills of a dashboard or report user, we must create insight that can be used in an operational decision. The results of descriptive analytic techniques can often be embedded represented as a set of business rules or an equation. Predictive analytic models can be described using calculated attributes or equations. Optimization models can be represented as code also and can also drive operational decisions but this is less common in practice. The key tools and techniques for embedding analytics in decisions, and thus automated processes, are therefore those related to descriptive and predictive analytics.

Descriptive analytics

For example, consider data mining or descriptive analytic techniques that result in customer segments or clusters. The classic approach is to take information about customers, including something desirable such as profitability or loyalty, and see which properties of a customer (number of products purchased, time as customer, age etc) divide customers up into groups with a similar profitability or loyalty. Clustering or segmentation techniques create different groups and this can be visualized in a BI tool. But it can also be turned into a set of rules—customers with a specified combination of properties/values fall into this segment while customers with a different combination fall into this other segment. These rules can be executed by a decision service so that the decision itself—which customers to retain and how, for instance—can use the segmentation as part of its decision making process.

Predictive analytics

Predictive analytic techniques are also embeddable. Using predictive modeling techniques one can create a formula that predicts how likely something is to be true—how likely a customer is to churn, for instance, or how likely they are to accept a particular offer. These formulae or equations are hard to develop (at least they are hard to develop if we want them to be usefully predictive) but they are easy to express once developed. They also typically calculate a value, a score, representing how likely something is to be true.

Such an equation can be used to populate a field in a database so it can be used as part of a record. For instance, a predictive model of credit risk can be executed against every customer record, populating a column in the database called "risk score." However, this makes the value static in between updates.

Alternatively a decision service itself can execute the formula or equation, calculating the predictive "score" as it is called and making that available as part of the decision making process. For instance, the decision service can make a different decision for those customers who are more loyal than those who are less so.

By adopting these analytic techniques, we can turn the data we have into insight that can be consumed by automated decision services.

BUSINESS RULES AND ACTIONS

The third issue with intelligent, automated processes is the need for them to keep moving: for them to make decisions take actions and proceed without waiting for human intervention. We may not manage this 100 percent of the time, but we want our processes to move on without intervention as often as possible. Even if we turn the data we have and our understanding of our business into executable insight, we must still act on that insight. A prediction about a customer is not a decision, it is just a prediction. A description of our customer is *part* of what we need to decide but it is unlikely to be *everything* we need to decide. We must be able to define the actions we take as a consequence, and the action we take must be legal and appropriate.

Decisions need more than analytics

Take an example. We have a process for onboarding customers that needs to support kiosks and website signups—so it needs to be automated. During this process we want to make a decision about cross-sell, up-sell or down-sell—we want to make sure the customer has the right product(s). In particularly we want to drive a decision that will maximize loyalty.

We can build a set of predictive models that allow us to see how likely it is that someone will be a loyal customer for each of our base products. In other words, we can build a model to calculate the likelihood that a specific customer (with these characteristics) will be loyal if he or she buys a specific product. To make the decision about recommending an alternative product, however, we need to be able to take those different values, see if the product the customer is trying to buy is the best choice and, if it is not, decide if the "best" choice is more or less profitable. If it less profitable but boosts the potential loyalty of this customer enough and if we can deliver that product to that customer (perhaps there is a capacity limit on our products), then we may decide to make alternative offer.

To keep the process moving it is not enough to calculate the propensities for this customer, we must be able to act on them. We must be able to define the business rules that determine which action(s) to take.

Don't code decisions

While we could just write code to do this, that would be a mistake. Decisions are often high-change components of a process with many factors causing the rules to change. For example new regulations can be issued or we can change our policy. Delay in being able to change our decisions to reflect such changes may result in lost business or fines.

In addition the logic of a business decision is very much under the control of the business, not of IT. Writing code to implement these rules will make it hard to change them quickly and hard to bring the business into the ownership role for the decision. Instead of writing code we can and should use a Business Rules Management System or BRMS to manage Business Rules explicitly.

Business rules

Business Rules in this context are logical, atomic statements of what can and should be done in different circumstances. Each business rules is independent and can be written, assessed and changed independently. A BRMS can manage all the rules that go into our operational decisions and make it possible for the business to "own" them while still ensuring that IT can manage them. A BRMS is an effective way to automate decisions while remaining understandable by the business. Modern Business Process Management Systems are increasingly delivering an integrated BRMS or providing interfaces to make integration with one straightforward.

In addition to this business control and agility, decision making logic in a BRMS is now explicit. When the decision service makes a decision it is possible to log exactly how it did so—which rules fired, what analytic insight was applied. Not only is this helpful for regulatory compliance, it is also a new source of insight into how our business operates.

More than just analytic rules

While some of the rules in a decision might be derived analytically as discussed above, business rules can also be derived from regulations, policy or experience. Regulations impose restrictions on what is allowed and insist on certain actions being taken in certain circumstances. Similarly company policy or expertise can lead to rules that constrain or drive actions.

Many decisions require a mix of all these kinds of rules. For instance, a loan pricing decision requires rules set by the lender based on its policy and experience, additional rules set by State and Federal regulations, rules about what can and cannot be effectively sold on the secondary market and rules derived from analysis of the current loan portfolio to characterize the proposed loan in terms of likelihood of pre-payment or default. A good decision will use all these rules.

INTELLIGENT, AUTOMATED PROCESSES

Using embeddable analytic techniques, both descriptive and predictive, in combination with business rules allows you to effectively automate operational decisions so they can be embedded in automated processes.

Decision services in the technology stack

As Figure 2 below shows, the technologies required to build decision services fit inside a standard service-oriented architecture. Controlled by a business process management environment and taking full advantage of data and performance management infrastructure, a Decision Service contains the right mix of business rules, descriptive and predictive analytics, and optimization to make the decision for which it is designed.

Adaptive control is an additional step for organizations with more complex decisions to make using decision services. Adaptive control uses test and learn or champion/challenger approaches to constantly test new rules and analytic models against the current approach to see if better approaches are possible. For more details, see Taylor & Raden, 2007[1].

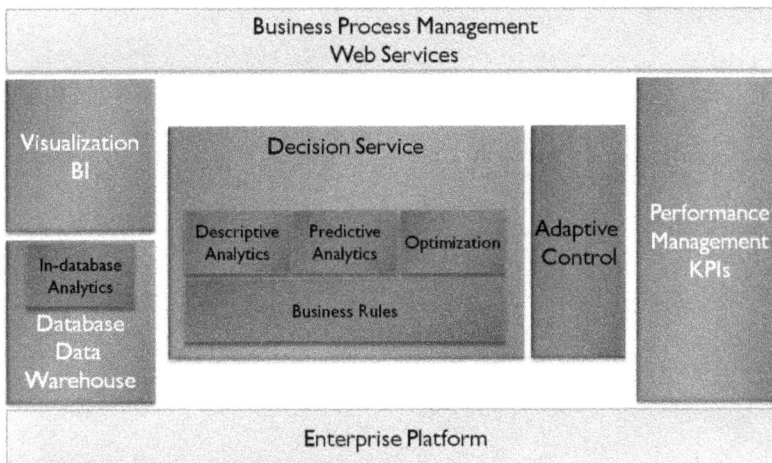

Figure 2: Technology for Analytics in Operational Systems

---

[1] Taylor, James and Raden, Neil. *Smart (Enough) Systems: How to Deliver Competitive Advantage by Automating Hidden Decisions.* New York. Prentice Hall, 2007.

Getting started

To get started with the approach, we begin by identifying the decisions that will make a difference to our processes and by understanding how they relate to our KPIs. We need to understand the decisions within and about our processes, we need to classify them and we need to put them in context.

When it comes to automating them we must begin with the decision and we must keep it in mind. We will develop analytics that will help with the decision or make it more accurate, we will find the rules that apply to the decision. We will use these analytics and rules to determine the data we need and then integrate and cleanse that data.

> ✓ *Consider business rules and analytics as linked decision-making technologies. There are problems that can be solved by one or the other but the combination is more powerful.*

> ✓ *Always begin with the decision in mind. There is a temptation to create infrastructure across all processes and this should be resisted. Focus on the decisions and drive infrastructure from the needs of those decisions.*

Intelligent, automated processes are not the stuff of science fiction. They can be developed by automating the decisions that are embedded in our operational processes.

Section 2:
Case Studies
Delivering the Customer-Centric Organization

Achievement Awards Group (Pty) Ltd, South Africa

1. Executive Summary / Abstract

Adaptive Case Management (ACM) is imperative in enterprises where the exception to process becomes the process! ACM, a topic widely discussed and analyzed by academics, professionals and IT specialists, is what is needed whenever processes must react to changing and diverse customer or client needs and interactions to ensure efficient and effective outcomes. This means that defined, rigid processes become responsive to circumstances that require fluid processes in order to address specific requirements.

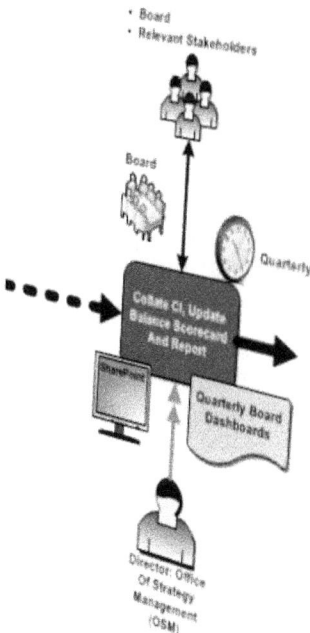

* Board
* Relevant Stakeholders

Board

Quarterly

Collate CI, Update Balance Scorecard And Report

Sharepoint

Quarterly Board Dashboards

Director: Office Of Strategy Management (OSM)

Achievement Awards Group (AAG), based in Cape Town, South Africa, recognized the benefits of adopting ACM as a critical success factor in attaining their strategic goals, and in response to their changing, diverse and unique customer requirements. The focus of AAG is to effectively and efficiently attain what they term "Customer Delight". The business of AAG includes predicting and responding to customer needs. No margin for error is allowed. Period.

This meant that absolute process agility had to be defined, designed, agreed upon and be continuously revisited. In the context of AAG, knowledge workers are the process executors, while stakeholders include customers and AAG shareholders.

A Customer Delight Framework, incorporating dynamic, unstructured process and process rules, was designed to deal with cases that require deviation from standard processes. These cases often require agility to ensure that desired process outcomes are achievable, regardless of the scenario.

Figure 1: A snapshot of VizPro® Process Step

The Customer Delight Framework was superimposed onto the business processes by using a collaborative, real-time and highly visual process mapping methodology called VizPro®. This easily understandable methodology clearly maps out who does what, why, where and how. It enabled role players to collaboratively design agile customer centric (outside-in) processes that are able to deal with a diverse set of cases or scenarios. In short, VizPro® facilitated an out-of-the-box mindset to design effective responses to customer needs.

What follows is a record of the roll-out of the Customer Delight Programme and the approach used to design dynamic processes which ensured quick management decision making, enterprise-wide adoption and execution of customer centricity.

2. CLIENT AND PROJECT QUICKVIEW

AAG (www.achievementawards.co.za) is a medium sized enterprise in the business of designing and delivering full-service incentive and performance improvement programmes for clients.

Profile

- It was established in 1980;
- the founder and current CEO is Geoffrey A. Amyot;
- the Head Office is in Westlake, Cape Town;
- the fulfillment centre/3260m² warehouse is also located in Westlake
- it has three certified Human Performance Technologists on staff;
- it is a single source provider;
- it has strong project management infrastructure;
- it has entered into a strategic partnership with Maritz Inc. (USA);
- it has produced more than 800 incentive programs to date;
- it has touched the lives of about 1.5 million South Africans to date; and
- its in-house services include a creative studio, a web/new media team, an IT development team, a banking/management information centre, a catalogue/supply chain team, an IATA certified travel agency and a VOIP enabled call centre.

Service portfolio

"Get a holistic perspective on your business; examine your cultural climate; support staff development through learning; motivate, recognise and reward performance; manage rewards and fulfillment requirements; and support back-end program requirements".

The project

The requirement was to partner in the development of an easily implementable Customer Delight Programme (CDP), based on the Disney Approach to Quality Management and Customer Care and effectively implement it by designing Customer Delight into process. The aim was to achieve customer excellence and continuous improvement.

The CDP comprised two aspects: First, the development of an operating model to address the requirements and challenges faced by the organisation. And second, an innovative design of customer-centric processes that would be easy to understand and implement, be aligned to business strategy, would be clearly defined, and would have the flexibility to deal with deviations that are part and parcel of the business of dealing with diverse customers groups. The CDP was to be infused into processes using VizPro®.

As one of the key outcomes, this programme created an AAG organizational-wide awareness amongst knowledge workers, support teams and management which resulted in buy-in that truly embedded customer excellence and a continuous improvement culture in all AAG activities.

Figure 2: A snapshot of Customer Delight Rules, describing what will need to be done to attain a state of customer satisfaction, and what needs to be avoided.

Pétanque Consultancy (www.petanque-c.com) partnered with AAG, deploying one Specialist Consultant, two process architects and one project coordinator. The IT applied included two consultant laptops, MS Visio™, MS Office and data projectors. Key processes were printed on AO paper and the final output was framed and displayed in the AAG offices.

3. RESULTS

The feedback from the AAG Project Office four months after the initial roll-out stated: "Through our Customer Delight programme, we have been able to implement improvements in the After Sales Support, Courier and Stock Handling areas. As a result, we have cut down on back orders and delivery times. This has led to slight increases in our Customer Satisfaction Index (CSI) scores and compliments and also a reduction in complaints. Quantifiable results will be made available at the end of 2011."

Results in the following areas have been realized, and continue to do so:

- Cost saving through reduced time-to-customer and cycle time, as well as reductions in returns and queries;
- quality Improvements in how call centre and customer contact processes are executed; and
- clear performance indicators have been implemented.

4. KEY INNOVATION ELEMENTS

The principal success factors for this project were as follows:

1. to ensure Executive and Management Support,
2. to participate in developing and adopting a workable Customer Delivery Framework (see below), and
3. realise or actualise this Framework in the day-to-day operations by making use of a process mapping and management approach (VizPro®) that ensures clarity and alignment, and most importantly deliver results through buy-in and enterprise wide participation VizPro® is highly customizable and ensures clarity by using a detailed, storyboard format that produces real time mapping whilst simultaneously engaging knowledge owners and stakeholders in high energy, high impact work sessions (similar to JAD sessions). Innovation, adaptability and engagement converged to produce a project that was delivered speedily and which resulted in immediate, as well as medium and long term benefits.

5. SUCCESS FACTOR ONE: SENIOR AND EXECUTIVE MANAGEMENT BUY-IN

Strong, visible sponsorship was essential for the enterprise roll-out of the Customer Delight Programme. A project kick-off meeting was held whereby senior management and the executive team were introduced to the Customer Delight concept and particularly, how this needed to be integral to the what needs to done; (i.e. process), by whom-, why-, when- and how-steps. Throughout the project feedback on progress, issues and stumbling blocks were shared and addressed.

The innovation was in the **way that engagement and consensus were achieved**, using the VizPro® methodology, described below.

6. SUCCESS FACTOR TWO: CUSTOMER DELIGHT FRAMEWORK

A two-pronged approach to imprint Adaptive Case Management in AAG was followed, based on the questions "What will we do?" and "How will we do it?" The "What" needed to be defined in terms of Customer Centricity and Delight and the "How" needed to be expressed in activities, or processes—hence, the focus on the AAG Customer Delight Framework and Processes.

First, the Customer Delight Programme (CDP) was conceptualized, discussed, developed and agreed upon, using the Disney Approach to Quality Management and Customer Care as the departure point, followed by designing the CDP into processes This programme would drive the Customer Delight Framework for each relevant process where Adaptive Case Management was needed.

The Purpose of the Customer Delight Framework

The Framework was developed to describe the general directives of what and what not to do when specific circumstances present themselves. The purpose of the Framework was to identify, for each relevant process, the customer touchpoints and link them to the relevant categories (see below).

How the Framework was applied

Once the Framework was agreed to, the customer touchpoints were identified, added to the Change Controller (a VizPro® artifact that ensures process focus, as described below) and each touchpoint in the process defined.

The touchpoints were categorized as follows:

Customer Touchpoint category	Definition
Customer Satisfaction	Meeting customer requirements or delivering what has been promised.
Customer Delight	Touchpoints that will provide opportunities for delight or exceeding the customer expectations.
Service Recovery	Based on the understanding that in a service industry, things WILL go wrong, this answers the constant question "What steps must be taken in the event of service failure?"

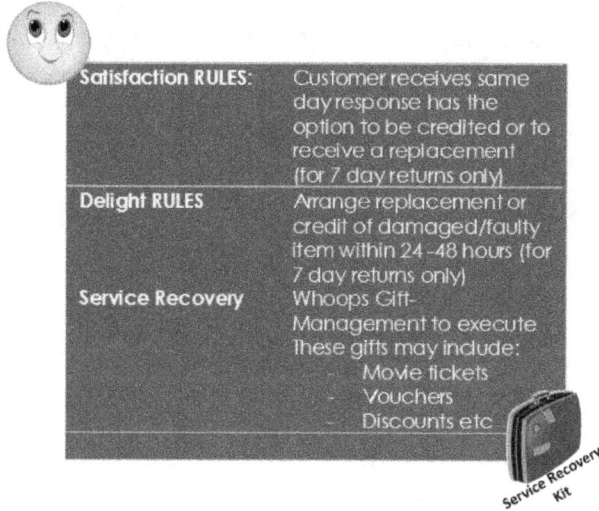

Figure 3: This is how a Delight Touch Point as referred to in figure 2 was elaborated upon.

Figure 3 shows how information was captured for one of the customer touchpoints. The touchpoint was split into the Satisfaction, Delight and Service Recovery categories, and rules developed to satisfy each category's definition.

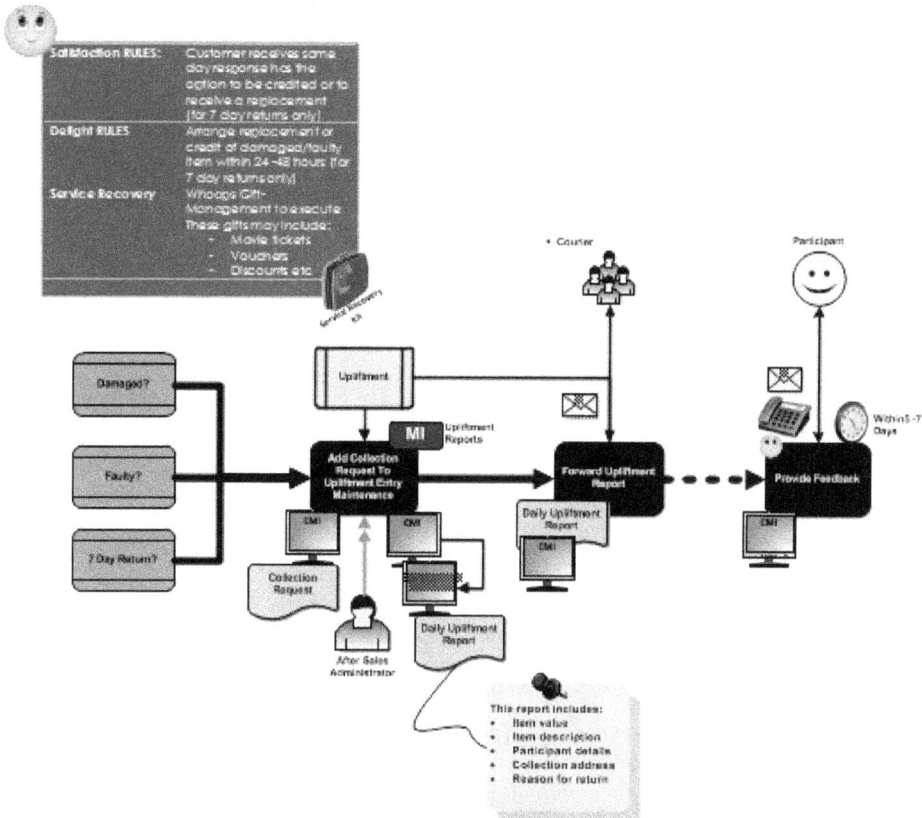

Figure 4: Snapshot of the After Sales Process, reflecting a Customer Delight Framework specific for this part of the process.

Figure 4 depicts how the Customer Delight Framework was applied. Each touchpoint was analyzed and through facilitated work sessions, agreement was reached on a) what to do in cases of Service Failure (Service Recovery), b) what practices would meet Customer expectations (Customer Satisfaction) and c) what opportunities and actions would exceed customer expectations (Customer Delight). The key customer information collection touchpoints (listening posts) were also identified. This enabled AAG to generate customer intelligence that ensured better understanding of their customers which, in turn, fed into the AAG processes for continuous improvement.

Benefits of using the Customer Delight Framework

The benefits include:

- identification of critical touchpoint directives, or rules, to design customer centric processes;
- identifying ways of improving the customer experience and formulating these into framework directives for process role players;
- agreeing on ways to re-design areas with the greatest customer service inefficiencies in order to improve on responsiveness and, ultimately, profitability through customer retention and cost savings;
- a clearly defined action plan to drive behaviour change; and
- identification of and alignment on customer information collection points to generate intelligence that would facilitate customer centricity, continuous improvement and the development of metrics to monitor progress.

7. SUCCESS FACTOR THREE: PROCESS MAPPING AS THE VEHICLE TO PLAN, DEFINE AND DELIVER CUSTOMER DELIGHT

The Customer Delight Framework needed to be "dropped" into processes that were deemed too structured for an effective and efficient Customer Delight focus. In particular, the project participants identified the following as being the result of rigid structures:

- stifled creativity and innovation;
- slow responses to market changes as case-based solutions were not possible;
- non-adherence to the processes.

In addition, the following problems were identified:

- existing processes were not a true reflection of what was being practiced i.e. processes were not aligned with practice;
- there was a lack of efficient and effective communication, especially when there were service breakdowns i.e. when things went wrong;
- there was a lack of process accountability; and
- management and front-line staff were not aligned on how to deal with specific cases as they presented.

As a result of these insights, the following needs were identified:

- the need for a clear collective understanding of customers' needs and how to "wow" them; and
- the need for an agile processes that were easy to manipulate and quick to respond to market changes and customer requirements.
- the need for a Centre of Excellence to manage and maintain templates, business processes, version control, action lists, business improvement projects, etc.

It became evident that the project needed to incorporate the Customer Delight Framework into existing processes. In cases where there were gaps, new processes either had to be created or current activities had to be enhanced to ensure the inclusion of those elements needed to bring about Customer Delight.

7.1 The Motivation for deploying Process Mapping to fast track ACM into the enterprise

Process is the vehicle that states what activities are needed for specific outcomes. It also states who needs to do these activities. To be effective, process must clearly tell the "story" of the activity, i.e. identify the role players, pinpoint the risk areas, determine how to address exceptions and define the controls to be built into the flow; to list only a few of the many elements that are needed for a process "story". Each of the process elements must converge to synchronize people, activity, systems and artifacts to achieve agreed-to outcomes. These outcomes or results per process, in turn, must support the enterprise goals.

The process mapping methodology applied in this project was, and will for the foreseeable future be, VizPro®. It was chosen due to its ability to:

- build easy to understand, highly visual storyboard format processes;
- obtain immediate buy-in and support;
- build agile processes quickly and efficiently;
- gather corporate knowledge and expertise into process maps through interactive and collaborative work sessions; and
- build Customer centricity.

7.2 How Process was applied

Business process architecture includes understanding (i.e. analysis), developing, modeling, documenting and improving business processes, end-to-end. Unstructured or ad hoc processes are processes that cannot be clearly defined, and allows process stakeholders to develop the "what to do" as they execute the process, within defined guidelines or "the how-to" when many different scenarios present to the process role player. These are typically used in environments where there are many ways in which to execute and activity and execution is impacted by each circumstance

VizPro® lends itself to this by being a process documentation and analysis methodology that enables and facilitates Business Process design, architecture and buy-in. It applies the power of pictures and the effective use of narratives to show how processes support the enterprise goals—process-by–process and step-by-step. It engages process participants, role players and stakeholders in high energy mapping sessions where knowledge is captured and immediately converted into step-by-step maps. Workshops engage all session participants, thus leading to lively discussions that are informative and aimed at building improved practices. As a decision on the "who" does "what", "why" and "how" is taken, the information is captured and projected, thus creating a clear understanding of each step, along with immediate buy-in.

The following innovative process development, assessment, alignment and **mapping elements** resulted in multiple benefits and facilitated innovation in ACM in AAG.

8. ORGANIZATIONAL POSITIONING MAP

The Purpose and Creation of a Positioning Map:

Similar to enterprise architecture, but focused on creating links between processes and strategic goals, the aim of this map is to **link enterprise vision, mission and values** to a Performance Profile in which the strategic direction and goals are mapped. It furthermore identifies how each process will and must be designed and managed to achieve a common set of outcomes.

Each strategic directive and goal is linked to one or more critical success factor (CSF), which is in turn linked to a balanced scorecard focus area. Next, the processes that will impact on achieving those CSFs are identified and listed. The indicators per focus area are then recorded using process icons.

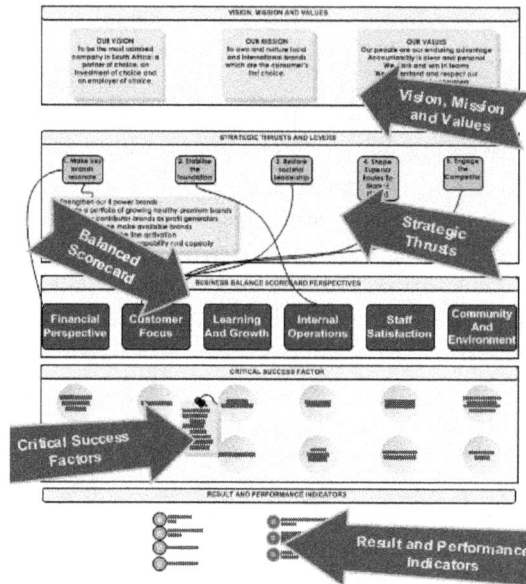

Figure 5: Snapshot of the Performance Profile

To complete the linkage between process, strategy and vision, a level one map is developed to show in five to six broad brush stroke steps what the enterprise "does". The processes to achieve these outcomes are then taken from the basket of processes defined in the Performance Profile (see figure 5). Having positioned the processes in the enterprise value chain, the group then agrees on which processes are critical to the outcomes and will bring the quickest improvement results if unpacked.

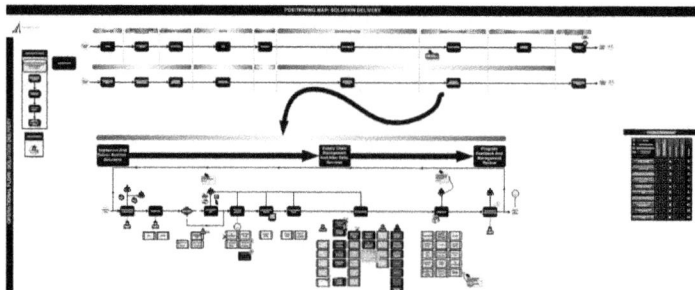

Figure 6: Positioning Map in which the processes that are needed to attain the value chain steps results, are identified and prioritised

How the Positioning Map was applied in AAG:

- The Positioning Map (figure 6) was developed with both the senior and executive management teams during a one-day work session. It depicts what value the organisation creates and required 8 hours to develop and complete.
- A key strategic objective for AAG is to actively manage the entire business to a customer focused value system. The management team agreed that the Solution Delivery Division should be "unpacked" as it would render the quickest and highest impact outcomes in respect of Customer Delight.
- The Solution Delivery Division contains many customer touchpoints, which means that this division needs to be highly adaptive and agile to each customer case that enters the process. Each of the Solution Delivery processes had to be designed to be fully aligned with the strategic objective(s) of being profitable, yet also being highly customer centric.
- The processes and activities thus needed to be designed to incorporate the characteristics of adaptability and agility whilst ensuring customer centricity, yet with enough flexible to deal with specific cases and enabling continuous improvement.

Benefits of using the Positioning Map:

The benefits included

- identifying and agreeing the key "must achieve" elements for each process that would collectively deliver results in support of enterprise goals;
- identifying the processes that make up AAG's value chain from start to end;
- identifying the critical processes needed in order to steer the business to being a customer centric organisation;
- providing direction in organising and developing a cross functional approach, instead of the traditional departmental approach;
- providing a high level view of the organisation and how all the processes interface to ensure effective service delivery; and
- identifying the scope, the process owners and stakeholders for each of the Solution Delivery Division processes and establishing the schedule for the Customer Delight Programme roll-out.

9. CHANGE CONTROLLER

Purpose of the Change Controller:

The purpose of the Change Controller is **to list those** minimum requirements that each process must adhere to in order to attain enterprise goals. These are derived from three sources, namely the CSFs and Performance Profile developed in the Positioning Map and from the "What Good Looks Like" (WGLL) statements developed by work session participants.[1]. These requirements are created by prefacing the source statements with the question "does this process..."

The Change Controller lists the "must do" elements in a matrix format. When reviewing each process against its particular Change Controller items, there are five status options (see Figure 7 and below). The status profile derived from the

---

[1] When defining desired outcomes, the term "What Good Looks Like" or WGLL, (pronounced "wiggle") is applied to guide responses in order to define what the desired process results must or should be.

Change Controller gives a good indication of the level of support a particular process lends to the enterprise goals.

CHANGE CONTROLLER		NOT CLEAR HOW TO ACHIEVE IT	IN ACTION LIST FOR LATER IMPLEMENTATION	IN PROGRESS	CONCLUDED	NOT APPLICABLE	CATEGORY
G	Growth						
C	Consumer Focused						
OS	Organisational Structuring						
OM	Organisational Management						
Does This Process Prompt And Promote Delight?		O	O	O	O	O	C
Does This Process Provide Sufficient Information To Manage And Improve On Customer Delight?		O	O	O	O	O	C
Will This Process Provide For An Optimal Solution For Our Customer?		O	O	O	O	O	C
Does This Process Comply To Delivering On Time, To Standard And Right Price?		O	O	O	O	O	G
Does This Process Allow For Innovative Solutions?		O	O	O	O	O	G
Does This Process Follow Project /Workflow Management Principles?		O	O	O	O	O	OM
Does This Process Clearly Define Roles And Specifically, Accountability?		O	O	O	O	O	OS

Figure 7: AAG Change Controller.

How the Change Controller was applied:

AAG's key strategic objective, as defined during the work session, included "to be excellent at servicing customers". To achieve this, the group agreed that it was necessary to address processes and align people and systems to:

- ensure that the organisation became more customer-focused;
- improve service delivery;
- develop customer centric business processes;
- develop agile processes that ensured quick management decision making;
- develop fluid processes that provided for innovative, creative and out-of – the box case-based solutions;
- create a customer excellence and continuous improvement culture;
- create a centre for excellence or Process Management Office (PrMO); and to
- create sustainable continuous improvement.

The Change Controller was developed to ensure that the Solution Delivery Division processes supported the company's strategic objectives. Each Case Manager had the opportunity to list their individual WGLL statements for the division. Once these statements were translated into goal definitions, the team agreed on what was critical for continuous improvement and to become a customer centric organisation. These prioritized goals were then added to the Change Controller. In the case of AAG, strategic goals were identified in the following categories:

- Growth;
- Consumer Focus;
- Organizational Structuring; and
- Organizational Management.

After each process mapping session, participants worked through the elements in the Change Controller to ascertain whether the process did indeed adhere to these requirements. These were categorised as such:

Status	Definition
"Not clear how to achieve it",	This means that there is a gap that needs to be addressed.
"In Action list for implementation"	This means that change actions have been defined, scheduled and assigned.
"In progress"	This means that it is incorporated in the "as is" or "to be" process, i.e. it forms part of what needs to be done and outcomes will reflect the process impact on the particular element.
"Concluded"	This means that the process outcomes are supporting the relevant element/requirement.
"Not applicable"	This means that the process is not intended to address the element.

Each Solution Delivery Division process map contained the same Change Controller against which the processes were tested to make sure that it contributed towards the strategic goals. A process would only be signed off once aligned to the Change Controller.

Benefits of using the Change Controller:

The benefits included:

- enabling Case Managers to list their process "WGLLS" and align these to enterprise goals;
- clarifying what each process should aim to deliver on;
- ensuring that there is a common direction when mapping processes in order to guarantee that the activities that occurred in each process would in fact bring about the desired results, as defined in the WGLLs and the CSFs; and
- ensuring final signoff of processes, since the Change Controller is the last step for final approval.

10. PROCESS MAPPING

The purpose of process mapping and processes

Each process clearly defines a number of related aspects, namely
1. what needs to be done,
2. who does it,
3. why is it done (i.e. "what outcome am I trying to achieve by doing this activity?"),
4. who is involved in each activity,
5. how does communication take place, and
6. how to achieve improvement where notes highlight specific "how" tips.

Each process step incorporates the value system of the enterprise by default and shows what needs to be done to achieve process outcomes. It also defines process management elements, such as what risks occur where, what controls are applied and where information is gathered with which to measure results (see figure 8).

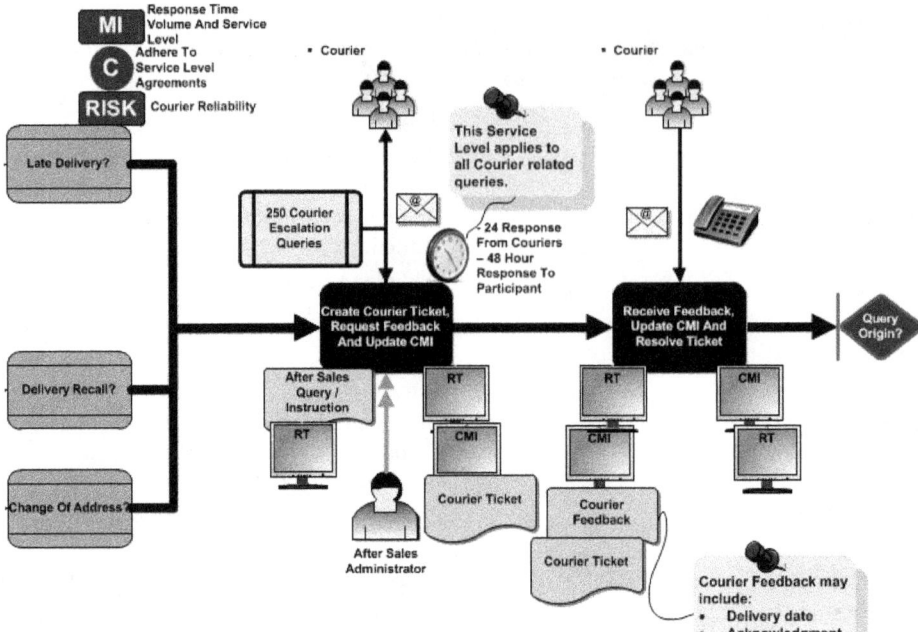

Figure 8: Snapshot of a VizPro® process map: section snapshot.

How the processes were mapped in AAG:

For each process the work session started with a blank screen. After agreeing the name of the map, the purpose and scope of the process was defined, discussed and recorded (refer to figure 9). From this starting point each process would be recorded, developed and improved upon—step by step.

The AAG Process Maps contained the following:

- customised icons;
- roles and responsibilities;
- customer touchpoints;
- opportunities for customer intelligence / feedback gathering; and
- areas where case-based solutions were needed and had to be executed according to response or activity Frameworks that incorporate Customer Delight Programme elements.

The Process Maps were developed in different versions:

Version 1:

Up to eight people were invited to unpack the "as is" (i.e. the status quo), adding notes on changes to be made, where needed. Discussion included subject matter experts, process stakeholders and management.

These sessions gave process stakeholders a forum to voice concerns and highlight challenges, problem areas and bottlenecks and to suggest solutions. It also aided in the collaboration of ideas and innovations whilst enabling the development of Frameworks on how to engage with customers in specific processes, and at specific points in the process. By doing this, the principles of Customer Delight could be built into each Framework ensuring the identification of the "do's" that would achieve the Customer Delights goals, as opposed to the "don'ts" that would compromise Customer Delight. Service recovery rules were developed to ensure sufficient guidelines for those occasions when service fails.

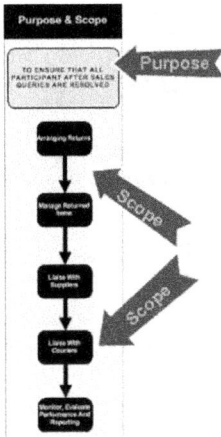

Figure 9: Snapshot of the Purpose and Scope of an AAG Process Map

The average time spent on each version one process map was between eight and16 hours per process.

Version 2:

Up to 12 people joined this version to discuss, challenge and debate each of the Version 1 Process Maps, with the aim of adding improvements. This session included subject matter experts, external process stakeholders (organisational staff that had an impact on the processes) and cross functional management teams. This session provided opportunity for further design, collaboration and agreement that was particularly impactful in terms of information sharing and clarifying process risks and ACM.

Specific emphasis was placed on the following during discussions:

- Customer Delight and Service Recovery rules;
- risks and control points, specifically defining risks and the relevant mitigations that could be implemented;
- defining management information (MI) points where information is gathered;
- locating accounting points where cash or stock enter or leave the process and may impact on ACM;
- quality assurance points;
- key performance indicator (KPI) points, what indicator is applied to measure which element of performance and linking this back to the Performance Profile referenced above;
- burning points that resulted in bottlenecks or breakdowns in delivering services;
- points of escalations where the process executor required relevant Delegation of Authority to authorise certain transactions; and
- governance elements, including statutes, policies, standards and directives, ensuring that these were considered during ACM instances.

The average time spent per version 2 of the Process Maps was between 4-8 hours per process.

Benefits of using this approach to Process Mapping:

The benefits include:

- fostering an understanding by process stakeholders of the end-to-end processes in terms of who does what, with whom, when and how;
- identifying and improving process efficiencies, which positively impacted on cost, time and quality;
- clearly defining roles and responsibilities through the creation of visual Process Maps;
- highlighting the flow of documentation within the organisation, which ensures a clear audit trail;
- providing a cross functional view of the business instead of the traditional departmental view;
- ensuring that MI and KPIs are relevant and that they provide the right performance information at the right time to the right decision makers;

- defining process risks and agreeing on the controls to mitigate them;
- clearly defining and linking interrelationships between processes (within the organisation and within the Solution Delivery Division), people and systems;
- identifying process inefficiencies, bottlenecks, gaps and weaknesses;
- increasing performance and staff morale as people understood the "big picture" and the importance of their respective roles in it;
- knowledge transfer taking place and improving teamwork;
- enabling the development of training and induction material by using the process maps as a starting point;
- identifying competency level gaps and developing training programmes to address them; and
- ensuring a high buy-in into business changes since the process stakeholders were involved in the design of the process and understood the background of the change.

11. THE ACTION LIST

The purpose of the Action List

The Action List records the drivers for change. Whenever an item or an activity is identified during a workshop as an issue to be addressed, it is added to the Action List. The "who" and "when" is then agreed to by the participants.

Achievement Awards Group

Action List

Issue #	Category	The issue	What must be done	What must be achieved	By whom	When	Status
1	Undelivered items	Participants not available to receive their delivery at the provided address which results in late deliveries.	Create/Reinstate an Attempted Delivery Notification card that can be delivered when the participant is not at the Delivery address.	* Customer delight point * Participants informed of attempted delivery and whether the item has been dropped at an alternative address * improve 3rd party reliability	Natasha Greg	2010/09/01	Closed
2	Service Recovery	Service failure is dealt with on an adhoc basis and is not formalised	*Create a Service Failure spreadsheet that lists the issues such as delivery to wrong addresses / non adherence to processes *Service Failures must be consolidated and reviewed on a mothly basis * Natasha to provide cost estimate for the implementation	* Standardised way of dealing service failures * Agents aware of consequences	Noori Tanzi	2010/06/01	Closed

Figure 10: Example of an Action List which records follow-on activities needed to ensure that change and improvement is executed.

How the Action Lists were used in AAG:

The Action Lists per process were populated and updated in real time during each mapping session. While working on processes, whenever a task needed to be recorded, the process architect would toggle to the Action List and record the action, stating:

- what the issue is;
- what needed to be done;
- what the desired outcome is;
- who needed to action the listed activity; and
- by when does it need to be done.

The benefits of the Action List:

The Action List:

- enhances ownership;

- it facilitates agreement of what activities or projects are needed to implement improvement, and
- it is a critical implementation management tool.

12. KEY BENEFITS

The key benefits of this process approach, which highlights the competitive advantages in addressing ACM as described in this case study, include:

- a saving of time—the work was concluded in 45.5 project days, over a period of six months utilizing one specialist consultant (six days), two process architects (31 and 7 days respectively) and a project coordinator (1.5 days);
- effective use of staff time, limiting the loss of work hours for the client—25 key people were involved in the project, impacting on approximately 150 co-workers, all of whom are part of the Customer Service delivery chain;
- it requires only low cost IT—MS Visio™ is used to produce the process maps and Microsoft Office Excel for the Action Lists. These documents are stored on the SharePoint Drive;
- recording a vast amount of knowledge in real time;
- enabling knowledge share and alignment through effective engagement;
- creating clarity on who does what, why and how and what the rules of each ACM instance are, as defined in the Customer Delight Frameworks;
- enabling a transfer of skills to update the process maps (1.5 days for training in AAG);
- aligning and linking each process to AAG's strategic direction and to specific business goals so that role players see the clear line between what they do and how it impacts on business goals;
- enabling group agreement
    - on actions to be implemented to ensure effective and efficient processes that are measurable;
    - on risks that need to be managed;
    - on how to attain Customer Delight; and
- agility as the tools and techniques are flexible and customisable to ensure that what is needed can be designed into processes and systems, provided that there is enterprise agreement and buy-in.

13. KEY CHALLENGES EXPERIENCED DURING THE PROJECT AND HOW THEY WERE ADDRESSED

Challenges	How they were addressed
Gaining senior management and executive buy-In ✓	Senior management and the executive team were key in the development of the Organizational Positioning Map. In this work session the focus was on the benefits of having customer-centric processes and how it would impact on the bottom line. By focusing on these elements, immediate buy-in occurred through discussion and collaborative verification of the benefits, along with the commitment to ensure continuous benefit realization.
Overcoming functional thinking ✓	Prior to the rollout of the project, AAG focused on traditional functional structures such as marketing, sales, operations, HR etc.
	The process sessions effectively communicated how approaching business processes from an end-to-end perspective would add value in service delivery. Once senior management and the executive team saw the outcomes of the

work session, which clearly identified the value stream from its origin to the end customer, there was immediate buy-in.

Business Change Management

✓

Process stakeholders initially showed resistance to the work sessions, but after having been exposed to the VizPro® methodology, there was effective buy-in. This resulted in excellent, enthusiastic and high quality participation as it provided a platform for stakeholders from different levels of the organisation to contribute to the design of the customer-centric processes in a manner that addressed their specific process-related issues.

Process stakeholder availability

✓

Many of the stakeholders felt that they had "more important" work to attend to. Once they experienced the VizPro® approach however, they saw the value it brought to their work lives. They also saw the project as being an opportunity to collaborate and develop innovative solutions to challenges faced on a day-to-day basis.

14. PITFALLS TO AVOID WHEN USING THIS METHODOLOGY

✗ Do not waste time. Deliver and show benefits and value as immediate value ensures continued participation and commitment from management all the way through to employees

✗ Do not underestimate the power of putting the right resources into the project. The relationships fostered in this way ensures the delivery of effective work sessions, and effective work sessions means delivering quick value to the client

✗ Do not waiver. Be secure and precise in the tools and techniques, be clear on the approach and explain in a way that every single person understands what is happening, why and what the end goal is

✗ Do not complicate matters. Keep it simple

✗ Do not underestimate the effort required. Prepare participants to what lies ahead and to the fact that it is hard work, with long, intense hours.

15. WHY THE INNOVATION IN THE PROJECT IS NOTEWORTHY

A number of reasons can be listed on why the innovation in this project is of significance:

- The approach was uniquely suited to introducing customer-centricity into the enterprise at every level as the easy-to-understand visible format conveyed the message in a simplified format which was easy to follow and implement.
- The approach fostered complete management support through its collaborative and interactive storyboard design work sessions;
- The project offered the holistic approach that was required by management and the relevant stakeholders to analyze the Solution Delivery Division processes in order to achieve realistic and practical customer improvements;
- The VizPro® methodology provided insight and a clear road map on how to achieve strategic objectives and organization-wide customer-centricity;

- The project required only simple, low IT to deliver a high impact methodology that enabled case-based solutions and highlighted essential customer touchpoints;
- The project, through its use of VizPro®, created participation and buy-in through interactive, high-energy workshops, resulted in user-friendly and information rich process maps. This moreover, led to the "wow" factor as abstract processes effectively come to life as visual storyboards through the use of icons that tell the story of each process in comprehensive detail. This is the unique characteristic of VizPro®.
- The project provided a voice to every knowledge worker participant that added to innovation and improved practices through effective collaboration.
- By facilitating discussions amongst process stakeholders from all organisational levels it enabled real-time collaboration of ideas and innovations that aided in designing, tailor-made customer-centric processes.
- The project ensured the best possible outcome by including stakeholders that lived the processes and its frustrations day-to-day, knew what to watch out for and have learned how to get past the hurdles. They have seen things go wrong and now had the opportunity to be part of the solution.
- The project provided clear programme elements. The Customer Delight Programme comprises the Customer Delight Framework, Customer Touchpoint Model, Positioning Map, Change Controllers, Process Maps and Action Lists which are all effective and easy access tools for the management of Corporate Knowledge.
- The project made smart use of technology by using MS SharePoint as the central repository system. The SharePoint was used to manage version control, process templates and to capture knowledge gained from lessons learnt in a timeous manner.
- A Centre of Excellence (COE) was established to design and document the core and supporting business processes.
- Skills were transferred to the COE team (Quality Champions) through on-the-job shadowing and formal training. The focus was on the VizPro® methodology and MS Visio™, and particularly, on how to effectively use technology.

The end result of the project was the creation of agile customer-centric processes allowing the AAG to embrace change rather than reject, control or suffer from change and the high demand on agility. The results included enhanced capability for knowledge workers and management to make quick decisions to ensure that processes generated the desired results.

Clear Programme elements:
- The Customer Delight Programme comprises the Customer Delight Framework; Customer Touchpoint Model Positioning Map; Change Controllers, Process Maps and Action Lists; effective and easy access to, and management of Corporate Knowledge;
- MS SharePoint was selected as the central repository system and is used to manage version control, process templates and the capturing of knowledge gained from lessons learnt;

- A Centre of Excellence (COE) was established to design and document the core and supporting business processes.
- Skills were transferred to the COE team (Quality Champions), through on-the-job shadow and formal training. The focus was on the VizPro® methodology and MS Visio™ on how to effectively use the technology;

Results: Agile customer centric processes were developed, allowing the AAG to embrace change rather than reject, control or suffer from change and the high demand on agility. The results included capability for knowledge workers and management to make quick decisions to ensure that processes generated the desired results.

16. CONCLUSION:

Achieving results through Adaptive Case Management is possible only when people, processes and system align and support one another. By creating a clear, easy to understand, management and staff supported Customer Delight Programme that includes a Customer Delight Framework and clearly defines in each relevant process "who" needs to do "what" to ensure that process outcomes *and* customer services are effectively and efficiently delivered, continued benefit is realized and results are monitored.

Abu Dhabi Commercial Bank
United Arab Emirates

1. Executive Summary / Abstract

Newgen provided the bank with a BPM-enabled workflow platform, which not only helped bank to automate its processes, but also allowed seamless integration of the BPM solution with its existing applications.

2. Overview

Abu Dhabi Commercial Bank (ADCB), with a strong presence in Consumer and Corporate is a leading provider of technology-enabled services. In its objective towards complete automation of processes, the bank was in urgent need for a solution that would enable end-to-end automation of their key business processes and also provide integration with its existing applications. Newgen provided the bank with a BPM-enabled workflow platform, which not only helped bank to automate its processes, but also allowed seamless integration of the BPM solution with its existing applications.

Some of the **key benefits** are:
- Reduced TATs, processing time and servicing time
- Customer Service Quality & Satisfaction for both existing and new customers
- Avoid dependency on the physical documents
- Large volumes of transactions handled on daily basis

Some of the key challenges are:
- Processing delays and low productivity
- Dependency on physical movement of documents between branches and departments
- Difficulty in verification process and error identification due to unavailability of documents
- Difficulty in tracking and monitoring of processes
- Major challenges in incorporating process change requirements using the existing application

3. Business Context

Starting its operations in 1985, ADCB has established itself as the bank of choice for a large number of customers in the UAE. The bank has been making steady investments in its IT infrastructure and business automation solutions. Along with a core system, the bank also uses a card management system for debit and credit cards, a courier system for dispatch and tracking of customer documents, and a Short Messaging System (SMS) application for customer communications. However, most of these applications and processes were operating without any integration between each other. The bank needed a solution which would provide the platform for complete automation and integration between processes and existing legacy system. This requirement was also in line with the bank's commitment towards technology adaptation for restructuring programme aimed at becoming the most preferred bank for both external and internal customers.

4. THE KEY INNOVATIONS

4.2 Business

The following section describes the impact of the project on the overall business scenario.

Benefits accrued to the bank were both direct and indirect. Reduction in operating costs, travel and communication expenses, office stationary and infrastructure usage were some of the benefits achieved by centralization and implementation of the BPM solution. The bank also achieved other benefits like increase in productivity and reduction in IT infrastructure costs through better utilization of the resources.

- Unified interface for all the underlying applications providing business users with enhanced ease of usage and perform multiple tasks through single system access.
- Enhanced performance was observed in terms of tracking of the business users, process and overall TAT.
- Extended availability by providing secured access to the bank's Direct Selling Agents.
- Scaling up of operational activities, enabling the bank to keep pace with business growth and demands.

4.3 Process

The following section describes the impact of the project on the processes involved in improving the overall system.

- Real time integration with the bank's core system and other applications.
- Reduced TAT for Account opening and other processes.
- Removal of work duplication, by restricting data entry at the branch operations only.
- Unified interface for all the underlying applications providing business users with enhanced ease of usage and perform multiple tasks through single system access.
- Identification of discrepancies at an earlier stage and their faster resolution through checking and validation utilities while doing data entry at the branch level.

4.4 Organization

The following section describes the impact of the project at the organizational level.

- Improved productivity and efficiency of employees with reduction in non-core activities, branch executives are able to cross sell other products.
- Improved customer satisfaction through quicker and better servicing, reduction in the requirement of physical forms, and reduced customer response timelines.
- Scalable solution that enables faster rollout of initiatives and handle increasing business volumes.
- Flexible solution, in terms of incorporating changes in short durations in accordance with business requirements.

5. HURDLES OVERCOME

Based on the bank's requirements, Newgen developed a customized solution, consisting of the following products:

- OmniFlowTM - workflow solution
- OmniDocsTM - document management solution

- OmniScanTM (OmniCapture) - image capture and indexing solution

In the initial phase, Newgen helped the bank automate one its most critical process, the Account opening process. Integrated with the bank's existing core application, the solution provides easier and faster data exchange across systems. Buoyed by the results achieved within a short time of deployment, the bank also implemented and automated a number of other key processes such as Customer and Account Maintenance, Term Deposit Initiation and Maintenance on the BPM platform. At present, the solution has been implemented across 43 branches of the bank and supports 706 users. Every month, more than 61,000 documents are scanned and imported into the workflow for processing. For Account Opening, the system processes approximately 245 applications every day, which can be easily scaled up to meet any future requirement of the bank.

The new system allows users to capture relevant information and customer signoff at the branches itself before the case files move to the Central Processing Department (CPD). Instead of customers having to submit complex forms, the system automatically generates the required forms. The branches update these forms online and take customer signoff before uploading in the system. On completion of the mandatory branch level activities, the files move to the CPD immediately for further processing. Through real-time integration with the core system, CPD users directly initiate the Account Opening process from the workflow solution. Through integration with the SMS system, the solution enabled the team to communicate to customers within 10-15 minutes of their account becoming operational. The solution also generates the welcome letter within 30 minutes of account activation. Post account activation, CPD is able to track and monitor the dispatch of the welcome kits to customers through the courier system, which has also been integrated with the workflow solution.

6. BENEFITS

6.1 Cost Savings

Benefits accrued to the bank were both direct and indirect. Reduction in operating costs, travel and communication expenses, office stationary and infrastructure usage were some of the benefits achieved by centralization and implementation of the BPM solution. The bank also achieved other benefits like increase in productivity and reduction in IT infrastructure costs through better utilization of the resources.

6.2 Time Reductions

Reduced TAT for Account opening and other processes.

6.3 Increased Revenues

Return on Investment of 230 percent.

7. BEST PRACTICES, LEARNING POINTS AND PITFALLS

7.1 Best Practices and Learning Points

✓ Consistently tracking prospects opens new opportunities for cross-selling and up-selling
✓ Greater customer satisfaction, which demands immediate and informed response to their queries, is effectively implemented using a BPM solution
✓ A BPM solution establishes explicit and specific responsibilities with the stakeholders, thereby ensuring greater drive to accomplish work at their end.

8. COMPETITIVE ADVANTAGES

- Scaling up of operational activities enabling the bank to keep pace with business growth and demands
- Compliance and Audit with easy KYC Process
- Incorporation of Islamic banking norms in very short duration due to Flexibility and improvisation of Processes

9. TECHNOLOGY

Opening of an account is the customer's first interaction with a bank. Newgen provided the bank with a BPM-enabled workflow platform for implementing an automated Account Opening process. The solution streamlined the overly complicated process. The customer approaches a Customer Relationship Officer or vice versa for opening an account. The officer captures the customer's details, verifies if the customer already exists, accordingly makes changes, captures the application form image along with the supporting documents and introduces it into the workflow.

Next, the officer submits the information to Customer Operations Manager for authorization. Once authorized, all the details arrive at the Central Processing Department (CPD), where the checks such as reviewing of customer and account information, verifying supporting documents, etc., are done. If cleared, the customer data is automatically pushed into the core system, else it is sent back to the branch for exception clearing. Information such as Account Information, Customer information including signatures, Cheque Book Request, Account Customer relationship, Account memo, etc., is pushed to the core system. Any new information is updated. CPD also generates a file for courier company for the welcome kits to be delivered.

Finally, a Welcome-kit letter along with other documents is generated and sent for dispatching through courier. Once, the kit is delivered, all documents related to the account opened are archived. If a kit is not delivered till a specified date, it is hand it over to branch for delivery to customer.

The BPM solution from Newgen has been integrated with the bank's Core Banking system, SMS system and Card Management system. The solution also enables generation of complete audit trail to view history of events taken place for any record.

The solution has been currently implemented at 43 branches of the bank, and is being used by 50 concurrent and 125 named users.

10. THE TECHNOLOGY AND SERVICE PROVIDERS

Other than Newgen no vendors were directly involved in the process except for the part where integration with the core banking system was done.

Other system interfaces to be exposed to the SMS gateway and Cheque Book System were developed by Newgen's delivery team. No external consultants were involved.

United Parcel Service (UPS)

1. EXECUTIVE SUMMARY / ABSTRACT

Founded in 1907 as a messenger company in the United States, UPS has grown into a multi-billion-dollar corporation by clearly focusing on the goal of enabling commerce around the globe. Today, UPS is a global company with one of the most recognized and admired brands in the world, managing the flow of goods, funds, and information in more than 200 countries and territories worldwide. As the global leader in its industry, UPS continues to develop the frontiers of logistics, supply chain management, and e-Commerce.

To support efforts to improve operational efficiencies and drive customer service excellence, the UPS Shared Services group identified that a pervasive BPM platform for rapid application development and deployment would solve a laundry list of challenges. Utilizing BPM, UPS has improved workload management and resource planning, improved IT's ability to measure and manage SLA attainment, and optimized the cost-to-serve model, ultimately decreasing operating costs while increasing employee and customer satisfaction.

2. OVERVIEW

UPS has achieved its position of global market leadership through a constant focus on reinventing itself and the technologies that drive its business. The IT services delivered to all UPS employees by UPS Shared Services are core to the company's ability to operate efficiently and provide service excellence and accountability to its customers.

UPS Shared Services had a wide range of challenges that it sought to resolve as part of an organizational focus on maximizing efficiency, productivity and quality. These issues included identifying and quantifying precisely "what its people do," modeling and automating existing web-based repetitive processes, identifying and eliminating process choke points, and revitalizing and consolidating work-driving forms.

Shared Services determined that solving these problems would require attaining greater process visibility. By seeing their processes as-is, optimizing them towards ideal states, and effectively managing them in real-time, the department could improve workload management and resource planning, improve its ability to measure and manage SLA attainment, and optimize IT's cost-to-serve model. Ultimately, this would not only decrease operating costs for UPS, but also improve overall satisfaction for Shared Services' 1,200 employees and their internal customers, while also having a positive impact on the quality of service delivered to UPS' external customers as well.

Shared Services deployed a BPMS as a pervasive platform within IT to develop, deploy, measure and manage shared services delivered out to the business. With more than 100 BPM process applications deployed to-date, using the BPMS platform has allowed UPS IT to identify, measure and optimize both process and people metrics, yielding improvements in labor efficiency and accountability, increased Service Level Agreement management, reductions in error rates and rework requirements, and enhancements in strategic planning capabilities.

3. BUSINESS CONTEXT

Although UPS is a technology-driven organization, with an appetite for innovation, the Shared Services group lacked a cohesive infrastructure to deliver end-to-end visibility across its processes. The department used a combination of disparate systems, from mainframes to COTS applications to spreadsheets. Following the mantra that "you can't improve what you can't measure," Shared Services needed a method to clearly measure existing processes. While SLAs were in place, there was no consistent method for ensuring that they were met. A new solution was needed to help Shared Services deconstruct the siloed approach of the past, where individual groups focused on process development and management without looking at the "big picture," and there was no end-to-end ownership as processes crossed groups.

Further, the team required real-time analytics and reporting in order to standardize the metrics for measuring process performance and people effectiveness. Its search for a solution led the group to investigate BPM technologies. However, an immediate roadblock became apparent in that most technologies UPS looked at required heavy outside services involvement due to the complexity of the platforms. Because UPS intended to internally own all solution development, deployment and management without the aid of any vendor professional services capabilities, extreme ease-of-use quickly rose to the top of the requirements list.

4. THE KEY INNOVATIONS

In keeping with recent economic conditions, the directive from UPS' CIO down through all of IT is to focus on the optimization of both cost and service. UPS IT is conscious that it must not only deliver today (in terms of meeting budget constraints, reducing risk and servicing customers), but position itself to deliver even more in the future (through more efficient business processes, improved agility and enhanced decision-making, and innovation in delivery of new services). While this requires a delicate balancing act, Shared Services' use of BPM has delivered on both counts across the organization, and by extension, out to external customers.

Customers:

The objective of Shared Services is a high level of customer support but at a reduced cost. BPM has provided a way to reduce cost by improving workload management (identifying opportunities to increase the productivity of existing headcount). This translates into better and faster service delivery for Shared Service's customers. The increased process status visibility has enabled (for the first time) management of Service Level Agreements. Identification and elimination of process bottlenecks has yielded a dramatic improvement in SLA attainment rates (as measured through ITIL reporting).

Process:

To-date, UPS Shared Services has deployed more than 100 BPM-based process solutions. While the size and scope of the solutions vary, all have contributed to the overall maturation of the department, and delivered key innovations to accelerate and improve service. Various examples are:

Circuit Disconnect Process

This is a high-volume process (roughly 90 requests per quarter). What used to be an 80-day process cycle time now takes 40 to 60 days (depending on geographical location). Process improvement yielded $30,000 in cost avoidance of circuit fees in three months. It improved customer service due to a more streamlined front-end process and faster end-to-end processing time, and improved efficiencies across the board during processing due to reduced manual steps.

Production Control

The more than 5400 annual production job schedule change requests were not adequately tracked. Multiple and disconnected systems were in use (Mainframe, Excel, Access). Customers had no status visibility and were not informed of progress. Through the BPM platform, an automated process was created to submit and track production change requests, fundamentally innovating the process. Information previously stored in multiple systems is now collected and tracked in BPM application. Complete and accurate audit trails and now easily accessed for improved Sarbanes-Oxley compliance. Customers are automatically informed of request status and completion dates.

Data Center Access

Thousands of annual requests for entry to a UPS Data Center were handled through a manual paper process. It was cumbersome and slow, requiring the requestor to physically locate the appropriate management for approval signatures. Through BPM, Shared Services automated the process to initiate and route requests electronically to the appropriate management. The time reduction was dramatic; what previously took 10 days is now done in less than 24 hours. In addition to improved customer satisfaction, the application yielded improved historical tracking and reporting, and enhanced security through a tracking database.

Production Control Mainframe Job Scheduling Requests

Shared Services receives an average of 450 requests per month. BPM shaved 15 minutes per process instance. This was a big win in customer satisfaction because duplication of information entries was eliminated by tying to the process to back-end databases and pre-populating forms.

Organization:

UPS's BPM program within Shared Services directly supports the organization's mission to deliver "The Best Service, at the Lowest Cost." It specifically corresponds to four key tenets:

- Improved Visibility: understanding how effectively IT budget is being spent.
- Prioritization: eliminating non-strategic, redundant projects to free up budget and staff.
- Streamlining: automating and consolidating comprehensively across IT.
- Innovating: being able to invest cost savings in strategic projects to drive competitive advantage.

The program significantly aids UPS' organizational goal to enhance process maturity efforts by standardizing processes and linking process modeling to execution. Through enhanced resource rationalization, workforce management, and end-to-end service and process management, it supports the maximization of organizational efficiency and effectiveness. By providing access to historical data it aids future program and capacity planning.

The program has also driven a top-to-bottom increase in UPS IT's ability to manage effectively and make better, more timely business decisions through personalized, role-specific real-time reporting, as illustrated below:

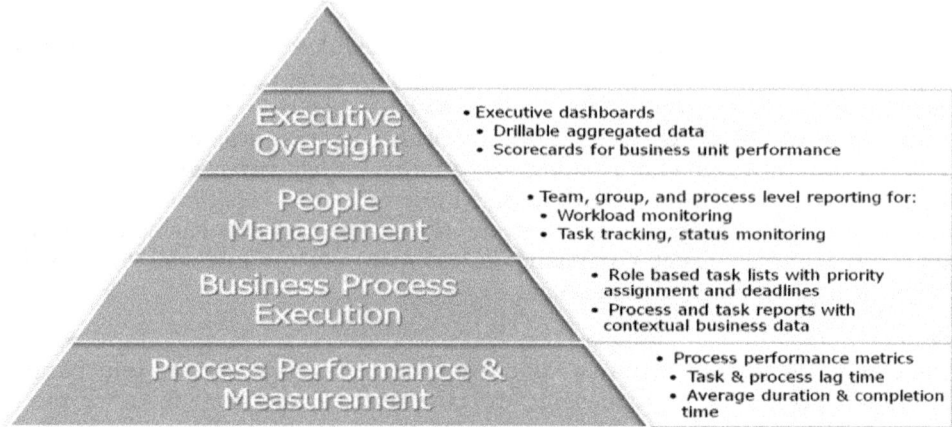

To facilitate change management and drive user acceptance and adoption, UPS Shared Services spearheaded a BPM Center of Excellence, driven through its BPM Governance Team. In addition to managing and prioritizing the flood of potential BPM projects, the COE has established standards and best practices, developed and leveraged lessons learned, and increased the organizational BPM footprint by promoting BPM successes and ensuring a steady stream of new, high-quality process implementations.

5. HURDLES OVERCOME

Management

A key hurdle was obtaining management buy-in. To do this, Shared Sevices developed in-house training and certifications to support an increase in BPM business acumen among management. It focused on defining the value BPM would provide. It fostered a "Process Culture" by highlighting how ever-evolving measures and metrics of process aligned with Key Business Objectives. These resulted in a definite "ah-ha!" moment among management. Initially people had to be mandated to identify process workflows for automation opportunities, but as more and more process workflows were automated, the benefits became obvious. Initial lack of understanding around what "process data" was gave way to acceptance of its value through education on how to use it.

Management was also swayed by increasing emphasis on the development and use of dashboards and reports as leading and lagging indicators to drive the business. Ultimately, the reporting of the information is what sold Senior Management. As the data repository built over time, it became easier to demonstrate the value of reporting on work volume and other trends such as resource utilization.

Business

Proving the link between BPM and key business objectives was a hurdle to overcome. Shared Services had to demonstrate that BPM was a tool to implement the concept of better business planning, to expand efforts around performance benchmarking, and to manage and continually support change for improvement in service, cost and quality. A big part of this was educating that the visibility and data delivered through BPM would help move the business to a proactive versus reactive operational environment, and change the behavior of rewarding "fire fighting."

Organization Adoption

Getting people to move to a process-centric attitude required helping them change the way they work and think. Increased accountability was perceived as an issue, with a clearer record now available for where and how employees were spending their time. It required a cultural shift for Shared Services' customers as well, as many would rather call or walk up than fill out a request form. To overcome these hurdles, the BPM team implemented the use of "RACI" models (Accountability, Responsibility, Consulting and Informing) as a method to ensure all participants understood their roles in a process. The team developed an in-house Train the Trainer program to help with the transition, and to encourage use of the process automation tool, leading to greater acceptance of a process "way of thinking."

Leading the organization to see the need for change was also crucial, and was accomplished by driving transition to a Service Management focus. By aligning all aspect of planning (Key Business Objectives (KBO) to Critical Success Factors (CSF) and Key Performance Indicators (KPI), the BPM team helped establish BPM as a cross-functional tool for governance.

6. BENEFITS

UPS has calculated a **$28M cost-savings** from process efficiency gains, user self-service, and data error eliminations.

In addition, the Team has identified an **additional opportunity pool of $23M** through better alignment of Incident Management processes. It is anticipated that this assessment will lead to further significant cost reductions.

Additional business benefits include:

- Workload balancing: improved more than 58%
- Resource allocation: more than 210 man-hours have been freed up and repurposed to more strategic initiatives
- Employee performance visibility: captured 85% - 90% of total hours and activities for 1200 employees
- Process cycle times: reduced from four, five or even 10 days down to 24 hours.
- Integrated tool sets: example – 5 Project Management systems consolidated to 1
- Function/Department rationalization: elimination of overlaps in roles and responsibilities between departments
- Increase standardization: establishment of BPM Governance group / Center Of Excellence
- Operational transformation: 154 Process workflows modeled

7. BEST PRACTICES, LEARNING POINTS AND PITFALLS

7.1 Best Practices and Learning Points

✓ *Define your problems first to avoid misinterpretation of purpose*
✓ *Secure Executive sponsorship and a dedicated, independent BPM team*
✓ *Establish strong communication to ease change management and bridge the user adoption gap*

7.2 Pitfalls

✗ *Don't underestimate the need for training upfront*
✗ *Don't fail to clearly define roles & responsibilities for all involved including stakeholders*
✗ *Don't try to move forward without a dedicated governance team*

> ✗ *Don't fail to celebrate wins loudly and often; this is a must for continued buy-in and motivation*

8. COMPETITIVE ADVANTAGES

UPS' BPM program has driven significant competitive advantage for the company. It has increased the efficiency and effectiveness of the underlying IT services that support the ability of the UPS workforce to carry out its duties. This ultimately translates to a direct customer-facing impact in enhanced quality and consistency of service.

BPM has provided an unprecedented level of visibility and data on which management can make better and faster business decisions. It has also supported UPS' strategic goal to increase overall organizational process maturity, increasing process flexibility to drive more agile responses to organizational, competitive and market changes.

UPS has a long-term perspective on the value of BPM. Its approach is that BPM is a journey, not a "one time effort." That's why shared Services and the BPM COE have specifically architected its program to be reusable and sustainable. By leveraging the experiences gained in each BPM deployment, the organization becomes better at driving maximum value from future deployments, more quickly.

9. TECHNOLOGY

The Appian BPM Suite is the technology platform for UPS' BPM program. UPS selected Appian after a thorough vendor evaluation.

Because UPS decided to do all BPM application development and deployment on its own, without vendor services assistance, it was imperative that the platform it chose be both comprehensive in terms of integrated functionality and easy to use for both developers and end-users. Appian's 100 percent web architecture, personalized user portals, and drag-and-drop graphical modeling were exactly what UPS was looking for. In addition, Appian's powerful SOA integration capabilities were crucial in tying together the various legacy systems and data sources required for UPS' vision.

Appian's real-time process architecture enables the immediate and unlimited reporting and analytics necessary to support Shared Services' drive for better SLA management, and for the management and executive visibility needed to drive the organization.

10. THE TECHNOLOGY AND SERVICE PROVIDERS

Appian is the global innovator in enterprise and on-demand business process management (BPM). Appian provides the fastest way to deploy robust processes, collapsing time to value for new process initiatives. Businesses and governments worldwide use Appian to accelerate process improvement and drive business performance. Appian empowers more than 2.5 million users from large Fortune 100 companies, to the mid-market and small businesses worldwide. Appian is headquartered in the Washington, D.C. region, with professional services and partners around the globe. For more information, visit www.appian.com.

BAA Heathrow, United Kingdom

1. Executive Summary / Abstract

At London's Heathrow airport, a new case is created by a system feed, every time an incoming plane is registered by air-traffic control, and closes when the plane is en route to its next destination. This event enabled case-management approach to aircraft turn-around has dramatically improved the overall efficiency of operations at Heathrow, including:

- An increase in on-time departures from 68 percent to 83 percent,
- A savings of 90 litres of fuel per flight, due to decreased time spent on the runway, yielding cost savings for airlines, and a positive environmental impact,
- A projected increase in retail revenues, by allowing passengers on faster-boarding flights to spend more time in the terminal rather than seated in airplanes awaiting take off.

The caseworkers in this case are the people responsible for the timely and efficient turn-around of airplanes—from airline teams, to stand planners, to air traffic controllers, to cleaning crews, to baggage handlers. With this new system, they are empowered with all of the information they need to make the right decisions—including a real-time visualization of planes on the runways—and to initiate the right processes, and allocate the right resources, based on the context of the situation from type of plane, to the plane's next destination. The imperative for adaptive case management is clear here, where the context is constantly changing due to external events such as weather or security alerts.

2. Overview

This example demonstrates just how broadly a case-based approach to work can be applied. In the most common applications of case management, people are the subjects of the work, whether they are customers, citizens, patients. Here the subject of the case is neither a person, nor even a business; the subject is an activity, a span of time—specifically, turning around an aircraft. Yet the approach is unquestionably case management. Personal experience tells us all how dynamic this type of case is; we know how many factors contribute to our flights taking off on time—or not. It is a true testament to the power of new adaptive case management approaches that case management can be applied to such a dynamic type of case.

Each case that is handled by BAA is like a performance of a well-coordinated jazz ensemble. In jazz, there are many sets of rules—tonality, rhythm, harmony—that govern what the players play. At the same time, the players improvise within this set of rules, constantly reacting to the actions of the other members in a perfect balance between structure and improvisation. At BAA, the different actors on the case whether people, departments or systems, are akin to the different instruments within an ensemble. Just as each instrument has a set range and sound that gives it a unique ability to contribute to the performance, so too each of these actors has a unique range of skills enabling them to contribute to the resolution of the case. Both the actors, and the skills they can apply, change with the context—one doesn't want a trumpet player belting out a fortissimo when the desired mood is pianissimo.

In the following pages, you'll read how BAA has harnessed this kind of controlled improvisation to substantially improve airport operations. Underpinning this was an undertaking by BAA to capture the rules of their operation, institutionalizing them such that every actor is able to perform to the best of his or her abilities in every situation. Because of the system-based nature, this is possible without years of training on what those policies and procedures are. In this way, BAA is able to fully empower the entire network of people collaborating to quickly turn around—literally—a jumbo-jet, without fear that regulations are being breached, or customer service is being overlooked.

3. BUSINESS CONTEXT

In 2008, over 145 million passengers passed through BAA's UK airports, including almost 70 million through the world's busiest International airport, London Heathrow. At Heathrow over 70,000 staff were engaged in helping those passengers to move through the airport as efficiently as possible.

Prompted by upcoming domestic and industry regulations such as the EU's Single European Sky ATM Research program (SESAR), in 2008 BAA initiated a program to simplify the complex set of operational systems that were used to manage the airport. One of the first goals of the program was to put in place a system that would allow the airport to optimize flight turnarounds, both in terms of time, and in terms of resources.

Prior to the program the resources that were employed to turn around a flight, including the stands, gates, check-in counters, refueling crews, cleaning crews, flight crew managers, and information from the systems—for example the air traffic control system—were managed by separate teams. Each of these teams was part of a separate line of business—or even part of a separate company. This organizational architecture yielded "optimization" at the department level, not at the airport level. At the airport level it was sub-optimal—on-time flight departures hovered around 60 percent. As one of the busiest and most inter-connected airports in the world, the ramifications of delayed flights extended globally.

Taking cues from other industries which have improved their customer service, BAA decided to take a case management approach, with the aircraft turn around being the case.

4. THE KEY INNOVATIONS

Describe the impact that resulted from the project (recommended).

4.1 Business

Since going live with this system, Airport Collaborative Decision Management or A-CDM, BAA has increased on-time departures to 85 percent from 68 percent which in turn decreases the amount they pay in penalties. The ability of managers to improve resource planning and allocation significantly improves the efficiency of terminal operations.

Because BAA now has visibility into which flights take the longest to board, whether based on how full they are, what the destination is, etc., they can optimize boarding to keep passengers in the terminal longer, rather than prematurely boarding them.

There are three benefits that arise from this practice:
- Passengers are happier, because they are free to move about rather than corralled in an airplane sitting on the tarmac.
- Passengers spend more time in the terminal shopping at retails outlets, or eating at dining establishments, improving the bottom line for these interests. Metrics for this are still being collected.

- The last benefit from this case-based approach to aircraft turnaround is that each airplane now spends less time on the runway, saving approximately 90 litres of fuel per flight. Not only does this decrease the carbon footprint, but—aggregated over time, it is a significant savings to the airlines flying in and out of Heathrow.

4.2 Case Handling

Case handling before implementation:

Prior to this program the resources that were employed to turn around a flight, including the stands, gates, check-in counters, refueling crews, cleaning crews, flight crew managers, and information from the systems—for example the air traffic control system—were managed by separate teams. Each of these teams was part of a separate line of business—or even part of a separate company. This organizational architecture yielded "optimization" at the department level, not at the airport level.

Case handling after implementation:

Now, when a flight bound for Heathrow enters British airspace, a system feed from air traffic control automatically creates the case. A template for how to handle it is applied based on a variety of criteria, including where the plane is coming from and going to, the size of the aircraft, etc. BAA thinks of these as resource plans. The template or plan that is used will also differ based on the current stress-level of the airport. The A-CDM system is then able to monitor the real-time aggregated volume of traffic in the airport and manage it based on pre-defined stress levels. These levels correspond to the amount of stress on airport resources and are constantly monitored to ensure that the current level reflects reality. The inputs to the level are various, but some are: weather, security status, daily and/or seasonal passenger volume. Each level has its own set of templates and policies that are applied for resource allocation, in order to ensure the optimal allocation given that particular stress level.

The key roles are:
- Airline Staff
- Air traffic control
- Stand planners
- Stand managers
- Flight crew managers
- Cleaning crews
- Repair crews
- Refuelling crews
- Baggage handlers
- Airport security

The assignment of a given crew or person to the turnaround of a specific aircraft at a specific stand is performed automatically by the system, based on the rules specified by the prevailing stress level. Up until the point that an aircraft is actually at the gate, these assignments (particularly the gate) are constantly in flux, ensuring the optimal resource allocation. Once the aircraft is at the gate, while the gate itself will not change, the allocation of other resources needed to turn the plane around will depend on the broader functioning of the airport, as well as any knock-on effects from air traffic at other airports. For example, an aircraft might be ready to turn around, Heathrow might have the capacity to send it on its way, but the destination airport may have an air traffic control delay in place. Given that situation, it may not make sense to deploy the resources to turn the plane around right at that moment, but rather to wait and address other turnarounds, whose aircraft may be in jeopardy of late departure.

The rules that are in force based on the stress level—which form the basis for the template, and the actions that are available—affect assignment and "routing" of aircraft and personnel. However, the actual work is still being performed by people, and their actions and updates impact how the system handles/allocates other resources, and what actions are available to others. The various managers of these resources act within the sets of policies that apply at that stress level. This means that they still have all the freedom they want to perform any action, as long as it isn't explicitly prohibited by the stress level. In this way, the case is extremely dynamic, as people and systems are constantly interacting to ensure the highest percentage of on-time flights, given the circumstances (or context) at the time. For example, an air traffic controller who decides to hold a plane on the ground automatically impacts the allocation and handling of all other aircraft at the airport.

"Caseworkers" also have a real-time view of the position of the various aircraft on the runway. This allows them to better understand how the work they are doing for a given turnaround case fits into the broader whole—the airport "case load" as it were.

Of course all of the rules need to be flexible and adaptable to manage situational flux. Firstly, different airlines want to manage their turnaround rules in a unique fashion, and therefore some of the rules within the case template are adaptable to define, for example, what the minimum turnaround time for each flight is. This automatically sets the goals and target times within the system for that flight. Also, as turnaround proceeds, some flights are delayed and others are ready ahead of the expected time. Therefore the airline has the ability to update its state of readiness and alert air traffic control that they will be ready to leave either earlier or later and the necessary processes (passenger boarding, pre-departure sequencing etc) can be amended accordingly. These are two examples of many functions in the system designed to allow the airport and the people working on its behalf to react promptly and consistently to constant change.

4.3 Organization & Social

Before the A-CDM system was deployed, the operating model was akin to moving from one "fire" to the next, as they were unable to anticipate, nor allocate work to address the flux in the amount of work. Now, while there are still certainly very busy times, in all except for emergency situations, they are able to plan for those, and staff accordingly. Even in emergent situations, the return to normal occurs in a faster and more orderly fashion. The appropriate policies for that stress level are applied, and these help to ensure that workers across the airport are able to handle the situation in the most effective way possible.

At the very outset of the process, BAA rigorously defined its business architecture, including a business capability and service map. This foundational work was necessary to being able to put together the resource plan templates, and also in meeting one of BAA's other goals—reusability. Further it has proven very valuable for helping BAA to manage the on-going changes being introduced by this new, ever-evolving, and expanding system.

5. HURDLES OVERCOME

Management
- Executive support throughout the project was essential, not only for requirements clarification but also to maintain the buy-in of the many external stakeholders. Executives were always aware of the importance of this project in the achievement of a range of BAA's corporate targets

Business (Operations)
- As above, this was achieved through clear and constant communication across the user community.

Organization Adoption
- The problems before CDM was delivered were that no one believed the information in their systems— everyone was looking at different 'versions of the truth'. This led to people putting poor data into the system or trying to use loopholes to their advantage. This system is coaching all users towards a more honest use of the system, including publicizing the accuracy of the data that each airline provides to the broader user community

6. BENEFITS

6.1 Cost Savings / Time Reductions
- Increases in on-time departures has reduced penalties paid to the airlines
- Save 90 litres of fuel/departure, as average time spent on the tarmac has been reduced
- Considerable reduction in system development, management and maintenance costs compared with off the shelf monitoring tools.

6.2 Increased Revenues
- Expected increase in retail revenues due to keeping passengers in the terminal as long as possible—without jeopardizing on-time departure.

6.3 Quality Improvements
- Increased on-time departures from 60 percent to 85 percent
- Airport running at 98.7 percent capacity

7. BEST PRACTICES, LEARNING POINTS AND PITFALLS

7.1 Best Practices and Learning Points
- ✓ Make sure you have clear definitions of your business services and business capabilities, and how these are used throughout your organization.
- ✓ Identify and communicate the responsibilities for all stake holders
- ✓ When selecting a vendor, have a clear set of requirements. Ask each vendor to implement the requirements (some) in 1 day, then on the 2nd day, change the requirements. This will give you insight into how easy it will be for YOU to make changes when you need to.

7.2 Pitfalls
- ✗ User adoption
- ✗ Change management

8. COMPETITIVE ADVANTAGES

Improving on-time departures ensures that Heathrow will continue to be a major hub for European and trans-continental travel. Without a demonstrated, on-going commitment to on-time departures and overall efficiency, BAA would run the risk of losing traffic to other major airports.

The A-CDM project is just the first step in a long-term plan to increase the efficiency of Heathrow.

9. Technology

The underlying technology infrastructure.

- The A-CDM system uses Pegasystems as its key technology. For the user interface, Pegasystems is combined with Microsoft SharePoint.
- In order to ensure that upgrades are easy, BAA has implemented a strict rule that only generally available functionality be used within the solution—no custom coding.

10. The Technology and Service Providers

Pegasystems; implementation was handled by a joint team of Pega professional services and BAA Information Technology staff.

Los Angeles County Department of Public Social Services (DPSS)

1. CHALLENGE

With over 10 million people, Los Angeles County is the largest county in the United States. The Los Angeles County Department of Public Social Services (DPSS) currently serves over two million participants each day and a caseload of over 1.6 million across its various public assistance programs—more than any other jurisdiction except the states of California and New York. Even though the County has developed standardized processes and workflow, the unpredictability of people and the sheer volume of cases in Los Angeles create an often overwhelmed situation. It is the goal of the Call Center personnel, who are classified as Eligibility Workers, to determine individual benefits eligibility.

Through DPSS, the County provides a range of programs including CalWORKs (California's Temporary Assistance to Needy Families (TANF) program), CalFresh, Medi-Cal (California's Medicaid program), and General Relief. Eligibility determination for all of these programs is provided through a case management system called LEADER (Los Angeles Eligibility Automated Determination Evaluation and Reporting). With demand for these programs and the complexity of administering them ever growing, LA County's DPSS needed a solution that would increase case worker accessibility, improve operational efficiency and enhance the overall customer service experience.

2. SOLUTION

In August 2006, DPSS selected Lagan to collaborate on the implementation of a centralized customer service call center for approximately 86 eligibility workers designed to service the San Gabriel Valley District Office with an annual caseload of 30,000. This was the first wave of a planned enterprise roll-out that ultimately will touch approximately 6,000 case workers and potentially, 600 to 800 Customer Service Representatives (CSR).

The Call Center went live in January 2007, achieving a key project milestone early on— integration with the existing LEADER system—thanks to Lagan's open interface toolkit. Lagan and LEADER created an interface that allowed case information to populate on the Lagan application and case comments to automatically populate on the LEADER system without retyping the comments.

CSRs have direct access to over a million eligibility case records in the County's LEADER system while fielding live calls in a contact center environment. Later that year, the County added two more district offices, and as of June 13, 2011 has expanded to eight district offices serving a combined caseload of 400,000 clients. Average monthly call volume is 110,000, with monthly tracking tickets averaging 35,000.

In January 2008, the County implemented a self-service component through an Interactive Voice Response (IVR) system giving callers 24 hour access to case information, such as benefit amounts and case status, as well as emergency hotlines. Today, the IVR system helps screen the calls that are purely informational in nature before ever reaching a Call Center agent. The calls that are taken are documented by the Computer Telephony Integration (CTI) and Requests for Information (RFIs) are supported by the software solution that front-ends the County's eligibility system (LEADER).

Actions that need to be performed by Case Workers or other District Office workers are initiated as tickets from the software solution that then assigns tasks that need to be completed in order to resolve case issues for a County welfare participant. Every case is unique because every family is unique. The number of family members, ages, relationships, parents, step-children, foster children, adopted children, locations, educational levels, etc., vary greatly from case to case. There may be similarities to case and the process workflow helps to identify those similarities to aid in greater efficiency. The LA County DPSS Customer Service Center (CSC) project team analyzes reports and data extracts through Business Intelligence (BI) reporting and utilize that data to make changes in the Business Process management (BPM) module of the software solution.

In June 2010, the County implemented an Outbound Dialing System to further improve communication and customer service. The system places reminder calls to DPSS participants and assists in reaching the most vulnerable participants in case of emergency.

Through the call center, participants have access to service information Monday through Friday from 7:30 a.m.–5:30 p.m. via an 800-number. Support is provided in five languages—English, Spanish, Mandarin, Vietnamese and Cambodian. As a result of a well-developed knowledgebase and system ease of use, approximately half of the calls received can be handled directly by the customer service center without the need to generate additional work for the case workers. The remaining calls are automatically routed via a tracking ticket to the district office for case worker follow-up. Supervisors have instant access to case files and can track progress in real time. Reports and notifications are automatically generated to inform supervisors where bottlenecks and issues may be occurring, making it far easier to manage the day-to-day work of the agency.

3. RESULTS

LA County DPSS deployed the solution in a fraction of the time it would have taken for a traditional solution; the initial phase of the project took less than six months from contract signature to implementation and rollout.

Today, LA County DPSS customer service center receives about 190,000 calls per month, of which an average of 74,000 reach a Customer Service Representative. Approximately 74,000 tracking tickets are generated each month, fielded by the 222 representatives in the call center.

There were several key factors that have made the deployment of Lagan Human Services and the expanded customer service center capabilities a success: defining processes up front; encouraging involvement of case workers, supervisors, customer service representatives and the technology department throughout the process; garnering support and buy-in from top administrators; and fostering collaboration between Lagan and the County.

The successful collaboration between department and vendor was critical to reach the goal. Defining the business process along with input and feedback from users was integral to the success of the project and will ensure success though expansion.

Preliminary customer satisfaction surveys have yielded a 99 percent satisfaction rate. Through the centralized call center, participant access to case information has increased from two hours a day to ten hours a day. The self-service option ensures that more questions can be answered with a single phone call, with fewer visits to the district offices. The response, both internally and externally, has been excellent.

The net results:

- For staff, the opportunity to excel by providing more responsive and accurate guidance to participants
- For supervisors, higher levels of accountability since all data is being tracked in real time
- For the County, a highly cost-effective means of improving accessibility to services through the application of non-invasive technology
- For the participant, a completely new way of interacting with DPSS—one which saves trips to the district office and yields positive outcomes in shorter periods of time

Today, the customer service center handles calls for eight line district offices. The goal is to expand support to handle calls for all 36 LA County district offices. Plans are also in place to extend the IVR system and expand county-wide with multiple full-service contact center locations serving as one virtual center. The customer service center has implemented an Electronic Document Management System (EDMS) which will allow DPSS to begin its transition to a paperless environment by scanning all case documents. Longer term, the county seeks to streamline its operations more strategically, incorporating other programs, additional customer service and hotline numbers, and internet-based automated services.

4. LA COUNTY DPSS CALL CENTER SUCCESS AT A GLANCE

- Access hours expanded from two hours/day to ten hours/day, 7:30 a.m.–5:30 pm.
- Self-service interactive voice response system adds 24/7 access to case information and program and emergency hotlines
- Eight district offices now supported with a combined caseload of 195,000
- Monthly call volume: 190,000 of which 96,000 are handled by the Customer Service Representatives
- Monthly tracking tickets: over 74,000
- Trained call center customer service representatives directly handle approximately 77 percent of inquiries
- Customer satisfaction survey rates are 99 percent.

5. ABOUT LAGAN, A DIVISION OF KANA SOFTWARE

Lagan, a Division of KANA Software, Inc., is the global leader in G2C (government to citizen) solutions connecting government and citizens worldwide. Lagan enables governments and citizens to communicate online, on the phone and on the move. With 200 public sector customers worldwide, Lagan helps local governments serve the everyday interests of more than 60 million citizens.

Lagan's solutions for Service Experience Management have been designed to streamline the service delivery functions of government, enabling improved efficiency and more citizen-centric public services. Lagan manages the interactions between citizens and government and provides full support for a wide variety of government service delivery processes. Lagan's solutions have proven utility for state and local governments and offer a range of flexible delivery methods: on-premise, on-demand and hosted. Learn more at www.kana.com.

Lincoln Trust Company, USA

1. EXECUTIVE SUMMARY / ABSTRACT

This paper describes the experiences of implementing an enterprise wide BPM program at Lincoln Trust Company. The program was constituted in early 2007 with an initial goal of managing core processes related to physical paperwork and an ultimate goal of using BPM technology to manage all strategic processes of the organization. When the program began the company was receiving over 100,000 client documents each month with limited to no control over these instructions. Initial, overwhelming success with an enterprise wide implementation of BPM technology to workflow-enable document centric processes led to the strong desire of company management to move quickly to our next goals of understanding, improving, and automating other strategic processes. By doing so we've been able to open our back office process for collaboration with a strategic outsourcing partner, drive processes to the web, reduce costs and risks, improve customer satisfaction, and completely turn around a damaged relationship between IT and the business.

2. OVERVIEW

Lincoln Trust Company (LTC) is a financial services custodian that provides individual retirement account (IRA) and employer sponsored retirement plan administration. Lincoln Trust differentiates itself among many of its competitors in that, as a custodian, in addition to offering traditional investments, the company specializes in offering administration of non-traditional assets such as private placements, promissory notes, offshore funds and residential and commercial real estate for investment in IRAs and other account types. LTC has approximately 350 employees and over $15 billion in assets under administration.

As the program started, the immediate challenge facing LTC were serious process problems related to customer instructions received via the mail. As mentioned previously, we were receiving over 100,000 customer documents each month. The gravity of the situation at this time cannot be overstated and we were quite literally sinking in our process problems. We had calculated the yearly weight of this incoming paperwork to be 18 tons and the weight of our filing cabinets was so much an issue that we had to continually relocate them throughout the building to keep the floor from sinking in spots. On top of all this each business unit had intensely manual, risk prone and costly paper-based workflow processes. The programs first priority had to be to "stop the bleeding" and implement a document workflow solution quickly. To accomplish this we choose to initially implement the workflow capabilities of a document management tool we already owned.

In early 2007, a roadmap was established with executive sponsors that identified 10 implementation phases to deliver document workflow to all business units. In order to move quickly across the enterprise a strategy was recommended that emphasized a common, standardized process approach and incremental 90 day deliverables.

The initial results were wildly successful. The BPM program was able to make a dramatic business impact that gained the attention of executives across the business and generated demand for higher-level process innovation. By mid-2008, after a series of phased rollouts, we were using workflow technology to electronically route and deliver nearly all incoming mail, faxes, checks, ACHs, and wires.

Benefits of these initial implementations included, for the first time, being able to leverage an outsourcing partner and have portions of our back office processing performed offshore. Documents were not lost, we had full tracking of their business status, quality control rules were enforced, and analytics were provided to the business for use in staff level planning. In this first year and a half of the program we experienced a 90% reduction in customer complaints, decreased processing times by up to 75% in some areas, and calculated an ROI of 120%.

A challenge we faced early on was the businesses desire to perform higher level process automation (beyond document centric workflow) involving straight through processing with our core trust accounting system and integration with our customer portal. We understood that, in order to meet these process innovation demands, along with changing business models within our organization, we would need a more robust BPMS, and after an exhaustive vendor search, selected an industry leading BPMS along with a leading Business Intelligence platform for advanced analytics. Since mid-2008 we have utilized our BPMS to implement processes as varied as Mutual Fund Trading to general Service Requests.

To date, the BPM program at LTC has implemented 15 enterprise-wide business processes impacting 10 different operational business units with 5-120 employees each. Some of the business processes implemented have only 4 to 5 activities while others have more than 20 activities. This variety of processes and solutions demands a tremendous amount of agility not only from the BPMS and supporting applications but the teams that conduct BPM projects and implement the solutions. Listed below are the BPM processes deployed, with their respective production date up to 04/20/2009.

- Transfers In, New Accounts – 5/4/07
- Transfers Out – 5/4/07
- Institutional Front Office – 8/11/07
- Deposit Processing – 2/14/08
- Cashiering and Customer Credits – 2/14/08
- General Trading – 7/14/08
- Pricing and General Maintenance – 7/14/09
- Mutual Fund Trading – 7/14/08
- Service Requests – 1/20/09
- Distribution Rejection – 1/20/09
- Quick Trades – 1/20/09
- Distributions – 3/25/09
- Transfer Tracking – 7/6/09 (This deployment and below listed but not otherwise considered because of recent deployment dates and award rules.)
- Corporate Retirement Services – 9/14/09
- Online Distributions – in progress

3. BUSINESS CONTEXT

Lincoln Trust is a newly formed private company that was recently spun off from a larger parent organization, Fiserv, Inc. As a result of the divestiture the company went from 950 employees to its current size of 350 employees. In order to be successful as a smaller, private entity, it was imperative that the business model change and it was understood that the previous business model could not be sustained in a smaller company. The risk to reward dynamics had changed in our market place for a smaller company. Segments of the IRA business have historically been in decline and there would be no ongoing entity without this BPM effort. LTC had to fundamentally change how we provide services, and the supporting business vision needed to change how we identify, attract, interact with, and process work for our customers. In order to be successful and profitable, and position ourselves for future growth, we needed to change our business model and chose to embrace BPM as an enabling discipline. Our BPM program was initiated to enable change to the business model and enable an all new architecture.

Prior to the initiation of the BPM program the process landscape was extensively manual. Most processes were tracked using desktop tools such as Microsoft Excel, Access, and Outlook. There was no visibility into processes and it would often take multiple phone calls and research to resolve a client issue or simply to provide them status. Skill levels of individuals performing work varied and often senior level employees were spending significant portions of their day performing non value-add work either maintaining process status or providing follow-up to customers because of rework and inefficiencies earlier in the process.

Also at the time we began there was a seriously negative perception of IT. The business did not consider IT to be a strategic partner and relationships were strained. There had been two significant attempts under different IT leadership to implement a workflow solution in the years prior to 2007 and they both failed at much expense to the company. An executive over one business area had even declared that she "would fire all of IT if she could." As a result new leadership was brought in and the program was restarted with the immediate goal being to workflow enable our document processes and eliminate as much paper as possible from the business operations. The anticipated benefits were to move some processes to an offshore partner, speed processing times, eliminate lost documents, improve client service, reduce risk, and provide complete visibility into our processes and customer documents. Our longer term goals remained to leverage a more full feature BPMS and establish electronic forms on our customer portal (eliminate paper in the first place) and use a BPM approach to streamline and automate all our strategic business processes.

4. THE KEY INNOVATIONS

4.1 Business

Our first processes implemented in our "common shared process" model allowed us to work with our offshore partner, Fiserv Global Services, to take on business operations work that previously could not be outsourced due to our work being driven by paper rather than a workflow system supported by imaged documents.

Subsequent process implementations have allowed us to move away from paper transactions entirely in some cases. We can now engage our clients over our web portal for transactions that previously could only be requested by paper forms. However, we still have the flexibility to support paper form requests for client base that does not have access to or the desire to use a computer to submit requests.

We have integrated our process data with our VOIP telephone system such that, when we receive a phone call from our client and they have keyed their account number into the phone system, a "screen pop" will automatically appear for the Client Service Representative (CSR) that shows all completed and in progress process data, along with any images that are attached to a process, in addition to other information that is pertinent to the client relationship. This visibility allows the CSR to resolve many phone call requests from clients on the same call, requiring no call back on the part of the client or the CSR.

We are now integrating customer profitability scores into our processes so that our most profitable customers receive the highest levels of service. This allows us to turn our processes into a way to generate additional revenue by encouraging our clients to "upgrade" their accounts to receive enhanced service. Having customer profitability scores built into our process helps us ensure that we're consistently providing the highest level of service systematically and retaining our profitable customers.

4.2 Process

In January, 2007, we formed a small executive steering group and a small BPM team comprised of one project manager, one developer and one business analyst. We needed a cost effective strategy to implementing BPM very quickly across the organization. We came up with a two-tiered strategy. We would first use a "common shared process" model that could be rolled out quickly across the enterprise. This model would deliver imaged documents in a business process workflow and discontinue paper delivery. After a significant concentration of the business was "paperless", we would initiate the second tier of the strategy, to implement true, or "first order" business process models for our most strategic processes. While there would be customizable features for each implementation of the common shared process, in order to provide the necessary speed of implementation, the executive steering group committed to ensuring that their business units would not demand highly specialized features that would slow down the implementations. Below is a diagram that outlines the features of the common shared process:

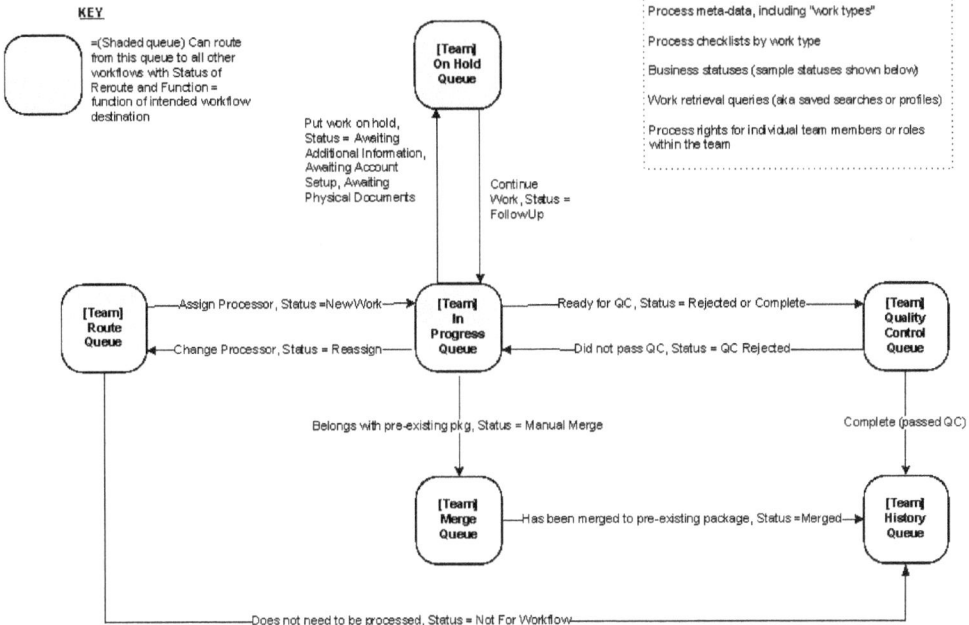

Overview of Common Shared Process Template

In February, 2007, we kicked off our first BPM project with the Transfers In and New Accounts business units and added several business unit employees to the project team as process owners and subject matter experts. In May, 2007, we implemented the New Accounts and Transfers In business processes using the "common shared process" model as the template. The project was a tremendous success and yielded many unexpected benefits.

By July, 2008, fifteen business units' business process documents, which initiated or supported over 145 business processes, were implemented using the "common shared process" to resolve the paper problem quickly.

As we implemented this process model across the business, we learned that adding new, seemingly simple or intuitive, features to the model was very difficult and required a good deal of custom software, which also added time on to our implementations. By extension, we were also learning that "first order" business process implementation and the analysis and automation it would require would definitely not be served by our existing workflow tool. After a good deal of research, we decided that we would be better served by acquiring a BPMS that we could integrate with our document management system (and any other line of business system) quickly and easily. Since we had demonstrated measurable benefits in our implementations since 2007, we were able to form the business case to justify the purchase of a BPMS (Lombardi Teamworks) in August, 2008.

Strategically significant business processes are now being carved out of the "common shared process" that hosted them previously and built into an individual business process model that manages all the activities of the process (not just those that are common to document workflow). As noted previously, this type of implementation is called a "first order business process" in our process architecture.

Both the common shared process and first order processes are now hosted in our BPMS and served with a shared set of document management web services that are integrated with our document management system, Oracle IPM.

As a principle in our process architecture, we make very limited modifications to our common shared process – only where required to prevent errors or reduce liability – limited improvements for efficiency and better visibility. We prefer to invest our limited IT budget in first order, strategic processes instead.

4.3 Organization

To help describe the impact of BPM and our implementations on the business, the following are a few direct quotes from managers:

- "We now have tools to map out, study and improve all our processes. They are user friendly and logical. I'm excited that we've embraced the BPM technology/culture that supports the way we want to manage our business." LaTeca Fields, Special Support Services Manager
- "We are able to use tools typically exclusive to IT. Amazing things have begun to emerge." Bonnie Lewis, Operations Vice President "The BPM Quick Trade component adds huge accountability to the trading process in that it requires one to route items timely and accurately." Brett Davis, Trading Manager
- "BPM has given us a way to dissect the manual cash reconciliation process, produce a plan to automate the reconciliation and report discrepancies." Cathy Maestas, Cash Services Manager

Evidence of BPM advancing as a discipline is literally written on the walls of the organization. Our BPM executive sponsors challenged their management teams to conduct BPM projects for at least five strategic business processes that operate within and across their business units. Many walls of the three floors of the building we occupy are now wall-papered with business process maps on long plotter sheets. Often you can find groups of employees standing around them and socializing about the processes. Many business units have invited all employees to scribble process problems and solutions feedback directly on to these maps by a certain date. These scribbles are later documented and used in BPM projects as inputs into sessions to identify process problems and solutions.

Another impact to the organization was that many employees now have the ability to telecommute. This became very important just recently during our business continuity planning and testing for the H1N1 flu pandemic. Without the implementations of the BPM program, our business continuity planning would have been extremely difficult, if not impossible.

As we mature our BPM program and framework, we are working towards a "practice center" model of organizing our program rather than a centralized business unit or single department ownership of BPM. When we discussed a "Center of Excellence", our organization struggled with the name and the idea that BPM might be "owned" by one area of the business. Our vision is very much to have BPM be a way of life in every business unit. The idea of the "practice center" resonated much better with our organization. The current evolution of the BPM Practice Center is a SharePoint site with links to our various project information, standards, articles, training materials, roadmap, etc.

5. HURDLES OVERCOME

5.1 Management

There have been many organizational challenges to implementation. At the time we began the program there were strained relationships between IT and the business that resulted in new IT leadership being brought in. The organization was going through a divestiture from our parent organization that resulted in a remaining workforce one fourth the initial size. Functional business teams were reorganized and consolidated as part of the divesture of business. Program credibility had to be established incrementally to get all business channels on board with the initiatives. Training and process mapping and analysis skills had to be provided to the business. We had also recently made the decision within IT that all development, configuration, and implementation for processes in our BPMS would be performed by an overseas outsourcing partner.

As would be expected, there have been technical implementation challenges as well. Internal standards and program framework were not in place when we started. There were learning curves for project staff on new technologies. Also, foundational architecture had to be established to allow for integration with Active Directory, SharePoint portal, the Oracle IPM document repository, and other host applications. Additionally, we did not have a well defined operational model for managing and supporting BPM technologies in production.

The biggest hurdle we had to overcome initially was an extremely poor relationship between IT and the business. This relationship was a hurdle for all projects requiring IT support. Resolving this issue was done primarily at a macro level outside of the BPM program, but the same principles were applied in BPM project implementations as well. These principles included taking to heart "the marketing of IT" as advocated by Forrester Research in (The Marketing of IT: A Core Element of Improving IT's Business Value by Laurie M. Orlov; delivering value as quickly as possible and working every day to build trust through using basic trust-building behavior keys.

The biggest management challenge we're facing now is BPM project prioritization. Demands for improvement are multiplied each time we implement a new process. Careful and thorough prioritization of small, medium and large BPM initiatives can get contentious. To resolve this, we apply BPM program governance in several contexts at Lincoln Trust Company. This governance is currently facilitated by the Business Process Automation team, which resides within IT. The program is led by Executive Sponsors that are all members of the company's senior executive team. The Business Process Automation team meets with this leadership group monthly to review the BPM Program Roadmap showing the major initiatives (1-3 month iterations) that are to be delivered during the year. The team also reviews a backlog, prioritized by the BPM Steering Group, of smaller process improvement solutions. The LTC BPM Steering Group is comprised of managers representing each business unit in the company. This Steering Group is also responsible for making key process implementation decisions, especially for processes that cross organizational boundaries, and for resolving organizational issues that arise during the implementation of a given process solution.

5.2 Business

As would be expected, the biggest hurdle we can encounter in the business is resistance to change. Change management practices are used extensively to manage this.

LTC's BPM program is fortunate in that our executive leadership has emphasized that nothing short of dramatic transformation, especially related to business processes, is expected of all levels of the organization. This is primarily due to being a new company, formed from the vestiges of an older company, with a desire to shed all baggage that might get in the way of achieving the new company's vision.

All employees are continually told through company meetings, phone mails, team meetings and their own leadership that they must continually challenge their business processes to create operational effectiveness. This direction and message is emphasized at the project kickoff and throughout a given BPM initiative.

Each BPM project team partners with a Human Resources representative that helps to assess the skills of the impacted employees. The representative also determines what will be changing as a result of the project and the requisite new skills and design and implement a training plan to help bridge the gap. Each business unit has a "super user" team that is responsible for ongoing assessment of the process and support of the employees on their team with respect to process questions and first line BPMS support.

Additionally, the BPM overall program and each BPM project conducted has a communication plan, identifying stakeholders, what they are interested in knowing, the best method for communicating this, how often they need to know it and who is responsible for communicating it. This keeps critical communications structured and effective.

5.3 Organization Adoption

Numerous strategies are employed on several fronts to drive organizational adoption of BPM. Central to this approach is communication about what the BPM program is, why it is being implemented and what is involved in conducting a BPM project. We have many "lunch and learns" and similar communication events in which the participants in a BPM project (current or past) talk about what BPM is and what it's like to work on a BPM project. Additionally, executive sponsors of the BPM program speak at these sessions to share why BPM has been chosen to help the company achieve its goals and how important it is to participate.

We also work on building up motivators for getting involved in the BPM program. Only the organization's best employees are selected for participation in BPM projects. When selected, employees are told that they were selected for their skills and valued contribution to the organization. This brings a level of esteem to BPM program participation. The performance of an employee working on a BPM program initiative is recognized and rewarded in employee performance reviews. Executives attend many project meetings throughout the project, giving the employees opportunities for exposure to a level of the organizational management they may not interact with very frequently and reinforcing the importance of quality participation.

We work hard to create confidence and passion around the BPM program. Those involved with the BPM program have seen repeated successes with multiple solution implementations over the past two years, which have been widely communicated throughout all levels of the organization. This credibility gives participants the confidence that their efforts will be effective; they will be making an actual change in the organization, leaving their mark and making their lives and the lives of others better at work.

Finally, and most importantly, the BPM program is led by senior executives. These executives set directions and priorities for the BPM program roadmap, provide resources to BPM projects, make key process architecture decisions and resolve any conflicts needing resolution at their level. Their involvement also models behaviour for employees at other levels of the organization. We feel strongly that the importance of the senior executive participation in the BPM program cannot be overemphasized as a "make or break" element.

6. BENEFITS

6.1 Cost Savings

We have calculated a year one ROI of 120% and an overall cost savings of $2.2M.

6.2 Time Reductions

We have decreased process cycle times in some areas by up to 75%.

6.3 Increased Revenues

Increased revenues have been difficult for us to measure, but we've seen a positive impact in our ability to attract and retain profitable customers.

6.4 Productivity Improvements

The fact that LTC is able to process 75% of our process volumes prior to a divestiture with 25% of the original staff has been directly attributed to our BPM implementations.

Quality control processes, which are critical in our audit-intensive business, are standardized and enforced through automated decision rules in our processes so that we no longer need to fear whether or not we have properly followed our operational controls in place.

Our service level agreements (SLAs) with our internal and external clients are now built into the process so that business units now have the ability to reallocate work load volumes to ensure these important agreements are met.

7. BEST PRACTICES, LEARNING POINTS AND PITFALLS

7.1 Best Practices and Learning Points

✓ *A major component of LTC's BPM discipline that we consider to be a best practice is our project framework, which provides a structured, repeatable approach for project success. LTC's BPM project framework is tailored from a variety of different prominent industry methodologies, primarily the 7FE BPM Project Framework and the Lombardi Teamworks Implementation Framework (for iteratively executing process solutions in our BPMS). This framework is helpful because it is used not only to train the resources that administer the BPM program's projects, but it is shared with project stakeholders so they can understand how a given project will work.*

✓ *We have also had success with our project team composition. The Business Process Automation team coordinates the work of multiple BPM project teams. To ensure that the highest quality process solutions are delivered, several roles are involved in a BPM project depending on the types of solutions that are to be delivered in a given project. A typical core BPM project team consists of process owners and subject matter experts from the business units impacted by the project, a BPM Analyst, a Process Architect, a Data Analyst and a BPM Project Manager. All development and technical process implementation work in Teamworks is outsourced to an offshore partner for delivery.*

✓ *Each BPM project team conducts a weekly update meeting with the projects stakeholders to review project progress, make any needed process decisions and resolve any issues that have arisen during the week. All project teams working on BPM projects meet for a daily standup meeting to review progress on BPM projects and resolve any roadblocks.*

✓ *It's been very important to us to maintain a backlog of new process/projects and continuous improvement ideas prioritized by the business and continually manage these items.*

✓ *For more complex processes, we have used "story boarding" of the solution/user interface as a companion to the process map to help users visualize and agree upon process automation solutions.*

7.2 Pitfalls

✗ *At different points in our program, while we were learning how to mature our BPM program and project approach, we have had the opportunity to bring on site two different BPM consultants to help us conduct BPM projects. While these individuals were very professional and knowledgeable about BPM, they tended to be adamant about spending most of the contract time on the current state business process analysis/process mapping and relatively less time in the creation of the future state process, especially in our BPMS. The end result was that we ended up having to explain to our project sponsors why it took two months to document a current state process where, in other projects, we would have been performing QA testing on a process solution by that point. They key lesson learned for us was that, while we understand the value of getting a clear, detailed picture of the current state – our organization is best served by "time-boxing" this work into a previously agreed upon time frame.*

✗ *In our initial projects on our first workflow system, we did not involve a data architect in our process design. This made subsequent business intelligence deliveries of process data very challenging. We now integrate this role into every project, which has made process reporting much easier and less costly.*

✖ *The BA Myth: All of the vendors that we worked with early in our evaluation processes touted how a strong BA in the business could implement their own BPM system solutions. Our experience has been that business and IT partnership is critical to successful BPM efforts. Particularly when getting started, IT architecture and technical staff were critical to successful implementations, especially with respect to line of business system integration and data architecture.*

8. COMPETITIVE ADVANTAGES

The asset custody, trust and back office support for self directed retirement plans is very competitive. It is a business based on large volumes with low profit margins. Our profit margins have seen unprecedented pressures from the global financial crisis. In addition, competitors in our market niche have struggled to innovate with such a manually intensive, paper driven segment of the IRA industry.

Investment in our BPM program has enabled Lincoln Trust to differentiate itself as an industry leader in the alternative assets segment of the IRA industry and better respond to the global financial crisis. BPM has enabled us to impact the entire value chain from our partners to our customers in innovate ways that reduce costs, improve profit margins and ultimately retain and attract the best customers.

This investment at a critical time for Lincoln Trust will enable us to emerge from the global financial crisis a stronger more agile company that will be well positioned to grow organically or participate in a possible consolidation of the industry.

9. TECHNOLOGY

The BPM solution architecture has been implemented leveraging the following core vendor technologies:

- Lombardi Teamworks BPMS- used for simulation, optimization, process orchestration and integration, process automation, team performance and SLA tracking.
- Lombardi Blueprint- used for process discovery, mapping, and inventory
- Microsoft SharePoint- used for internal and external portals including dashboard and scorecard capabilities
- Microsoft SQL Server- used for BI capabilities including Reporting Services, Analysis Services, and Integration Services
- Cisco VOIP – used for integrated with portal screen pop of customer information including process details when a call is received from a customer
- Kofax Capture – used for document capture and indexing
- Oracle 10g RDBMS- used for operational data store and active data warehouse
- Oracle IPM- used for customer document imaging repository
- Top Down Systems, Client Letter – used for customer correspondence management and tracking

We have implemented a SOA and WOA architecture and Lombardi Teamworks is being used to enable process integration activity between multiple systems leveraging web services. Our BPMS is an architectural standard to orchestrate customer processes initiated from our external website.

All internal form development is done using Teamwork's coaches and external forms are built using .Net and presented on our portal.

Example of an internal process form:

In addition to, and in support of BPM process initiatives, LTC has developed an active data warehouse. The warehouse supports customer interaction and process initiatives in several ways. First, as processes are initiated in Teamworks the warehouse scores the customer based on customer profitability and value allowing everyone interacting with the process to be aware if the customer is a high-level Tier 1 client. Additionally some BPM processes have OLAP cubes designed within the warehouse that provide process analytics. Process data is loaded into a data warehouse using Microsoft's SQL Server Integration Services (SSIS) and the business now has business intelligence tools from Microsoft to analyze data using analytical cubes.

Information is delivered using a "My Workspace" concept through Microsoft SharePoint Portal, ProClarity, and SQL Server Reporting Services Reports (SSRS). Critical data regarding current staff workloads, overall processing volumes, and SLA management is obtained. In addition, through SSRS, all end users have the ability to run secure, Web-based, interactive reports, designed with multiple filtering and drill-down options to view all the imaging and process data needed to conduct their jobs and service clients.

We've also gotten a surprising amount of benefit from the Blueprint process mapping technology we've licensed. We have trained business staff members and they are initiating BPM projects by documenting their processes along with process problems, duration, and severities within the tool. The business then presents their findings to the BPM program team members, using the tool, for collaboration on solutions.

Here is an example of the Claims process as documented by a line of business manager.

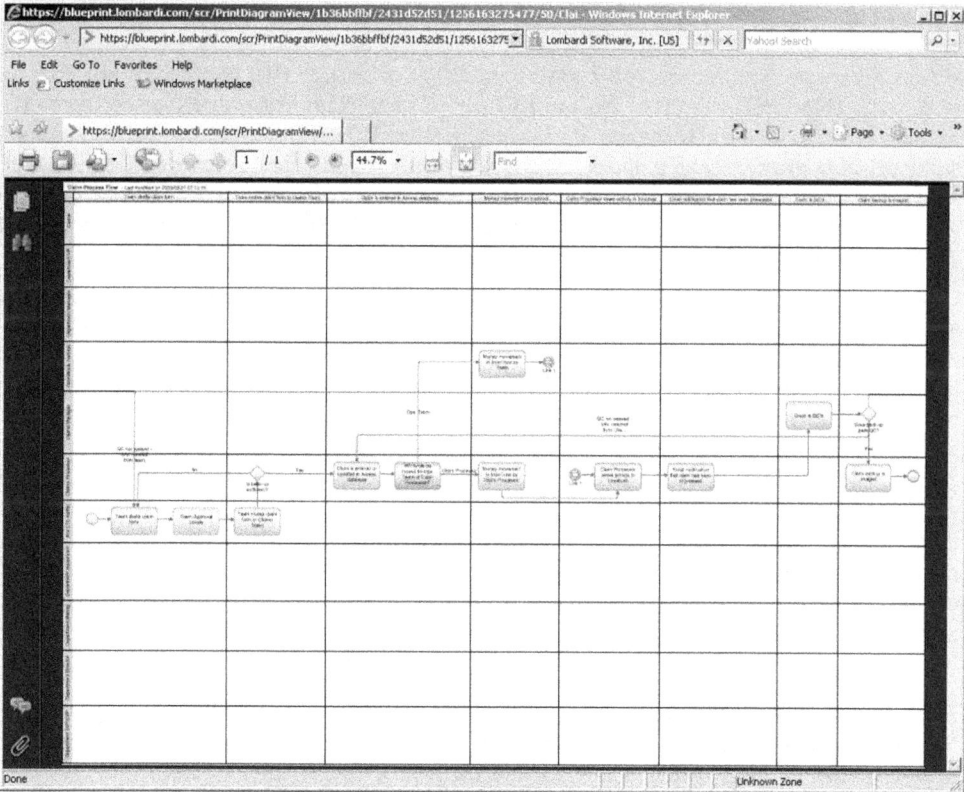

10. THE TECHNOLOGY AND SERVICE PROVIDERS

Lombardi Professional Services were utilized to assist on installation and configuration of Teamworks BPMS in our environment. They were also utilized to assist us in implementing our first processes in Teamworks and with knowledge transfer to our internal BPM team members. www.lombardi.com

Twinstar Inc. professional services were used initial to assist with our imaging system setup and integration.

Nokia Siemens Networks, UAE

1. EXECUTIVE SUMMARY / ABSTRACT

Nokia Siemens Networks was created in 2007 through the merger of the former Networks Business Group of Nokia and the carrier-related businesses of Siemens. Today, NSN is one of the world's largest network communications companies – with 60,000 employees, a leading position in all key markets across the world, and total sales of more than €15 billion a year. The Consulting and Systems Integration (CSI) unit within NSN is an organization of 4,000 staff, with sales of over €500 million a year.

CSI's particular business is an unusual mixture of high-volume/low-revenue engagements (i.e., consulting projects) and low-volume/high-revenue projects (i.e., major value-added service rollouts within large network implementations). The "mish-mash" tools landscape resulting from the NSN merger fundamentally did not meet the needs of CSI's dynamic business requirements. In addition, NSN's formation from two companies with, in many respects, polar opposite corporate environments created friction in operational execution. CSI desperately needed to get an established set of processes in place very quickly because without end-to-end visibility, fast and effective decision-making to drive the business was hampered, if not impossible. CSI looked to BPM technology to drive quick, highly-configurable, higher-value/lower cost process solutions to meet its business goals.

2. OVERVIEW

Nick Deacon assumed leadership of CSI's Business Process Management team when NSN was founded. Since that time, he has been responsible for the creation and implementation of the CSI process framework and the development of effective business process management suite technology use within CSI. Through previous professional experience, Nick has dealt first-hand with working environments that lacked robust processes and tools aligned to a process framework. His mission within CSI is to create a working environment that speaks one common process language, utilizing a business process management suite to manage the business effectively and support growth. From the start, this mission has been driven by Nick's vision to use BPM to transform the way NSN operates as an organization.

The basic tenet of this vision is that a competitive, industry-leading business needs to have full visibility into its fundamental business components (Sales, Delivery and Resources), as well as the ability to drive and maximize its business performance through effective portfolio management, knowledge management, remote capability and overall business management. This data needs to be accessible in a holistic environment that supports not only business management but also Consultant's, Engineers, Project Managers, and other employees.

Due to NSN/CSI's heterogeneous technological landscape, the end-to-end business could not be viewed at any stage. NSN's infrastructure housed large enterprise systems such as ERP from SAP, and other rigid and disconnected sales workflow, resource and knowledge management applications. These tools, designed for large (and largely inflexible) enterprise needs left CSI to manage its dynamic business by spreadsheet. This resulted in the inability to conduct real-time business management, limitations on Future Planning capability, inaccuracy of data both within CSI and the wider NSN, and significant overhead wasted on reporting, training and data entry. CSI desperately needed to get an established set of processes in place very quickly because without end-to-end visibility, fast and effective decision-making to drive the business was hampered, if not impossible.

CSI set a very aggressive timetable for success in its BPM program. Through a modular delivery approach, CSI targeted initial BPMS services rollout in 4-6 months, and complete end-to-end business operational management within one year. As Nick had expected with such a grand vision and journey ahead of him, there were minor set-backs and hurdles to be crossed along the way, but the resulting BPM solution, named "ZEUS" after the Greek God of Control, achieved pan-CSI rollout and effectiveness a mere 90 days behind schedule.

The results of ZEUS have been staggering. For a €1.8 million investment, CSI has calculated a €12 million annual productivity savings through the system. This impressive and transformational Return-On-Investment has been carefully benchmarked. For each principal role or function, CSI used 15 specific measures to compare time spent before and after the delivery of ZEUS. These benefits span all levels of CSI employees (Global and Regional Management, Consultants, Project Managers, Technical Support Managers, Solution Architects, etc.), the business as a whole, and across the value chain to customers.

3. BUSINESS CONTEXT

NSN inherited an array of inflexible and disconnected tools – SAP for logistics, a workflow solution for Sales, COTS solutions for Resource Management and Financial functions, and primarily local hard drives for knowledge management. Areas such as Delivery, Technical Support, and Reporting had no systems support at all. CSI was forced to use EXCEL to off-set the limitations of the enterprise systems, and to fill the large gaps. In addition, CSI had limited ownership of data entry and was reliant on others to populate CSI's needs. This left CSI with poor visibility into its Sales Funnel, Projects Delivery, forecasted Revenue, Cost and Margin and Demand and Supply Planning. CSI did develop and actively communicate a strong Process Framework, but with no holistic underpinning technology platform, it was difficult to manage and enforce. Additionally, that Framework was inherently dynamic, constantly changing and updating to reflect new business needs and new personnel/contractors joining the organization. The lack of embedded process created an inability to govern effectively, and poor visibility of business data led to inaccurate decision making and planning.

The "work" to be addressed by the ZEUS BPM solution covered CSI's entire business, from highly human-centric functions across sales, technical support, delivery, etc., to back-end system-to-system processes. This meant that all CSI employees were potential users of the system, necessitating an intuitive and flexible technology approach that would enable business-level user adoption.

4. THE KEY INNOVATIONS

Customers:

ZEUS is a comprehensive BPM Program encompassing multiple process solutions targeted to all three core elements of CSI's business: Sales, Delivery and Resources. CSI's customers have been directly and positively impacted by the ZEUS rollout. By allowing CSI employees to focus on what they do best, and giving management the real-time data to make better decisions, ZEUS ensures that customers receive the highest possible service from their CSI team.

Process:

CSI achieved complete end-to-end business visibility in 15 months, with periodic modular deployments of ZEUS application solutions for Service Delivery, Resource/Competency Management, Sales Management, Technical Support, Product & Portfolio Management, and Remote Delivery & Offshoring. Just two examples of ZEUS process transformation are:

The Resource & Competency Management application allows Resource Managers (RMs) to understand, for the first time, the skill sets of all employees, forecast accurate project close dates, and identify the required resources. All employees now rate themselves against the NSN portfolio of service products and general skills. A custom interface allows RMs to search this user store, filtering by skill sets and other criteria. Extended user profiles and reports give RMs a 360-degree view of resources and competencies, and detailed SQL Reporting delivers insight into current and predicted staffing needs, staff availability, and allocation ratios segmented by regions and sub-regions.

The Sales Management application enables Solutions Consultants to track and manage all of their sales opportunities throughout a well-defined series of sales phases. The application tracks the weighted value of each opportunity, enabling the business to accurately forecast potential and future revenue from sales across operational regions and lines of business. During the Sales process, resource needs anticipated for potential new projects are requested in the **Resource Management application**, with secured deals transitioning into the **Project Delivery application**.

ZEUS will continue over the next 6-12 months with the optimization of each of the modules to 'mould' ZEUS to the exact needs of the business. This optimization is greatly enabled by real-time process architecture and "on-the-fly" process modification capabilities of the Appian BPM Suite, upon which Zeus is built. Real-time data visibility on process performance and bottlenecks can be used to modify process models in-flight, with the changes deployed in real-time into the production application.

Appian's 100 percent web-based software and Service Oriented Architecture are also important factors in achieving NSN's BPM vision. Both significantly ease the integration challenges posed by such a large-scale BPM program. Appian's "Smart Services" also make SOA a useful tool outside of IT, giving end users drag-and-drop simplicity in employing web service components within their composite applications and mash-up portals.

Organization:

The solution touches all functional areas within CSI, as well as suppliers and customers.

- Projects Module: 400 users, Live since Sep 08, 2000 projects
- Technical Support Module: 150 users, Live since Jan 09, 600 contracts
- Socio-Business Networking: 2,400 users, Live since Feb 09, 800 pages
- Resource Management: 2,400 users, Live since Mar 09, training
- Competence Management: 2,400 users, Live since Mar 2009, 47% completion
- Sales Management: 500 users, Live since May 09, training
- Solution Management: 500 users, Live since May 09, training
- Business Management: 300 users, Live since Jun 09, training
- Remote Delivery/Offshoring: 1500 users, Live since Jun 09, training

The system receives an average of 240 log-ins per day at present from a 'real' user base of approx 1,500 users. As training is completed on the final modules it is expected that these needs will increase dramatically. All CSI employees now benefit from the efficiencies and lowered learning curve of standardized and repeatable workflow processes, managed by exception. CSI management also now has improved its business-critical decision making based on real-time data.

5. HURDLES OVERCOME

CSI faced the dual challenge of moving NSN towards a process-centric approach to business, while also developing and deploying ZEUS without generating negative attention from IT (with its entrenched reliance on enterprise systems such as SAP) and other business units in the company.

For these reasons, CSI chose to stay "under the radar" in communicating about ZEUS until it was up-and-running with a proven success. With its success benchmarked, CSI began intense, but selective, "selling" of its BPM story to other NSN business units at the management level. Since then, myZEUS portals and Zeus Regional Champions (ZRCs) have succeeded in building a highly-visible "ZEUS community" that has positively influenced senior NSN management to embrace the system and support improvements to service delivery. Technical implementation challenges have also been par for the course, but Appian's SOA support has greatly eased those expected issues.

Success Strategy to Overcome Challenges:

Quarterly ZEUS Champions Workshops bring together program champions from each of the seven regions and four Lines of Business and Practices to conduct planning, communications, and brainstorming activities. This is particularly important to achieve user buy-in and ensure alignment of the program across the complete business. **Monthly**, there is the Steering Board / Change Management Review involving Directors and VPs from across the business. A **fortnightly** communications session with the complete ZEUS Champions Community keeps them updated on program progress. Program teams hold **weekly** reviews. **Daily** project review meetings and Functional lead meetings maintain progress and address issues to keep the program on track.

A key to success has been creating the complete ZEUS Champions Community which covers the regions and Lines of Business/Practices. It has also been vital to get senior buy-in from the business unit leadership teams – 'convincing' them of the benefits of the program to them in order to get their full support. That said, having the 100% support of the Head of the Business Unit, is an absolute 'must have'.

Governance routines are operationalized through repeated communication sessions, the employment of the Champions Community (which is embedded throughout the business), and from having the 100% support of senior management.

CSI intends to use the Process Enterprise and Maturity Model (PEMM) to measure process maturity and to drive process improvement across the business. Significant agility is required as NSN and CSI are still just over 2 years old and there are constant changes and improvements that need to happen in order to drive progress and improvements. This has been difficult to achieve with only a small centralized team and requires the full support of the business which is a constant effort to maintain. Communication campaigns are important to try and keep this support, improving awareness and understanding at all stages.

6. BENEFITS

The measurable benefits of ZEUS include:

- Improved repeatability and reusability of solutions
- Improved business-critical decision making based on real-time data
- Maximized productivity for current business, and to drive/support future growth

These objectives are all being realized. Senior Management now has end-to-end visibility into the state of the business. Real-time reporting provides details on profitability, project status, and actuals versus forecast on margins and more.

Based on the above, the system is delivering **repeated productivity savings of €12 million a year**, which have all been benchmarked. For each principal role or function, CSI used 15 specific measures to compare time spent before and after the delivery of ZEUS. These benefits span all levels of CSI employees (Global and Regional Management, Consultants, Project Managers, Technical Support Managers, Solution Architects, etc.), the business as a whole, and across the value chain to customers. These benefits can be summarized as:

Benefits for Management

- On-line, 'Real-time' visibility of the business
- End-to-end control
- Portfolio and Product management
- Governance of processes

Benefits for Users

- A satisfying 'user experience'
- Enhanced inter-working between functions
- Clear visibility of responsibilities and status
- Re-usability and repeatability of Knowledge

Benefits for Customers

- Real-time Visibility of Project Status
- Improved CSI response time to bids and projects
- Benefit from CSI's global experience and knowledge

Benefits for the Business

- Cost reduction against reporting
- Cost reduction in data entry
- Cost reduction in bid preparation
- Optimization of processes
- Improved utilization
- Measurement of this value as a driver of top-line revenue has not been done.

7. BEST PRACTICES, LEARNING POINTS AND PITFALLS

The most valuable lessons learned through CSI's BPM program include:

- ✓ *Invest at the start in a Project Manager with a track record of successful BPMS Delivery*
- ✓ *Create sufficient branding for the solution so that future users can relate / refer to it easily (this enables more effective selling / marketing of the solution)*
- ✓ *Build a BPM community right out of the gate, and leverage it to influence senior management as the program evolves*

✓ *Leverage an experienced technology partner that emphasizes comprehensive, but easy-to-use BPM Suite technology*

✗ *The biggest pitfall to avoid is in how you get started with BPM and the initial process selection. Although the conventional wisdom has been "Think Big, Start Small," if you don't start with something meaty for the business (high enough value to make an impact, with enough risk associated to keep management engaged) your efforts are not likely to blossom into a full and successful BPM program.*

8. COMPETITIVE ADVANTAGES

ZEUS has allowed the CSI division of NSN to significantly drive competitive advantage and alter the playing field. It allowed CSI, early in its existence, to establish a common process language that enabled it to quickly ratchet up skills and delivery capacity to be more competitive in the market it had entered. It has also armed CSI management with a level of visibility and real-time control over all mission-critical business aspects and resources that surpasses the industry standard. ZEUS acts as CSI's system for operational business management, and the ongoing optimization/continuous process improvement inherent in the ZEUS program will support continued market advantage.

9. TECHNOLOGY

The Appian BPM Suite acts as the foundational platform for all of ZEUS. CSI selected Appian after a thorough vendor evaluation. In addition to technology strength, Appian won because of its commitment to a true partnership with CSI.

Nick knew that CSI was not exactly sure how to solve its end-to-end visibility and control problem, and that its BPM experience would be a journey of discovery. To ensure success on that journey, and to deal effectively with the inevitable unexpected detours, CSI needed its BPM vendor to be as much a business partner as a technology provider, helping to guide solution development and facilitate knowledge-transfer to move the organization towards BPM self-sufficiency.

Appian satisfied CSI's technical criteria based on the comprehensive features of natively integrated process, analytics, content and collaboration capabilities; Appian's extreme ease-of-use (including tailored user interfaces, personalized portals and information targeting, drag-and-drop process modeling, and ease of user and group administration); and Appian's flexible architecture (100% web-based with zero client-side downloads, service-oriented architecture and ease of integration). Appian's expertise in the human-centric side of BPM was an essential qualifier as collaboration and knowledge management play a central role in effective operations for CSI. The Appian platform acts as the single point of management for processes, process artifacts, stored documents and other electronic content (reports, task lists, images, video), plus associated metadata. Appian allows for the collaborative creation of all process artifacts and electronic data, as well as effective distribution, archiving, and protection. Features such as Single Sign-On throughout the entire system, and native search enhanced by integration with Google Search Appliance further extend the ease-of-use. Users interact with a rule- and role-based portal that facilitates CSI's need to capture, share and disseminate information in a flexible yet secure environment.

10. THE TECHNOLOGY AND SERVICE PROVIDERS

Appian is the global innovator in enterprise and on-demand business process management (BPM). Appian provides the fastest way to deploy robust processes, collapsing time to value for new process initiatives. Businesses and governments worldwide use Appian to accelerate process improvement and drive business performance. Appian empowers more than 2.5 million users from large Fortune 100 companies, to the mid-market and small businesses worldwide. Appian is headquartered in the Washington, D.C. region, with professional services and partners around the globe. For more information, visit www.appian.com.

Swisscard AECS, Switzerland

EXECUTIVE SUMMARY / ABSTRACT

The liberalization of the credit card market in Switzerland in 1997 paved the way for American Express and Credit Suisse AG to establish the joint venture company Swisscard AECS AG and to merge their credit card activities. Swisscard ideally combines the complementary strengths of the founding companies, with American Express being the global leader in card management and Credit Suisse providing strong national sales channels. On behalf of Credit Suisse, Swisscard offers the world-famous American Express card within Switzerland. It is thus the sole issuer in Switzerland with all three major brands (American Express, MasterCard and Visa) in its product portfolio.

In 2007, Swisscard issued its one-millionth credit card. Swisscard employs approximately 500 staff in total. We aim to offer the best possible card solutions to all our customer groups. In order to meet this challenge, we continuously analyze the needs of our customers and develop new products and services based on these findings. Innovation and its time-to-market are thus crucial: the foundation of our success lies in the permanent alignment of our business requirements with best-of-breed information technology. Our business is to act as a service center provider for our corporate and private customers. The quality and processing time of our former transaction-processing platform and host systems were not sufficient to serve our new products and services. We were also confronted with increasing regulatory and risk issues concerning internal credit card application processing, from both consumers and customers placing orders using handwritten, signed paper forms.

To improve these situations, we initiated a project to implement electronic workflows for the business processes involved – covering external document scanning with integral handprint recognition and data exchange services, as well as host and robotics integration – with the final objective of end-to-end automation, thus reducing human intervention to a minimum. This resulted in what we call electronic participant-to-participant (P2P) workflow, whereby workflow participants are treated uniformly whether they are humans or machines. Today we are capable of integrating, or rather socializing, host and robotic systems in such a way that they act as software agents just like human actors in SwisscardNet, the Swisscard workflow system.

This case study presents new methods and inventions that combine business process management (BPM) principles and software agent technology to minimize the costs, time and management overhead disadvantages faced when extending workflow boundaries to include external customers. Furthermore, we discuss the management of business process management with a generic meta-case approach as a valuable alternative for defining processes and activities.

OVERVIEW

Credit Suisse AG hired Swisscard AECS AG to handle the product development and management, marketing and sales, customer services, risk management, card processing and development/management of additional services and customer loyalty programs for all credit cards offered by Credit Suisse and its co-branding partners. Consumer Services ensures that our more than 30 card products are offered, acquired and marketed optimally. Corporate Services helps national and international companies to significantly and sustainably reduce their expenses, travel and purchase costs by optimizing processes, preparing reliable management reports and making invoicing more efficient.

As merchant acquirer, Swisscard is responsible for expanding and handling the American Express network of participating businesses in Switzerland. We ensure that American Express customers can use their cards wherever they want to. At the same time, our contracting parties benefit from the advantages of cashless payment transactions and access to attractive new customers. Altogether this makes us the current market leader in Switzerland:

- 25% market share
- No. 1 in frequent flyer and business traveler cards
- No. 1 in the discerning private customer business
- No. 1 in the corporate customer business
- No. 1 in the co-branding business (TCS, Miles & More)

To realize and strengthen this leadership, the Swisscard CEO, who had been a key stakeholder in the award-winning ServiceNet application at Credit Suisse, thought to replicate ServiceNet's cost, speed and quality benefits within a substantially smaller organization. The result of a process improvement study produced an action plan that electronically extended workflow support to our external contracting parties and automated overall processing as much as possible, thus reducing human intervention to a minimum. The close integration of our external contracting parties into our internal processing maximizes customer retention and reinforces our market leadership.

This report to the Workflow Management Coalition discusses the results of Swisscard's unique participant-to-participant BPM system.

BUSINESS CONTEXT

Swisscard responded to its substantial growth by increasing centralization, maximizing work automation and extending internal business process boundaries to our external contracting parties.

Optimizing was required for complicated processes with many media breaks, the permanent growth of informal communication with order nature, and inefficient monitoring due to complexity and physical separation.

In addition, we were confronted with increasing regulatory and risk issues, especially concerning the back offices' internal processing of credit card applications from consumers and contracting parties, which were made using handwritten paper forms. Furthermore, business process implementations were too slow and insufficient to fulfill our business demands for flexibility, agility, time and cost. We were forced to radically change the way we implemented and deployed our business processes.

Spawning process boundaries and integrating third-party technology (such as document scanning, handprint recognition and rule-based application validation) into the workflows was a key decision for successfully managing and orchestrating the new business-processing platform.

Out-sourcing Paper intensive Procedures

We outsourced the document management procedures, including scanning and handprint recognition, to a third-party company. We did so in order to completely automate data entry from paper forms, thus increasing throughput and the quality of credit card application processing.

Automating Data Exchange with Partners

In general, all application-related message interactions and processing between the contracting parties are fully automated. Contracting sales channels such as the remitting bank forward their credit card application forms to SwisscardNet automatically. The signed paper forms are sent to the Document Management Center, another contracting party, for scanning, while at the same time, customer information is forwarded independently to SwisscardNet from the remitting bank's internal front-office application. Managing the asynchronous messages from these heterogeneous external systems clearly requires business and conversation rules that are able to act appropriately depending on the actual situation.

Optimizing internal Message Processing

Software agents, wrapping the functionality needed of more than 200 different applications running as services or functions on the legacy, make it possible to automate internal message processing as much as possible. Human users will be involved only when the business rules demand it. The majority of the credit card applications can be processed fully automatically based on rules. This even includes embossing and sending credit cards by mail in the best case (lucky path) or sending rejection letters when declined. This automated processing approach boosted productivity and quality tremendously, thereby allowing us to focus employee capabilities on investigating risk-related issues and interacting with customers, which in turn improved data quality and customer service.

Initial Project Scope

It was important from the outset to integrate the internal processing platform (Legacy) with the new workflow platform and at the same time to eliminate manual data entry, i.e. the initial retyping of paper-based application forms. It is widely known that integration costs often exceed project budgets and are limiting factors for many good ideas. Nevertheless, we found an innovative way to empower existing host functionality; embed our contracting parties; set up the reflection of our organization including roles, competences and responsibilities; and coordinate all of this using software agents and the new electronic workflow platform as kind of a glue between people and machines. These were all prerequisites for success, and we completed the set-up within only three months. The initial project started in January 2008 and went live with the new credit card application processing for 30 different credit cards in April 2008. This included successfully integrating the host functionality needed for the different validation checks as well as document scanning and recognition, thus replacing manual data entry from the very beginning. Furthermore, we also integrated the call center and the in-house letter printing facility. Various organizational and people management processes were also developed in parallel, including new employee management, new organizational unit management, employee critical change management, organizational unit critical change management and, finally, user profile management.

Extended Project Scope

After setting up the new participant-to-participant (P2P) business-processing platform, new processes were implemented that focused on extending our processes to include our major contracting parties. Between May 2008 and April 2009, we developed and deployed a new process every two months, including any integration of legacy functionality that may have been required. This was the ultimate proof of the successful implementation of the new P2P-workflow system, coordinating people and machines uniformly as participants. One year after going live with the first process, the SwisscardNet workflow portfolio covers the following processes:

- ✓ Credit card applications for private and corporate customers
- ✓ Control accounts for corporate customers
- ✓ Detailed accounts for employees of corporate customers
- ✓ Applications for credit card bundles for private and corporate customers
- ✓ Employees and organizational units life cycle management
- ✓ Fraud and chargebacks

Expected Improvements for the Future

With the new workflow platform, existing and future host systems can be leveraged and integrated as active participants within the new workflows. Introducing the ActionWorks® "language of business" as the common protocol for all of the workflow participants, separates business from technology and will enable Swisscard to improve business and information technology in the future with minimum risk and dependency.

Needless to say, the new platform fulfills many business expectations for process optimization such as increasing productivity, increasing transparency and mitigating operational risks.

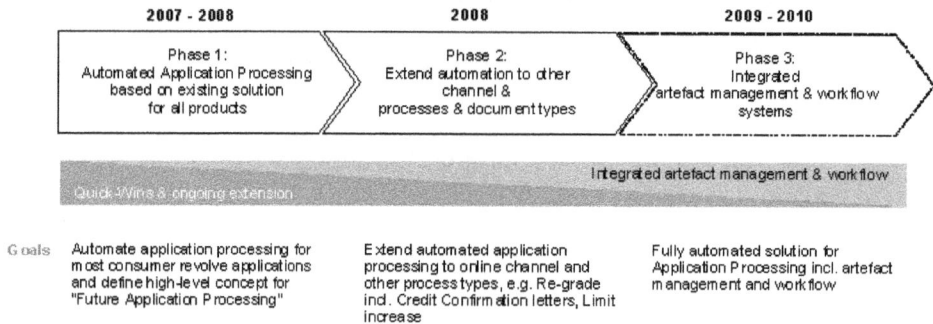

2007 - 2008	2008	2009 - 2010
Phase 1: Automated Application Processing based on existing solution for all products	Phase 2: Extend automation to other channel & processes & document types	Phase 3: Integrated artefact management & workflow systems

Quick-Wins & ongoing extension | Integrated artefact management & workflow

Goals	Automate application processing for most consumer revolve applications and define high-level concept for "Future Application Processing"	Extend automated application processing to online channel and other process types, e.g. Re-grade incl. Credit Confirmation letters, Limit increase	Fully automated solution for Application Processing incl. artefact management and workflow

Figure 1: SwisscardNet road map

The major objective of **end-to-end automation** of the core application processes is achieved by the end of phase 2. The original plan was divided into three major steps: in the first phase, we concentrated on the functionality of existing systems; we then extended it to optimize the processing of new products in a second phase; and finally, we homogenized and introduced new services according to our business requirements in a third phase.

Thanks to the software agents, new systems can be introduced without affecting SwisscardNet's current case processing. A number of the plan's key steps are already complete, while phase 3 steps are still in progress.

THE KEY INNOVATIONS

We decided to purchase Action Technologies' Metro software as a people-to-people BPM system, which uses a closed-loop human interaction model to manage negotiations, agreements and customer satisfaction with work performed. The system also provides real-time monitoring of every step of every process, as well as the status of work within every commitment. Action Solutions and Systems Integration Center AG added inventions to this underlying system that dramatically reduced the integration time of third-party systems, which was key to extending process boundaries to our contracting parties. The patented interaction model from Action Technologies has been adopted as the communication language for the software action agents, which use a wrapping approach that enables them to deal with legacy software. In essence, we injected code into the legacy interface programs to allow them to collaborate in the business processes like any human actor. The SwisscardNet's software agent infrastructure helps to offload repetitive tasks from end users and guarantees compliance with our business policies. This resulted in what we call the participant-to-participant workflow system.

4.1 Business

The SwisscardNet innovation was driven by a combination of market expansion as the strategic business goal and service excellence as the essential competitive differentiation, with constantly increasing cost-efficiency requirements always in the background. Solutions to the challenges of growth, service and cost reduction often move in a direction that runs counter to much of the financial services industry, as these people-intensive services are very expensive to provide. "Straight-through processing" aims to shift the "people focus" away from repetitive work and onto value-added risk and customer service activities by automating as many business rules for processing as practical. Our strategy uses technology to augment people.

Paradox of Job enrichment thru Job enlargement

SwisscardNet improves the award-winning ServiceNet concept from Credit Suisse, the "case approach," by providing a unified platform for internal and external participants, such as the people and agents involved, to fulfill customer requests through distributed case management. Cases can be created by humans (manually) or by agents (automatically). Case processing, closing and archiving is structured by business rules and performed by humans and software agents cooperatively. The look and feel of the generic case user interface puts users' business models into terms they understand. This resulted in an average training time of two hours, and in several instances users adopted the system on their own initiative with no training. Management was thus able to introduce job enrichment for the human users (generalization instead of specialization) and delegate the burden of work to the agents (job enlargement).

Federated Business-to-Business (B2B) Platform

SwisscardNet actively incorporates contracting parties, e.g. remitting banks, into the case processing through both agents and automated data exchange. Relationship managers at the remitting bank can request credit cards without even recognizing that the processing is done by SwisscardNet. They are fully bound into the credit card processing but technically still loosely coupled and thus not highly dependent on the SwisscardNet's availability as vice versa.

Semi structured Information System

SwisscardNet ensures accountability, coordination, "visibility," end-to-end tracking and feedback – all of which are critical to delivering superior, swift service with reduced costs. One important benefit is that unstructured information – like free-text documents or images (e.g. scanned paper forms) – as well as structured data, such as recognized content from scanned paper forms represented in electronic forms by field/value pairs, are all visualized in a powerful and easy-to-use graphical interface. It is thus possible for users to visibly verify that the scanned and recognized data conforms to the original document with a single mouse-click. Users can easily process structured and unstructured information in formal, predefined or not formally specified ways.

Communication and Interaction Whiteboard

SwisscardNet also accommodates the existence of unexpected and unstructured information by providing a whiteboard system that allows agents and human users to share the results of their efforts in the form of instructions and comments. When a human user opens a case, he or she immediately sees if an agent or another user has reported any instructions or comments concerning the problem-solving state, e.g. while scanning and using handprint recognition the ZIP code did not match the location, or while validating using the legacy application the cardholder's solvency or credit worthiness was not sufficient. Human users' and agents' communication and interaction during case processing takes place solely through the instruction/comment whiteboard.

Visible reasoning

Another important aspect of SwisscardNet is that the reasoning of the current state of a case or business object is visible through the audit trail, which monitors all actions, both human and non-human. In fact, the user can even see which condition was fulfilled as a part of which rule on which business object – and has thus led to the current state of the business object or case.

4.2 Process

Previously, processing at Swisscard was time consuming and inefficient. There were various tools to support execution within each of the processing steps, but most had to be operated manually and were not integrated, or even capable of being integrated with each other. Before SwisscardNet, users needed to know and use several systems. During the course of their daily work, they would have to log in several times to several systems and copy/paste data between systems. Feedback from external systems needed to be copied back and forth in order to proceed with process execution. Users had to know the relevant rules governing each credit card's application process. Updating the rule handbook required significant amounts of time. Today, software agents take care of these issues and only relatively few people (line managers) have to know about the legacy systems in detail.

When activities on behalf of external systems are required as part of process execution in SwisscardNet, the software agent takes care of them. As soon as the external system comes back with an answer, the software agent acts on the content of the response and according to the rules defined. The burden of knowing all of the rules is now delegated to the software agents.

The following subsections discuss the results of implementing people-to-people BPM principles in service-oriented architecture with action software agents.

Morphing People-to-People and System-to-System Approaches

Extending process boundaries to third-party companies and automating the burden of work and complexity in such a way that only exceptional or decision-making tasks need to be processed by human users requires the two extremes of people-to-people and system-to-system workflow paradigms to be brought together. When morphing these approaches, we first generalized the terminology used to describe the two players involved, people and systems, henceforth calling them "participants." Participants in our new workflow paradigm should communicate with each other as linguistic equals, sharing data where necessary and yielding processing control to whichever participant requires data for manipulation at a particular point in time.

In information technology, software agents have been proposed as one way to help people better cope with the increasing volume and complexity of information and computing resources. Using the patented interaction model from Action Technologies as the common interaction protocol for our participants allowed us to both *systematize* the way in which people interact on the one hand, and *socialize* systems interaction behavior on the other.

Because people already used this underlying model to interact with each other in the SwisscardNet workflow application, the major effort was to leverage the different systems involved to make use of this. Instead of implementing this for every system involved and ending up in a never-ending integration story, we introduced software agents: we wrapped third-party systems functionality where needed, aligned them with business activities and adapted Action Technologies' interaction model as the default core speech-act-based agent-to-agent protocol shared among all software agents ("action agents"). Action agents now use the same protocol as human agents, and the communication between participants takes place through the use of semantic messages in the context of business conversations via an event channel. Semantic messages represent more abstract, higher-level and business-process-related actions. They hide the clutter of proprietary application-specific details and provide business-like semantics. Semantic messages are exchanged through an event channel service, which supports different connectivity standards, provides different interfaces and enables synchronous and asynchronous message passing – thus realizing the advantages of loose coupling in complex cooperating systems.

Channeling Conversation between Participants

The event channel adopts the OMG's CORBA event service specification and extends it in such a way that its implementation provides semantic message brokering between participants. The service supports various available interface definition languages (IDL), such as web- or Microsoft Windows COM-services. Unlike most communication architectures, the event channel takes into account not only the individual message in isolation, but also the various sequences in which a particular message may occur. We believe that social interaction among participants is more accurately modeled by taking conversations – rather than isolated speech acts – as the primary unit of interaction.

As Winograd/Flores (1986) observes: "The relevant regularities are not in individual speech acts or in some kind of explicit agreement about meanings. They appear in the domain of conversations, in which successive speech acts are related to one another."

In the event channel, a conversation is defined as a sequence of messages between participants that takes place over an arbitrarily long period of time (long transactions), but which is still bound by certain termination conditions described in conversation policies as conditions of satisfaction. Conversations may give rise to other conversations as appropriate. As semantic messages come in, semantic events are triggered automatically. In contrast to method invocations, semantic events provide a form of messaging that the event channel service can use to dynamically request services and information from each of the parts contained in the message. Semantic messages use a common vocabulary of requestable business activities grouped in suites of related events and associated conditional actions. These business policies, combined with the conversation policies and the abstraction of people and systems as participants, form the building blocks of our new participant-to-participant workflow model.

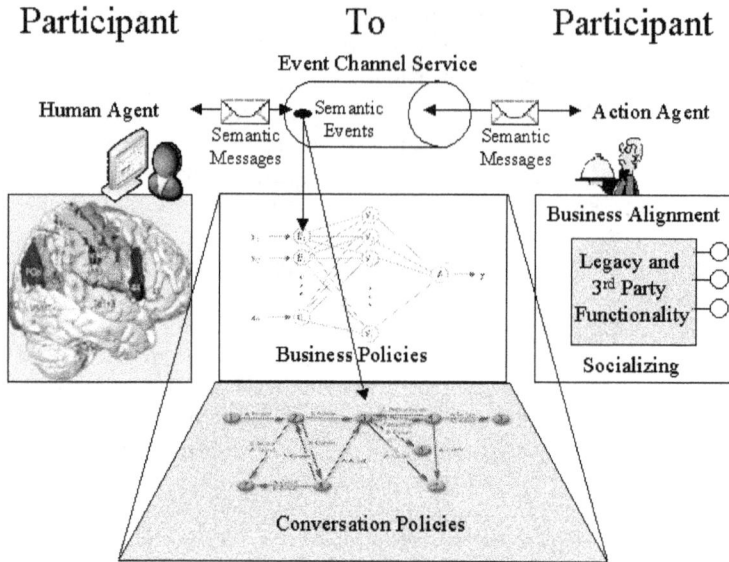

Figure 2: Participant-to-Participant (P2P) Communication Model

This federated system model is the architectural foundation for orchestrating the different participants in a uniform way. Specifically, this helps to overcome the limitations of passive artifact interface-based architectures in the following ways:

- *Scalability.* Agents are equipped with rule-based capabilities that run in the background to help people to perform case processing. They take into account the context of the person's tasks and situation as they present information and take action.
- *Scheduled or event-driven actions.* Agents are capable of executing tasks either at specific times or automatically in response to system-generated events.
- *Flexibility and opportunism.* Because they are instructed at the level of the business and conversation policies, they help to solve problems such as host system unavailability.
- *Abstraction and delegation.* Agents communicate with us, and we can delegate tasks to them. Rather than simply processing our commands, they share our goals and show us the state of work or what went wrong.

Participant-To-Participant (P2P) Workflow Model

SwisscardNet's participant-to-participant (P2P) workflow model deduces the reference model from the workflow management coalition group (WfMC) as described below. The lack of the process definition and activities building blocks from the WfMC reference model in our workflow model is because we integrated the modeling into the execution component (see also Jablonski and Bussler, Workflow Management: Modeling, Concepts, Architecture and Implementation, 1996). As a result, SwisscardNet process definitions will be composed dynamically at runtime and just before their usage (see also Kammer/Bolcer, Technique for Supporting Dynamic and Adaptive Workflows, 2000). This approach is also called "just in time" execution. For quality management purposes, this definition's agility can be further formalized using meta-cases, which take care of change management activities like testing, accepting and deploying new and existing definitions.

Business Process
↓ is managed by
Workflow Management System
↓ via
Process Instance
↓ include one or more
Activity Instance
↓ assigned via
Work Item
is ↓ stored in ↓ to
Case — Work Participant ← contains one or more
List
is ↓ is ↓ is
MetaCase Person Agent Role

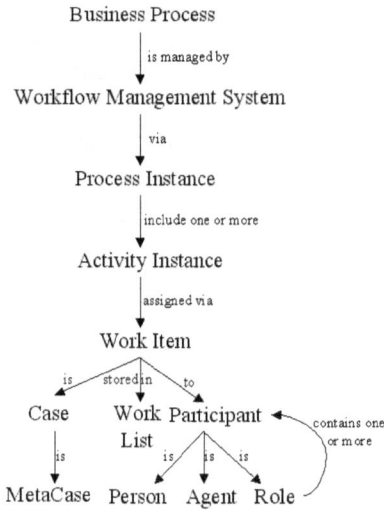

Figure 3: P2P Workflow Model

What makes SwisscardNet both simple and effective is the core concept that lies behind the design of the system: every work item becomes a *case*. Thus a case is the general unit of work, rather than individual messages, tasks, transactions or assignments. In order to define cases in advance, meta-cases are used. They do not simply define the details of the case, rather they guarantee testing, deployment and definition-versioning as well using a meta-data repository. Ad-hoc case definitions are part of every normal case and can be done by participants by entering processing instructions. The other important extension is that a workflow participant is a resource that performs the work represented by a case. This work normally involves taking one or more actions on information objects contained in a case and is assigned to the workflow participant via the work list. A participant is either a person, an agent or a role. A role is an abstract user containing one or more persons, agents or other roles. An agent is a virtual user, while a person is a human user.

Basic Characteristic of Action Agents

In the context of SwisscardNet, action agents can be thought of as virtual users. They respond appropriately to a basic set of speech acts (e.g. request, decline) and in a way that is consistent with certain desirable conventions of human interaction, such as commitments. In SwisscardNet, the whole organization – consisting of organizational entities (OE) and people with their profiles (roles, rights and obligations) – is reflected in an underlying subsystem called "user administration." By default, every organizational entity has at least one virtual office. During case processing, tasks that are not assigned directly to a person can be sent to the virtual office of the organizational entity required. People who have access rights to this virtual office can now enter it to check out work and take ownership of further activities.

CSG-OEBASIS
KIOS-O
Filler
DIV9-BET
CSG-J
  Kielholz Walter B.
  New
  Agent office - Chairman Board of Directors
CSG-JG
CSG-JV

In addition, we have also added an action software agent for every organizational entity by default, which can act as a kind of virtual assistant for all people assigned to this organizational entity. These agents inherit all of the profiles of their organizational entities, including roles, rights, restrictions and obligations. They have their own workboxes, where all messages sent to them can be placed.

Figure 4: Agent-Workbox in OE Tree

Forwarding messages can be done manually by human users or automatically as part of the execution of a conditional activity. Agents are embedded into the organizational structure in a very natural way. They work in a virtual office, where human users with permission to enter can monitor the cases that the relevant agent is currently working on and what the state of the work is. Drill-down to the current case is possible, as is a summarized view of all cases assigned to the agent. As long as agents are working on the cases, the cases are blocked, i.e. read-only views are the only views available. Only administrators have the rights to manipulate the cases currently being processed by the action software agent, e.g. to change ownership or cancel the current activity.

Our assistant agents significantly reduce the workload for their human counterparts, respecting policies and processing rules at the same time.

Open Cases by Responsible: Agent office - Running Applications   Back..   Forward..

⬥ Task	⬥ Fallnummer			⬥ Priorität	⬥ Document Date	Document Type	Document State	⬥ Marketing Code
Status: En Route								
Case	SWC-10182682	○	☝	Normal	01.04.2009 11:43:06	MasterCard	NEW_CHECKED_AUTO	
Case	SWC-10182686	○	☝	Normal	01.04.2009 16:14:07	American Express	NEW_CHECKED_AUTO	
Case	SWC-10182687	○	☝	Normal	01.04.2009 16:18:07	American Express	NEW_CHECKED_AUTO	
Case	SWC-10183345	○	☝	Normal	18.06.2009 11:38:46	Visa	FINALIZING	

Page Size: 20 ▾

Figure 5: Agent's virtual office showing the current state-of-work

Building SwisscardNet Workflows

SwisscardNet provides a framework for managing the following:

- All different types of workflows, whether fuzzy and not-well-understood or deterministic and highly repetitive, using **cases**.
- (Un-)structured data (forms, text, images) as **information objects**.
- Data exchange, long transactions, third-party and legacy systems integration through **agents**.
- The behavior of cases and business objects, two special types of information objects, with **business and conversation policies**.

SwisscardNet is an enabling technology for the end user programming paradigm that views workflow applications as cases containing collections of information objects. These information objects can be tied together via business rules. The framework includes a semantic messaging facility that defines high-level messages used to communicate the requests. With semantic events, the participants, human users and agents can act not only on cases but also on the information objects they contain. Information objects can be simple structures, e.g. e-mail messages, or more complex ones such as compound forms containing lists, embedded objects, single-choices and fields. An information object's dynamic defines the operations that can be invoked via semantic events as part of a business rule using scripts. Scripts are programs executed by interpreters. The scripting language is able to translate human-readable scripts into semantic events and activities. This allows a business user to create scripts that fire semantic events, which result in collaborations among information objects and cases. Scripts combined with information objects are pure dynamite: they let business users assemble flexible information object combinations in record time, they provide tenfold productivity improvements over compiled languages and they allow non-programmers to automate all sorts of tasks. Scripts provide the basis for agent technology because agents "like" to be self-sufficient. It is for this reason that events and activities are made available to agents by default when setting up a SwisscardNet case, and as a result are fully automatable. The conditions in the business rules decide when and whether human users need to be involved. Furthermore, chaining event/act pairs allows case processing to be simulated without the involvement of human users.

Setting up a SwisscardNet case can be done in different ways. Ad-hoc case processing is done by human users in defining instructions at run-time and decides ad-hoc who will be involved in further processing and how. Pre-defined case processing requires the definition of policies (business and conversation rules), business objects involved with their dynamics (state-transition model) and the layout of the graphical user interface. All this is done using scripts for just in time execution or meta-cases, which generate the scripts as part of the case processing.

Managing Business Process Management (BPM) using Meta Cases

Separating business from technology has much justification and is one of the SOA principles we used at the process level, introducing the scripting approach to define cases. Nevertheless, this end-user dynamic requires close monitoring of the change management process for process definitions. To ensure the quality of delivery, meta-cases come into play. Meta-cases describe case definitions and can be used both to define new cases as well as to maintain existing ones. Because all of the major SwisscardNet building blocks (cases, information objects, policies and participants) can be defined using scripts, this can easily be done within a meta-case, too. A meta-case creates ad-hoc test plans, based on the condition definitions, for all of the business rules' alternative paths, including traces of test results. They ensure quality reviews, generate the necessary set-up packages, enforce visas for deployment, enforce feedback from the IT department of successful installation in the production environment and, last but not least, update software releases/meta-repository. Depending on the security, policies and environment, even the installation of the definitions package can be done automatically as part of the meta-case process. Because of the availability of data exchange functionality, such case definitions could be sent by e-mail, automatically triggering the corresponding change management meta-case.

This allows change management to be done in the same way as all other business processing, using the same techniques and bringing the same advantages.

4.3 Organization

In the past, interactions surrounding client requests were very paper-intensive and all coordinated via phone, e-mail, fax, mail and face-to-face meetings. Because clients normally interact with customer relationship managers from our contracting parties, the propensity for misunderstandings and miscommunication was very high. Moreover, there was no inter-company visibility into the process, no formal accountability on who had agreed to perform which tasks by when, and no consistent audit trail. Introducing the electronic participant-to-participant workflows was key to bridging and reorganizing the way people worked together across company boundaries. Of course, we cannot dictate the way our contracting parties process their clients' requests, nor the availability of their service infrastructures. We therefore introduced a federated case processing approach, where event communication was standardized and decoupled for the first time. At the same time, we reorganized the front office data exchange taking place in our contracting parties' branch offices all over the world, and also made it paperless. The SwisscardNet workflow system made it possible to channel all of the different media (phone, fax, paper, electronic documents and e-mail) and to use a case approach to streamline the business requests from the front offices to our middle and back offices. SwisscardNet's federated system approach maximizes our independence and the quality of service in terms of availability, flexibility and self-government, while at the same time optimizing the collaboration and cooperation with our contracting partners.

Standardizing the Information Supply Chain thru Cases

The availability of the right information – presented to the right participant at the right time and in the right format – is key to successfully coordinating process execution across companies, people and systems involved. The SwisscardNet workflow system design meshes system-to-system, system-to-people and people-to-people interfaces through the same interface, using software agents and the underlying patented interaction model from Action Technologies. The generic user interface implements the case concept from Credit Suisse's award winning ServiceNet application, which has been extended and modified such that agent interactions and notifications are embedded, the structured information from attached documents is made actively available in dynamic forms, and the rules which are responsible for the current state of work are made visible to human users.

This case view provides the information needed for both extremely efficient processing of standard service requests, such as credit card applications, and effective responses to non-routine requests, such as acts of fraud and chargebacks. A routine case is moved quickly and completely through the different processing steps (internally or externally), while non-routine cases are also moved quickly and completely through the approval and collaboration steps. The case is always kept in view and no type of interaction, including third-party system events or notifications, is ever left open. Every case has a complete process audit trail managed by the system and updated automatically. The audit trail shows all of the activities within a case and thus significantly reduces the operational risk of violating rules and/or regulatory policies.

Overall, this solves one of the single largest and most widespread problems in process coordination, the lack of "visibility" into the processes across the enterprises involved. In traditional workflow systems, no single person has an overall view of the system, but only sees his or her own part of the process. As a workflow moves through the network of interactions and interdependencies, it disappears from view. There is no direct and simple way to track statuses, reviewing which workflows are pending, completed, due or delayed. There is no overall history attached to the workflow as it moves through the complete process swamp, and no flexible feedback on it or its progress. In contrast to the individual tasks and operations carried out within a given workflow, the workflow itself has no built-in metrics showing the status of the process. Swisscard's workflow remedies all of this. It is in this sense a distributed management system. It ensures that the steps in the process and responsibilities for carrying them out are handled within the context of a distributed case, whereby all information is captured and managed centrally in SwisscardNet's case structure: in the right context, format and time, and visible only to the right participants.

Users and What Their Jobs Entail Now, Compared to Pre-Installation

Our middle office's direct "customer" is the front office – people like relationship managers and their assistants from third-party companies, our contracting partners. The external relationship manager acts on behalf of the bank client and initiates a request in the bank's own proprietary application environment, knowing nothing about the existence of SwisscardNet; the software agents together with their human colleagues from the middle and back office, our human agents, ensure that the request is honored. It sounds simple – but of course, being able to fire off a request externally and with the assurance that it will be fully handled internally is not at all simple.

Customer care has to be provided in a business context that is extremely complex, time-dependent, global, varied and demanding in terms of operation speed, quality and efficiency. For our human users in the middle and back office, the differences between working with the old, semi-manual system and the new workflow solution have radically transformed their jobs in several ways. First and foremost, repetitive and error-prone tasks like the massive amounts of data entry have been automated and delegated to a third party (scanning and handprint recognition). Time-consuming tasks such as printing documents, routing them for approval and monitoring the review process through e-mails and phone calls have been eliminated by automating and delegating them to software agents for normal processing. Today, only exceptional tasks require the intervention of human users. It is thus that individual job enrichment has become a way of life among our human user professionals. In addition, the codification of rules and procedures for processing the different business scenarios ensures that everyone, human and non-human agents alike, is acting within Group policy.

Agents that reduce Work

In essence, the use of software agent technology is the key to successfully implementing the major objective of end-to-end automation, involving people only when policies require doing so. Furthermore, because we are talking about bridging the gaps between organizations' electronic interfaces, the need for more socialized system-to-system interfaces is evident. We are not just exchanging data; rather the interfaces have to manage long transactions and thus "commitments" between the different partners in a conversation-like manner. This applies especially to effectively managing exceptions, e.g. interruptions, and to becoming a pleasant working partner, notifying human users only when appropriate due to service level agreements, which are reflected in the business and conversation policies. Today's action agents successfully manage repetitive tasks with respect to defined policies, and notify their human colleagues through the instruction/comment whiteboard (see Figure 6) about what went wrong and why.

This way human agents are always up-to-date and can manage exceptional situations extremely effectively and delegate further processing back to the action agents. Action agents periodically gather publicly available information from third-party companies over the Internet and update internal information accordingly, for example ZIP code data mapping, which is used to validate address information. They verify the result of the handprint recognition of the scanned credit card applications and act according to policies for further case processing. They forward data to external subsystems, wait for the answer from the processing and automatically take the next steps according to policy rules. Action agents prepare and export letters to be sent to applicants, including semantic wording (text blocks) in the required correspondence language and according to the specific context, e.g. reminders or rejection letters. Furthermore, action agents ensure that all of the asynchronously exchanged electronic messages for the next processing act are available as well as checking their structural consistency.

| AECS SWC-10183977 | | Betreff: | | Sprache: | Deutsch ▼ |

| Mail versenden | Print | | PO auswechseln.. | Fall annullieren.. | Fall schliessen.. | Change state.. | Speichern.. | Senden.. |

Auftraggeber:		Erstellungsdatum:	17.09.2009 14:24:47
Problemowner:	Daniela Marchese, ,	Status:	Offen
Send To Name:		Priorität:	Normal ▼ □ e-Mail beim Schliessen des Falls
Instradierung:		Erledigen bis:	17.10.2009 14:24:00
Marketing Kampagne:		Geschäftsart:	Application ▼
		Geschäftsbereich:	Consumer revolve ▼
		Geschäftstyp:	One Account ▼

| ❶ Instruktionen | ∂ Anhänge | Attributes | Subtasks | Audit Trail | Fehler Analyse |

17.09.2009 14:24:47   System Notification

Mapping failed: Mapping not possible because of unknown value N for tag signaturesupp

17.09.2009 14:24:47   System Notification

File 300130062009000009.pdf has been added by ActionWorks

14.10.2009 11:19:36   Instruction by
Tel.: 044 111 11 11,   **Daniela Marchese (A123456)**

Please ▮▮▮▮▮▮! Need **feedback asap**! Thank you!

14.10.2009 11:20:08   System Notification

IncompleteReason1: Jahreseinkommen unglaubwürdig

| Add instruction | Add Comment | ▼ ▲ |

| ✂ 🖺 🖺 **B** *I* U x₂ x² | ▤ ▤ ▤ | ▤ ▤ ▤ ▤ | **A** ◇ | Arial ▼ 3 ▼ |

Figure 6: Whiteboard for Human and Action Agent's information exchange

This is what makes action agents a bit like digital butlers – the people at Swisscard successfully run their office life with the help of a gaggle of well-trained butlers.

The Implementation Team

The Swisscard core project team consisted of four people: a project manager, two business analysts and one IT professional (plus three developers from Systems Integration Center AG). Specialists from systems engineering and the data center also contributed to the project. Systems Integration Center AG and its adoption of Action Technologies' business interaction model as the common shared conversation protocol between participants were critical to the success of the project. Project launch was in January 2008 and the going live with the first workflow was on of April 1, 2008. This already included the integration of all the involved sub- and host systems. After the first launch, a new workflow has been deployed every two months, whereas the integration focus was more on integrating new functionality using the techniques already in place. All together, we delivered seven complex workflows in only 14 months, ending in March 2009.

HURDLES OVERCOME

5.1 Management

There were no big management hurdles – rather a member of the Swisscard executive board initiated the project. He knew about the success of the ServiceNet application (previous, award-winning solution) at Credit Suisse and enriched this solution with his own ideas – the outcome being that we have, in addition to

ServiceNet (one generic process), one generic business language for both people and machines, who are treated uniformly as participants in business processing and respect the same conversation and business policies. The members of the SwisscardNet project team were charged with finding new ways of improving the middle and back offices' effectiveness and efficiency. The reorganization to introduce automation started in 2007; the automation was extended and external contracting parties embedded in the business process automation between 2008 and now; and finally, newer and more powerful back-end systems will be introduced and optimized by 2010 in order to service and leverage the middle and back office agents.

It was evident that for the successful implementation of all of these new processes, an innovative and unique workflow system was required that could not only service people in their daily work but also understand how people interact when carrying out their work. One prerequisite for automating business with external parties is closely monitoring the fulfillment of service level agreements and thus quality management. From the outset, it was evident to the management that automated quality management is an integral part of the new workflow platform, not only on a technical level but also specifically relating to business events. It is thus that cases are sent to specific quality assurance places by policies and that error analysis (good or bad) is included by default in SwisscardNet, as well as integrated reporting and statistical analysis. All this is critical for delivering superior, swift service with reduced costs.

5.2 Business

There was at the time a strong belief among Swisscard operations and IT people: what was needed was a "better" technology system. This led to problems that held up the deployment of the Swisscard concept of process and service, leading instead to a focus on replacing the technology platform rather than improving the process and service performance. In the end, these issues were resolved through a combination of the two: improving the process and service performance first, and afterwards starting to evaluate systems improvement.

The development of SwisscardNet started in January 2008. Only three months later, SwisscardNet was up and running. Systems Integration Center AG was able to build the first process quickly, including human agents as well as software agents, thanks to its use of the proven ActionWorks® business interaction model as the conversation protocol between people and systems. While setting up further processes, the major issue to overcome was that process design was surpassed by the speed of process implementation. This was primarily due to the software agent's generic approach: after implementing them once in the first workflow, we could simply tell them about new business and conversational policies. There was no need to extend them in any way, mainly because of the closed interaction loop of the underlying business interaction model from Action Technologies. To overcome this, we needed a way to improve process definition time without losing quality, which led us to the technique of defining case processing policies using cases known as meta-cases. This approach is extremely valuable because cases are defined in the same way as business cases are processed in SwisscardNet, just in a different context. Furthermore, change and version management came to be an issue because of time pressure. Prerequisites of releases, which had not yet been tested and thus not installed, were missing in production and were the reason for several support calls. All of these issues can now be managed and automated as an integral part of the meta-case processing, thus improving the quality of deliveries and guaranteeing change and version management.

5.3 Organization Adoption

The objective of the SwisscardNet initiative was end-to-end automation that would enrich human users' jobs and use automation to relieve them of the burden of certain types of work and needing to know all of the processing rules by heart. People were naturally looking forward to trying out such a new tool, yet it was not always easy to sell them on this approach, mainly for two reasons: First, the term "automate" almost invariably triggers fears of job loss. Secondly, nobody was really able to imagine what it would be like to collaborate with software agents. Responding to the first question is never easy, but most of us can understand that automation boosts corporate productivity and quality and thus, in the long term, guarantees jobs as well.

The other question wasn't as straightforward, because when people think about software agents, everybody has his or her own ideas and expectations. The most well-recognized software agent for people working in offices is probably Microsoft's Office animated paper clip. This guy is a fun novelty in the beginning, but after a while he always seems to appear at the wrong moment telling you something you already know, and thus most users sooner or later deactivate the feature. It must be said that in the beginning our own software agent was far from what it can do today, mainly because we have taken actual users' experiences with the agent as the inspiration for new features we hadn't thought to implement in the beginning.

One good example is that we initially had only one software agent in place, and because the agents are integrated into the organizational structure of Swisscard as virtual employees, the agents earn rights and obligations just like human employees do. This forced us to assign the agent to the highest level in the organizational hierarchy, thus giving it the right to see everything – but of course the agent's work then became invisible to most other people. This was intended by design, but after a while people started telling us that they were "surprised" by the agent's actions or that they don't understand why the agent "(re-)acted" in a particular way.

This led us to introduce the same user interface for software agents as for all human agents when it comes to ad-hoc instructions or comments: the instruction-comment view, where software agents notify human users about what happened and why. To overcome the obstacle that human agents could not see the workloads of their software counterparts, we created a software agent for every organizational entity (OE), thus endowing the local software agent with the corresponding OE-specific rights and obligations. From then on, human actors were able to check the workloads of their assistants using the virtual office views. This is extremely helpful for long transactions, when the agent waits for a reply message from an external partner or host system and the customer asks for the status of his or her credit card application entry. In fact, we developed the agent's user interface together with the human users, which provides a model of ideal collaboration between human users and their assistants. When users have the subjective sense that the application and live processes have a positive impact, then the application tends to be accepted and adopted very quickly. But the key to good acceptance was, in the end, improved functionality and performance.

As a result of this, teams at Swisscard could be reorganized such that individual teams now process all of the credit cards for specific cases. Previously, credit card applications were processed by several teams, but only for specific credit cards.

This was mainly because of the complex and card-dependent rules for processing applications. Today, thanks to the guidance and assistance of software agents, people can manage all of the credit cards/products within a given process. This is why management was able to introduce job enrichments for human agents and why it could even be said that it was the employees themselves who benefited the most from the introduction of SwisscardNet.

SwisscardNet Workflow Configuration

Hardware:

-1 dual CPU application Server
-1 dual CPU process manager
-2 quad CPU database servers
 configured in a fail over cluster
-1 dual CPU test server for unit and
 integration testing

Software:

-Microsoft Windows 2003 Server
-Microsoft SQL Server 2005
-Microsoft IIS Web Server
-ActionWorks® Metro 5.2
-ActionSolutions® Software Suite 2.0

BENEFITS

Until recently, it was not affordable for mid-size companies to implement process improvements across multiple companies and business areas. Nevertheless, even now the challenge is how to provide the impeccable financial services customers require on the one hand, and on the other hand how to keep pace with larger companies when it comes to enforcing compliance rules and fulfilling continuously increasing legal requirements, while simultaneously cutting costs. Many financial institutions have attempted to follow strategies that involve charging transaction fees or segmenting the market and reducing the level of service for particular client segments. Swisscard has bucked this trend by offering all of its customers the same level of service. Moreover, Swisscard provides services to its customers far faster than its competition, and at significantly reduced costs. *Mastering the information supply chain* was the key to improving business process excellence and to tremendously boosting both productivity and quality.

6.1 Cost Savings

Within the first fourteen months, seven different processes were deployed. The business case presented here focuses exclusively on the economic benefits of the first process, the *credit card application* process. This business case only takes into consideration the benefits resulting directly from the improved process design, i.e. cost savings from optimized process execution. Increased revenue or other earnings are not included, whereby initial investment costs for the software agent implementation are covered. All the other workflows were able to benefit from the existing software agency and thus have far exceeded the management's financial expectations. It is likely that as documentation of these additional business cases is completed, an additional white paper documenting the above-mentioned economic benefits will be submitted to the WfMC. The cost savings of the first year already amounts to over one million US dollars; the net present value (NPV) in 2009 nears the one million mark. The ROI of 338 percent fulfills the Swisscard management's expectation of having the business case in positive figures **within the first year**. Needless to say, the successful business cases of the other six workflows are grounded on this initial investment.

6.2 Time Reductions and Productivity Improvements

Reduced cycle time of 40%. Credit card application processing times could be improved by an unbelievable 40 percent through improved business and conversation policies. The availability of the right information, at the right time, in the right format and presented to the right (human or software) agent made these advances possible.

Increased productivity of 30%. The paradox of job enrichment through job enlargement has ended up with productivity increases of 30 percent. There were many critical when the SwisscardNet initiative was first announced. But now, one year later, the same number of employees can manage 30 percent more credit card applications and at the same time tremendously increase the quality of processing.

Increased quality of 10%. The number of withdrawals because of missing or incorrect information has been reduced by 10 percent thanks to the end-to-end automation paradigm, where human agents focus only on the activities which cannot be delegated to their counterparts, the action agents.

BEST PRACTICES, LEARNING POINTS AND PITFALLS

7.1 Best Practices and Learning Points

- ✓ Flexible design – Semiformal systems like SwisscardNet are most useful when we understand enough to formalize in a computer system some, but not all, of the knowledge relevant to acting in a given situation. We believe that this includes almost all real-world situations. The trick to designing semiformal systems, we believe, is to design flexible systems that allow us to exploit the patterns and knowledge we understand when they are useful, without getting in the way when they are not. And this is precisely the goal of the design principle used in SwisscardNet.

- ✓ Assistant Agents – Rule-based software agents perform active tasks for people without requiring the direct attention of their users. Agents can be triggered by events and act according to policies (rules). Agents assist users in different ways: they hide the complexity of difficult tasks, they perform tasks on the user's behalf, they help different users to collaborate and they monitor events and procedures. Agents work when you don't, and work where you aren't, and never get tired. Agents monitor events and always respect conversation and business policies when acting.

- ✓ Simplifying legacy integration – Requesting services through software agents at a higher level corresponds more to user *intentions* than to specific service *implementations*, thus providing a level of *encapsulation*, analogous to the encapsulation provided at the level of communications protocols. It is thus, that agents help to socialize existing system's functionality and in combination with a service-oriented architecture many of the standard services for distributed computing don't have to be reinvented.

7.2 Pitfalls

- ✗ Reliability – We should not assume that agents are infallible or perfect. They should be robust to inappropriate or malformed messages and should be able to support reasonable mechanisms for identifying and signalling errors and warnings.

- ✗ Visibility – Make everything relevant to agent's operation of a process (case) visible to people involved. When software agents do something, show the effects immediately. Otherwise people are confused and surprised at the results of actions.

- ✗ Responsibility – At every moment, human agents are in a position of authority and human actions affect the case's processing situation. If human agents just sit there for a time, letting software agent's activities go on in the direction they are going, that in itself constitutes an action, with effects that human agents may or may not want. At the end, human agents are solely responsible for the quality of process execution – this cannot be delegated.

COMPETITIVE ADVANTAGES

We have stepped ahead of our competition, both in terms of the technology, which is not available to any of our competitors, and in our combination of the business focus on a relationship management-centric strategy to embed external contracting parties in our business process execution. SwisscardNet provides the glue between external relationship managers and their clients, and between our internal middle and back offices. The technological edge is that we've modernized our IT people-to-people platform and applications ahead of our main competitors, thus enabling Swisscard to compete on financial service and specialization without incurring disadvantages faced by small and mid-scale organizations.

We have also reduced our operational risk by making sure that internal guidelines and external regulatory requirements are fulfilled. The integrated rule management in the new participant-to-participant platform allows us to adopt new requirements quickly, which in turn simplifies effective collaboration across enterprise boundaries. This is an advantage that should not be underestimated in the advent of stringent regulatory requirements, because the highest risk for companies today is rarely in routine operations; rather it is in informal, unstructured interactions among people working together. As a result, Swisscard is able to set the industry standard for service, grow our volumes and expand our client base without eroding our margins or cutting back on service. It will be very difficult indeed for most of our competitors to achieve the same results.

TECHNOLOGY

The SwisscardNet system consists of four basic building blocks: the SwisscardNet agency, the human user interface policy, the business policy and the conversation policy. All of these subsystems have been built on the foundation of the ActionWorks® process engine from Action Technologies Inc., using the Action Solutions Software Suite® from Action Solutions AG in Switzerland as the implementation framework. This framework consists of pre-built application parts and components for managing the various working styles in a generic, case-oriented manner, as well as a meta-data repository for storing all of the relevant policy, definition and configuration information needed at run-time to process the cases within SwisscardNet.

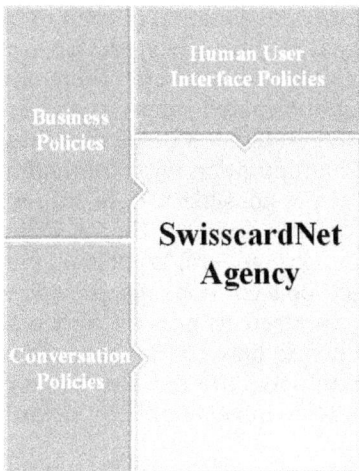

Figure 7: SwiscardNet system overview

SwisscardNet Agency

SwisscardNet agency is the core building block for all agents working with SwisscardNet, including human and action agents. In a purely Aristotelian sense, an agent is one who takes action. In social and legal terms, an agent is one who is empowered to act on behalf of another. In our case, action agents exercise SwisscardNet agency – on behalf of the human Swisscard agents and in service of Swisscard. A key aspect here is that both the people and their agents use and modify the same information base of linked information objects. Although the initial focus of BPM was on the automation of mechanistic business processes, it has since been extended to integrate human-driven processes in which human interaction takes place in series or parallel with the mechanistic processes. Whereas human agents focus on tasks where human intervention or collaboration is required on an ad-hoc basis or according to policy, the action agents focus on automatable tasks and systems interaction.

For example, when performing certain individual steps in the business process requires sophisticated intuition or judgment, these steps are assigned to appropriate human agents within the organization. The agency creates a single integrated environment out of many different kinds of formal and informal information and many different applications, which allows people to use a simple and consistent interface for all workflow activities and applications to interact with each other. Thus, the action agent's major effort is toward leveraging the function call or message-oriented third-party interfaces in a way such that they follow the business policies as well as the conversation policies used in the agency.

The action agent's approach to dealing with legacy systems is to implement wrappers. The wrapper can directly examine the data structures of the legacy program and modify those data structures when necessary. At the host-side, existing entry forms are manipulated with screen scraping, views and the programmable mouse approach using the Rational Robotic System. This allows existing host functionality to be integrated without the need for low-level software integration, using a kind of manual input emulation.

Human User Interface Policies

SwisscardNet provides a direct manipulation, graphical and fully web-based interface to human users. Since direct manipulation requires information objects to be visible, users are constantly informed about the types of things they can act upon. Anyone with experience of iconic desktop interfaces knows that there are times when sequences of actions are better off being automated rather than performed directly by the user in overly simple and therefore tedious steps. Combining the expression of user intention through direct manipulation with the notion of an indirect management style of interaction makes it possible to free human users from the obligation to spell out each action explicitly. Instead, the flexibility and intelligence of the action agents allows humans to give general guidelines and forget about the details. These human user interface policies not only provide a general, dynamic graphical user interface that can be used to present and manipulate all kinds of information objects; they also define how the action agents have to react to system-generated events when human users are not present, e.g. *what went wrong and why* through the whiteboard, which is available by default in the generic case's GUI.

Business Policies

Rule-based systems implement a model of processing based on logical constructs called production rules. Production rules have two parts: the antecedent (often called the left-side or the *IF* component of the rule) and the consequent (the right-side or *THEN* component of the rule). The antecedent specifies some condition to be satisfied, and the consequent some action to be performed when the antecedent is true. In a rule-based system, the production rules are organized and collected in a structure called a knowledge base. As the conditions of given production rules in the knowledge base are satisfied, the rule is fired to produce actions that direct the behavior of the system. Scripts can be used to represent some consistent sequence of events. They must include a set of entry conditions that need to be satisfied before the script can be invoked, as well as a set of information objects with their corresponding actions representing the sequence of events themselves. All this information is managed through business policies.

Conversation Policies

One major issue when designing agent-oriented systems is how to implement policies governing conversational and other social behavior among agents. A conversation policy explicitly defines what sequences of which semantic messages are permissible between a given set of participating agents. Since the ActionWorks® business interaction model is well suited to all of the thinkable request scenarios that both action agents and human agents can make of each other, we've chosen to make use of the ActionWorks® business interaction model as the default core-speech-act model; it thus provides the common base for all of the interactions between agents, human and non-human, in SwisscardNet. The conversational state is represented by a simple finite state machine, which models the sequence of interactions that occur in the conversation. For each conversational state, the state machine has an action associated with every input event type. The finite conversational state machine of ActionWorks® coordinates commitments and interactions between individual agents or groups of agents. The conversation policy of SwisscardNet currently supports various conversational patterns, all of which are shared among the agents and based on the business interaction model of Action Technologies.

THE TECHNOLOGY AND SERVICE PROVIDERS

Action Technologies Inc., Alameda, www.actiontech.com

Action Technologies has delivered for more than 20 years award-winning Business Process Management (BPM) software that reduces the time and cost of decision-driven processes by 40-60% and typically generates returns of more than 300%. The ActionWorks® Suite enables leading global customers to analyze, redesign, implement and continuously improve their operations through a patented system for managing negotiations and commitments.

Action Solutions AG, Zug, www.actiontech.ch

Action Solutions has delivered the ActionSolutions® Software Suite, an application framework based on the ActionWorks® BPM suite. The ActionSolutions® Suite is a unique Business Activity Software Suite consisting of different frameworks reflecting the way people work together. These frameworks and it's unique way of assembling workflows using generic work-style patterns were the base for the successful, rapid development and deployment at Swisscard.

Systems Integration Center AG, Zurich, www.sicenter.com

Systems Integration Center was the IT-Implementation partner for this project. They implemented the Action Agents and adopted the patented ActionWorks® Business Interaction Model as the universal language of business between the participants of the SwisscardNet P2P-Workflow in just 3 months. This was only possible due to the patented ActionWorks® Business Interaction Model that acts as a universal translator between the language of business and the language of technology.

UVIT–Financial Services, Netherlands

EXECUTIVE SUMMARY / ABSTRACT

The Univé-VGZ-IZA-Trias group (UVIT) is a Netherlands-based insurance company. During recent years, the people of UVIT have been facing increased challenges from Internet insurance competitors. Because of this, a main objective was to automate outdated processes that were primarily paper-based. To do this, UVIT chose EMC Documentum xCP for the creation of a case management application to process claims. The xCP platform is seamlessly integrated with the UVIT capture platform to digitize all incoming mail, especially the vast quantity of doctor and hospital bills customers forward for payment. The system is used by UVIT service, field, and insurance agents, while in the office, at home, and on the road.

With the new xCP system, UVIT staff now has instant access to customer documentation, which has helped improve customer response rates as well as overall processing efficiency. The amount of case documents they are now able to process is also huge– about three million in 2010, and they expect that figure to reach 50 million in the near future.

"EMC Documentum xCP has streamlined our claims processes substantially. Since using the new system, we have reduced costs by approximately 10 percent. We are very satisfied with the solution, and are expecting more added value when we begin using all of the features", said Pierre Kraakman, business analyst at UVIT. Documentum xCP orchestrates information through the process, end-to-end, while providing a 360-degree view of the case, in addition to supporting and documenting all human decision processes.

OVERVIEW

The Univé-VGZ-IZA-Trias group (UVIT), is an insurance company based in the Netherlands, with more than 150 satellite offices and about 4.2 million customers throughout the country. The company has its roots in the late 18th century and employs more than 5,000 people, 3,500 of whom work at the central organization and focus on product creation. The remaining employees are based in other locations, serving and consulting with customers. In 2010, UVIT revenue was approximately 11 billion Euros.

BUSINESS CONTEXT

UVIT's mission is to offer its customers top-quality products and services. As a partly profit-oriented entity, the insurance provider is always searching for ways to improve its business processes and provide better services to customers at lower cost. The company realized it needed to automate processes, many of which were paper-based and error-prone. It was definitely time for a change, as it often took hours, if not days, to locate all relevant documents needed to process a single claim. For compliance reasons and in order to strengthen competitiveness, Univé Health Insurance, one of the group members, decided at the end of 2003 to introduce a document management system that would store multiple resources, such as fax, paper, web, and e-forms, as well as a variety of document types. "At the same time, we wanted a scalable solution that we could use enterprise-wide for different processes. The system also had to offer a Dutch-language front-end, authorization rules, and version control, as well as full-text indexing. And it had to automatically control retention periods," said Mr. Kraakman.

The Dutch archive law stipulates that all bills, letters, and contracts must be retained for seven years. Documents relating to corporate-level decisions from the board of directors, however, have to be kept for ten years. And certain medical files must not be deleted for a full 15 years after an employee has left the company. Therefore, it was crucial for Univé to select a system that would be reliable and stable enough to guarantee compliance with such legal regulations.

After a thorough evaluation of the most highly rated systems on the market, the organization selected EMC Documentum as its enterprise content management (ECM) platform and Documentum xCP for building BPM/case management applications.

THE KEY INNOVATIONS

4.1 Business

The new solution immediately began reducing the time required to locate claims and enrollment documents and it substantially improved customer service. Instead of lengthy document retrieval processes in response to a customer call, service agents now locate relevant documents in less than three seconds. The incidence of misplaced documents decreased as well. Providing the right person with the access to the right information in the right timeframe dramatically improves decision making processes. Tracking and documenting how information is processed and decisions are made is vital.

Decisions regarding a case is digitally recorded and stored, where management information can be easily extracted. Every case has a number of standard metadata that need to be filled; in addition, there are a large number of fields that contain information about why and how the decisions around this case have evolved. Any amount which is paid and details of how the case manager arrived at this amount are also saved.

4.2 Case Handling

The first deployment phase started at the beginning of 2004, with the implementation of EMC Documentum 5.3. With the help of EMC Consulting, the system went live in September 2004, and has been productive ever since. It is connected to Univé's old back-office Health system which has to be kept until 2015, when all data stored can be disposed of. It is also seamlessly integrated in the selected capture platform to digitize all incoming mail, especially the vast quantity of bills customers forward for payment to the respective doctors and/or hospitals. After scanning, the paper bills have to be kept for another three months before they can be destroyed, reducing physical storage costs.

Initially, Documentum served as a stable archiving solution. Univé then set up the first workflows, and initiated the process to digitize all application handling roughly one year after implementation. Finally, Univé included all contract management for doctors/hospitals. At the end of 2007, due to a merger with three other health insurance companies, Univé and the other members of UVIT decided to initiate phase two and to upgrade to EMC Documentum xCP.

"We wanted to set up the new system from scratch and connect it to the new back-office system. The goal was to include both incoming and outgoing document streams, which was clearly going to be a large project, so we split it into two parts: part one related to all health insurance cases, part two, to the claims management," said Pierre Kraakman. Implementation of part one started in January and took about ten months, while deployment of part two began in February and finished in December 2008.

In winter 2008, UVIT began using EMC Documentum 6.0 with Documentum xCP, which provides highly granular access control and includes various services. Content Services provides essential features for organizing, controlling, and delivering repository content. Process Integrator allows UVIT staff to gain integration with external applications through a service-oriented architecture (SOA) implementation; so far, it is connected with Oracle and Printnet. Microsoft Office and UVIT's HR solution were integrated in July 2009.

The repository is accessible through two clients: "Our claims adjusters, who use the Documentum xCP environment, have access through TaskSpace, which can be easily configured to our needs," said Pierre Kraakman. Additionally, it enables the service agents to rapidly build and deploy intuitive applications for functions such as case management. Agents, who work with Documentum 5.3, use the browser-based user interface Webtop, which handles insurance forms, faxes, e-mails, and paper-based correspondence. Field agents can also access Documentum from their home offices, via a Citrix environment.

To assess material damages, UVIT often receives short electronic videos and/or photos from car dealers. So, the insurance provider has to process many different image and office formats, including TIF and PDF, which are supported by the integrated IGC Brava Viewer for TaskSpace. Depending on the cost estimate, UVIT decides to either meet the costs or to send one of their claims adjusters to assess the damages on site. Another essential criterion to accelerate the business processes is the quick and flexible creation of intuitive, standards-based electronic forms. Forms Builder, part of Documentum xCP Designer, provides both high-accuracy and HTML-based e-forms. "By using TaskSpace or Webtop, our operators reduce costly paper handling. They can also add or remove fields or change the look and feel, according to their preferences," said Mr. Kraakman.

With Documentum Retention Policy Services, UVIT no longer has to ask itself how long it has to keep the various types of documents and when to clean up the files. The system automatically takes care of revision-secure content retention and disposition.

In order to increase transparency, agents must have an overview of the workflow or lifecycle states of documents at any time. Documentum Reporting Services provides control of the underlying workflows and the number of documents handled. The services mentioned were deployed at UVIT's selling and consulting department, the operational back office as well as the customer contact centers.

Each claim is considered a case and the claims process has several roles that are strictly divided. This is done because UVIT wants the "simple and laborious" tasks done by people who do not have or need extensive skill or specific knowledge.

Besides that, UVIT has legal and organizational rules about which step in the process is done by whom. The claims are processed by information workers who can then focus on the content of the claim and not about the process of collecting the correct documents or indexing metadata. After the claim is processed, the claim is checked and authorized for payment.

Documentum xCP greatly improves decision making because the claims worker only has to focus on the claim, not on administrative tasks. The claims can be processed by any number of specialists who can collaborate and work together because the claim information is digitally available instead of in a paper file. In this particular process, case managers can not influence the process steps, this is a design decision made by the organization. Case managers can invite specialists (damage specialists or legal specialists) to collaborate within the process. They are invited to look into the case with a specific question.

On the way to paperless case management and claim processing, UVIT's overall goal is to achieve virtually paperless transactions. Currently, approximately 12 scan operators are busy with scanning all incoming mail, such as applications, bills, or letters. The capturing system automatically delivers all documents scanned to the repository as index files in PDF or XML format. The documents have a view-only access. UVIT employs about 150 people to manage the processing of the relevant claims documents, plus 1,900 employees for the outgoing letters for health insurance, which are automatically stored and can be dynamically recalled from the repository if necessary.

4.3 Organization & Social

The impact of Documentum xCP-based application on the employees and their jobs is significant. Instead of working with paper files, people have had to reorient to working with digital files. Every document is scanned at entrance and if there is no claim for this document a new claim is created. This has had a definite impact on the mailroom. There are now scan operators and workers who fill in the first metadata and verify if the claim is complete and can go to a case manager. The internal "mailman" has very little to do and several people with this role now have a different function. The people responsible for archiving have been reassigned.

HURDLES OVERCOME

Management

UVIT's management is very pleased but they did need to get used to the system. Digital case management works differently than paper case management. Before, a manager would have to walk the floor to see who was busy and who was not. If a case manager has a lot of paper on his desk he was busy, but now the manager can see if someone is very busy if he looks at the system reports.

Organization Adoption

After having had a half-day training session in order to familiarize themselves with the main features, about 1,500 employees now use Documentum xCP for their daily work. "We involved the users in the change management project at a very early stage, and showed them both the design and prototype, so they knew what to expect. What they appreciate most is the user-friendly interface, and the fact that they don't lose papers anymore," said Pierre Kraakman. UVIT plans to train more users in the course of the year.

BENEFITS

"EMC Documentum xCP has streamlined our claims processes substantially. Claims adjusters now have access to the documents they need within a few seconds only, and the incidence of misplaced documents has decreased. Since using the new system, we have reduced costs by approximately ten percent. We are very satisfied with the solution, and are still expecting more added value once using all of the features," said Pierre Kraakman.

6.1 Cost Savings / Time Reductions

Quantifiable benefits include:

- Claims process goes quicker, average one day
- Claim cases (or document belonging to a case) no longer get lost
- Quicker response to questions since everyone knows where the case files are and the right information and guidance is available to support the decision maker
- No personnel nor cupboards nor external contracts required for physical archiving
- Reduction of mailroom staff, reduction of administrative staff
- Reduced time-to-market and increased cycle time
- Higher availability and transparency—lower costs

6.2 Increased Revenues

Although difficult to measure at this time, improved customer service should improve competitiveness and expand the customer base.

6.3 Quality Improvements

Quality improvements include:
- Improve customer responsiveness–Case managers receive a message if a response from the customer is overdue
- The claim is paid quicker as well, so the customers are more satisfied
- Case managers can work from home; improves employee satisfaction and reduces facilities costs
- Management has better insight to process and they receive a message when a case is overdue
- Cases can be redirected more easily and quickly, allowing flexibility to reassign based on skills needed or availability.

The new solution dramatically reduced the time it took to locate claims and enrollment documents and substantially improved customer service. Instead of lengthy document retrievals in response to a customer call, service agents can now find relevant documents in less than three seconds. The incidence of misplaced documents decreased as well. Employees now have instant and simultaneous viewing access to customer documentation, which contributes to improving customer response rates as well as the overall processing efficiency.

The amount of data is huge: altogether, UVIT processed about two to three million documents last year but there is an upward trend. The insurance provider expects the figure to rise up to 50 million in the near future.

BEST PRACTICES, LEARNING POINTS AND PITFALLS

7.1 Best Practices and Learning Points

   ✓ *Digitization allows for more effective processes. Consider adapting the manual business processes along with the implementation of the system.*

At first, the business wanted a direct one-to-one transformation from paper to digital. Very quickly, we learned that this didn't work very well. We needed to adapt the business process along with the implementation of the system.

COMPETITIVE ADVANTAGES

Today's challenging economy requires all organization to be lean, quick, agile, and responsive to customer and market demands. "During recent years, we have been increasingly challenged by Internet-based insurance companies. That's why our main objective was to automate our processes, which were mainly paper-based.

We selected EMC Documentum xCP because we felt that it would help us best achieve our objectives," says Kraakman.

TECHNOLOGY

UVIT choose EMC Documentum xCP as the foundation for building their case management application for claims processing. Built on the industry's leading ECM offering, EMC Documentum xCP provides a graphical toolset for building case-based composite applications. Providing enterprise-class information orchestration throughout the organization, xCP can accelerate process development to resolve many different business challenges.

UVIT is currently busy with adding the HR files to the system. In parallel, all medical files of its personnel will be included in the system as the insurance company also offers medical services to its staff. Another project has been set up to digitize all incoming mail in the new head office in Arnhem, which is designed to be an office mainly for knowledge workers. All employees will also have access to the system from home. The Web Content Management and SharePoint integration services are to be added soon. This will enable external users to log in to the UVIT web portal. Insured persons will be able to access personalized data and check the status of a process. They will be more and more involved in the whole case management process, and customer satisfaction will rise. All these changes will help avoid paper-based case management, in particular, and thereby generate cost savings.

THE TECHNOLOGY AND SERVICE PROVIDERS

EMC Documentum xCP automates knowledge-intensive processes and delivers information in context to reduce cycle time, improve business decisions, and ensure compliance. xCP is built on industry's leading ECM platform, which provides critical content management and control to all of your information assets. EMC Documentum features and offerings leveraged in this solution include:

- EMC Documentum Consulting
- EMC Documentum xCP
- EMC Documentum TaskSpace
- EMC Documentum Webtop
- EMC Documentum Retention Policy Services

Section 3:
Appendices

WfMC Structure and Membership Information

WHAT IS THE WORKFLOW MANAGEMENT COALITION?

The Workflow Management Coalition, founded in August 1993, is a non-profit, international organization of workflow vendors, users, analysts and university/research groups. The Coalition's mission is to promote and develop the use of workflow through the establishment of standards for software terminology, interoperability and connectivity among BPM and workflow products. Comprising more than 250 members worldwide, the Coalition is the primary standards body for this software market.

WORKFLOW STANDARDS FRAMEWORK

The Coalition has developed a framework for the establishment of workflow standards. This framework includes five categories of interoperability and communication standards that will allow multiple workflow products to coexist and interoperate within a user's environment. Technical details are included in the white paper entitled, "The Work of the Coalition," available at www.wfmc.org.

ACHIEVEMENTS

The initial work of the Coalition focused on publishing the Reference Model and Glossary, defining a common architecture and terminology for the industry. A major milestone was achieved with the publication of the first versions of the Workflow API (WAPI) specification, covering the Workflow Client Application Interface, and the Workflow Interoperability specification.

In addition to a series of successful tutorials industry wide, the WfMC spent many hours over 2009 helping to drive awareness, understanding and adoption of XPDL, now the standard means for business process definition in over 80 BPM products. As a result, it has been cited as the most deployed BPM standard by a number of industry analysts, and continues to receive a growing amount of media attention.

WORKFLOW MANAGEMENT COALITION STRUCTURE

The Coalition is divided into three major committees, the Technical Committee, the External Relations Committee, and the Steering Committee. Small working groups exist within each committee for the purpose of defining workflow terminology, interoperability and connectivity standards, conformance requirements, and for assisting in the communication of this information to the workflow user community.

The Coalition's major committees meet as required per calendar year with meetings usually alternating between a North American and a European location. The working group meetings are held during these days, and as necessary throughout the year.

Coalition membership is open to all interested parties involved in the creation, analysis or deployment of workflow software systems. Membership is governed by a Document of Understanding, which outlines meeting regulations, voting rights etc. Membership material is available at www.wfmc.org.

COALITION WORKING GROUPS

The Coalition has established a number of Working Groups, each working on a particular area of specification. The working groups are loosely structured around the "Workflow Reference Model" which provides the framework for the

Coalition's standards program. The Reference Model identifies the common characteristics of workflow systems and defines five discrete functional interfaces through which a workflow management system interacts with its environment—users, computer tools and applications, other software services, etc. Working groups meet individually, and also under the umbrella of the Technical Committee, which is responsible for overall technical direction and coordination.

WORKFLOW REFERENCE MODEL DIAGRAM

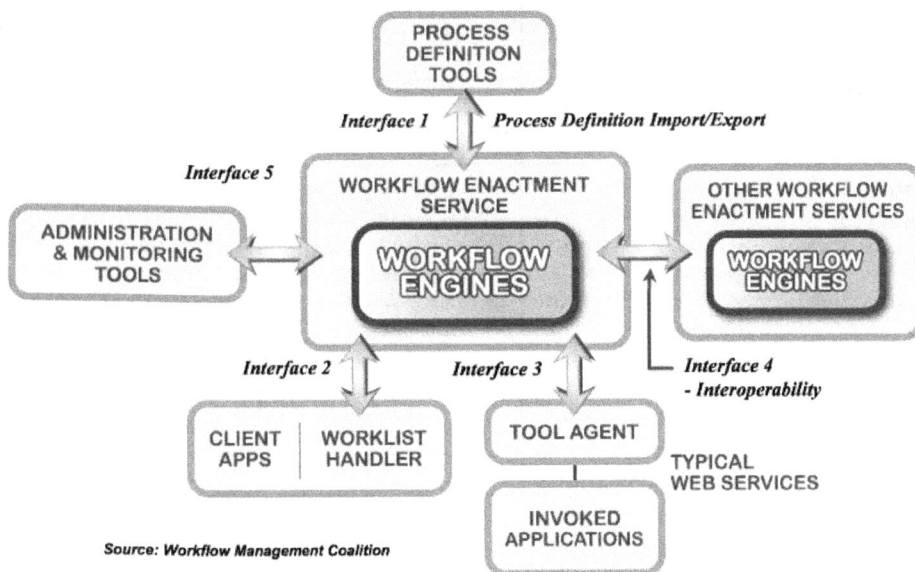

PROCESS DEFINITION TOOLS

Interface 1 — Process Definition Import/Export

Interface 5

WORKFLOW ENACTMENT SERVICE

OTHER WORKFLOW ENACTMENT SERVICES

ADMINISTRATION & MONITORING TOOLS

WORKFLOW ENGINES

WORKFLOW ENGINES

Interface 2   Interface 3   Interface 4 - Interoperability

CLIENT APPS | WORKLIST HANDLER

TOOL AGENT

TYPICAL WEB SERVICES

INVOKED APPLICATIONS

Source: Workflow Management Coalition

WHY YOU SHOULD JOIN

- Gain Access to Members-Only Research and Q&A Forums
- Participate in Members-Only "Brown Bag" Networking Sessions and Industry Speaker Series
- Receive Free Admission to Business Process Focused Events and Programs (a Benefit Worth $1,000s Annually)
- Access to the Industry's Largest Research Library on Business Process Modeling, Workflow, BPMS
- Assistance in Product Certification and Conformance, as well as Requirements Analysis and Procurement Strategy

Being a member of the Workflow Management Coalition gives you the unique opportunity to participate in the creation of standards for the workflow industry as they are developing. Your contributions to our community ensure that progress continues in the adoption of royalty-free workflow and process standards.

MEMBERSHIP CATEGORIES

	Full Member	**Individual Member**	**Observing Member**
Annual fee	$3500	$500	$100/year or $10/month
Hold office	Software Vendors, IT & Professional Services Firms, Government, Non-Profit & Commercial	Open to Individuals	Open to Individuals; Limited to Observer Role; Not Eligible for Committee or Officer Participation
Limitations	Eligible for All Offices & Committees	Eligible for All Offices & Committees	Observer Only
Events/ Research	Full Admission to WfMC Events (up to 3 individuals) and Full Access to the WfMC Research Library (up to 3 log-ons)	Full Access to the WfMC Research Library (single log-on) and Free Admission to Select WfMC Events	Full Access to the WfMC Research Library (single log-on) and Free Admission to Select WfMC Events
Promotional Benefits	Logo on WfMC Pages; Free Use of WfMC Banner Serving; Detailed Company Profile in WfMC Publications	N/A	N/A

ADDITIONAL BENEFITS OF MEMBERSHIP

This corporate category offers exclusive visibility in this sector at events and seminars across the world, enhancing your customers' perception of you as an industry authority, on our web site, in the Coalition Handbook and CDROM, by speaking opportunities, access to the Members Only area of our web site, attending the Coalition meetings and most importantly within the workgroups whereby through discussion and personal involvement, using your voting power, you can contribute actively to the development of standards and interfaces.

Full member benefits include:

- Financial incentives: 50 percent discount all "brochure-ware" (such as our annual CDROM Companion to the BPM and Workflow Handbook, advertising on our sister-site www.e-workflow.org), $500 credit toward next year's fee for at least 60 percent per year meeting attendance or if you serve as an officer of the WfMC.
- Web Visibility: your logo on all WfMC pages, inclusion in the WfMC web banner network, a detailed company profile in online member directory as well as in all WfMC publications.
- User RFIs: (Requests for Information) is an exclusive privilege to all full members. We often have queries from user organizations looking for specific workflow solutions. These valuable leads can result in real business benefits for your organization.
- Publicity: full members may choose to have their company logos including collaterals displayed along with WfMC material at conferences / expos we attend. You may also list corporate events and press releases (re-

lating to WfMC issues) on the relevant pages on the website, and have a company entry in the annual Coalition Workflow Handbook

- Speaking Opportunities: We frequently receive calls for speakers at industry events because many of our members are recognized experts in their fields. These opportunities are forwarded to Full Members for their direct response to the respective conference organizers.

INDIVIDUAL MEMBERSHIP

Individual Membership is appropriate for self-employed persons or small user companies. Employees of workflow vendors, academic institutions or analyst organizations are not typically eligible for this category. Individual membership is held in one person's name only, is not a corporate membership, and is not transferable within the company.

OBSERVING MEMBER ($100 PER YEAR OR $10//MONTH)

Open to Individuals and participation is limited to observer role. Members are not eligible for committee or officer participation. This is an excellent and cost-effective way to learn more about WfMC and have access to our huge database of books and reference materials.

HOW TO JOIN

Complete the form on the Coalition's website, or contact the Coalition Secretariat below. All members are required to sign the Coalition's "Document of Understanding" which sets out the contractual rights and obligations between members and the Coalition.

THE SECRETARIAT

Workflow Management Coalition (WfMC)

www.WfMC.org

Nathaniel Palmer, Executive Director,

+1-781-923-1411 (t), +1-781-735-0491 (f)

Additional BPM Resources

NEW E-BOOK SERIES ($9.97 EACH)

- Introduction to BPM and Workflow
  http://store.futstrat.com/servlet/Detail?no=75

- Financial Services
  http://store.futstrat.com/servlet/Detail?no=90

- Healthcare
  http://store.futstrat.com/servlet/Detail?no=81

- Utilities and Telecommunications
  http://store.futstrat.com/servlet/Detail?no=92

NON-PROFIT ASSOCIATIONS AND RELATED STANDARDS RESEARCH ONLINE

- AIIM (Association for Information and Image Management)
  http://www.aiim.org
- BPM and Workflow online news, research, forums
  http://bpm.com
- BPM Research at Stevens Institute of Technology
  http://www.bpm-research.com
- Business Process Management Initiative
  http://www.bpmi.org *see* Object Management Group
- IEEE (Electrical and Electronics Engineers, Inc.)
  http://www.ieee.org
- Institute for Information Management (IIM)
  http://www.iim.org
- ISO (International Organization for Standardization)
  http://www.iso.ch
- Object Management Group
  http://www.omg.org
- Open Document Management Association
  http://nfocentrale.net/dmware
- Organization for the Advancement of Structured Information Standards
  http://www.oasis-open.org
- Society for Human Resource Management
  http://www.shrm.org
- Society for Information Management
  http://www.simnet.org
- Wesley J. Howe School of Technology Management
  http://howe.stevens.edu/research/research-centers/business-process-innovation
- Workflow And Reengineering International Association (WARIA)
  http://www.waria.com
- Workflow Management Coalition (WfMC)
  http://www.wfmc.org
- Workflow Portal
  http://www.e-workflow.org

More Unique Books on BPM and Workflow from
Future Strategies, Publishers (www.FutStrat.com)

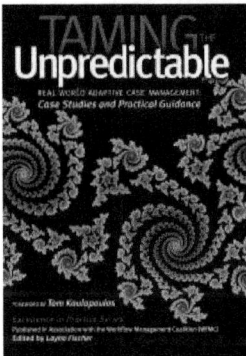

TAMING THE UNPREDICTABLE

http://futstrat.com/books/eip11.php

The core element of Adaptive Case Management (ACM) is the support for real-time decision-making by knowledge workers.

Taming the Unpredictable presents the logical starting point for understanding how to take advantage of ACM. This book goes beyond talking about concepts, and delivers actionable advice for embarking on your own journey of ACM-driven transformation.

Retail #49.95 (see discount on website)

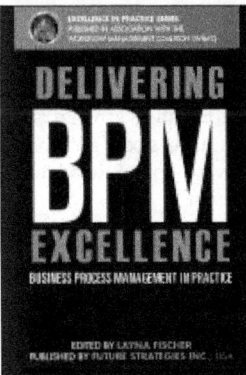

DELIVERING BPM EXCELLENCE

http://futstrat.com/books/Delivering_BPM.php

Innovation, Implementation and Impact

The companies whose case studies are featured in this book have proven excellence in their creative and successful deployment of advanced BPM concepts. These companies focused on excelling in *innovation, implementation* and *impact* when installing BPM and workflow technologies. The positive impact to their corporations includes increased revenues, more productive and satisfied employees, product enhancements, better customer service and quality improvements.

$39.95 (see discount on website)

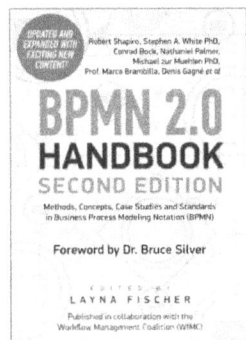

BPMN 2.0 Handbook SECOND EDITION

(see two-BPM book bundle offer on website: get BPMN Reference Guide Free)

http://futstrat.com/books/bpmnhandbook2.php

Updated and expanded with exciting new content!

Authored by members of WfMC, OMG and other key participants in the development of BPMN 2.0, the BPMN 2.0 Handbook brings together worldwide thought-leaders and experts in this space. Exclusive and unique contributions examine a variety of aspects that start with an introduction of what's new in BPMN 2.0, and look closely at interchange, analytics, conformance, optimization, simulation and more. **Retail $75.00**

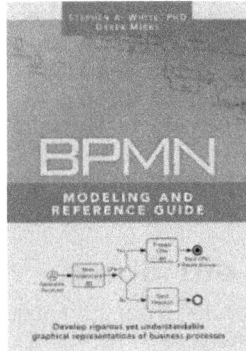

BPMN MODELING AND REFERENCE GUIDE

(see two-BPM book bundle offer on website: get BPMN Reference Guide Free)

http://www.futstrat.com/books/BPMN-Guide.php

Understanding and Using BPMN

How to develop rigorous yet understandable graphical representations of business processes.

Business Process Modeling Notation (BPMN) is a standard, graphical modeling representation for business processes. It provides an easy to use, flow-charting notation that is independent of the implementation environment.

Retail $39.95

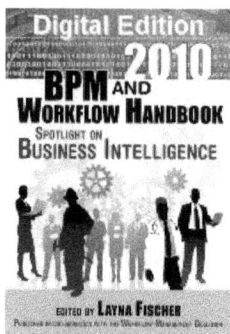

BPM & WORKFLOW HANDBOOK: BUSINESS INTELLIGENCE
HTTP://FUTSTRAT.COM/BOOKS/HANDBOOK10.PHP

Linking business intelligence and business process management creates stronger operational business intelligence. Users seek more intelligent business process capabilities in order to remain competitive within their fields and industries. BPM vendors realize they need to improve their business processes, rules and event management offerings with greater intelligence or analytics capabilities.

Retail $75.00 (see discount offer on website)

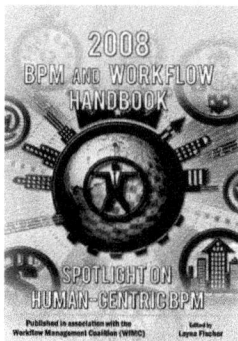

BPM & WORKFLOW HANDBOOK: HUMAN-CENTRIC BPM

http://www.futstrat.com/books/handbook08.php

Spotlight on Human-Centric BPM

Human-centric business process management (BPM) has become the product and service differentiator. The topic now captures substantial mindshare and market share in the human-centric BPM space as leading vendors have strengthened their human-centric business processes. Our spotlight this year examines challenges in human-driven workflow and its integration across the enterprise.

Retail $95.00 (see discount on website)

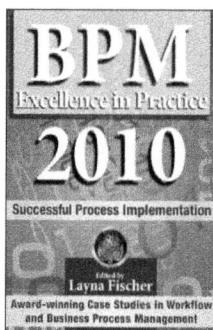

BPM Excellence in Practice: Successful Process Implementation
http://futstrat.com/books/eip10.php
Award-winning Case Studies in Workflow and Business Process Management

For over 19 years the Global Awards for Excellence in BPM and Workflow have covered virtually every economic environment, from bubble to bust and back again. The first modern process era emerged from the economic downturn of the early 1990s. Then, after years defined by relentless cost-cutting, the new charter for business shifted toward enhancing capacity to address the return of customer demand.

Retail $49.95

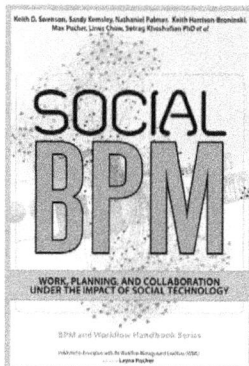

Social BPM
http://futstrat.com/books/handbook11.php
Work, Planning, and Collaboration Under the Impact of Social Technology

Today we see the transformation of both the look and feel of BPM technologies along the lines of social media, as well as the increasing adoption of social tools and techniques democratizing process development and design. It is along these two trend lines; the evolution of system interfaces and the increased engagement of stakeholders in process improvement, that Social BPM has taken shape.

Retail $59.95 (see discount offer on website)

Get 25% Discount on ALL Books in our Store.

Please use the discount code **SPEC25** to get 25% discount on ALL books in our store; both Print and Digital Editions (two discount codes cannot be used together).
http://store.futstrat.com/servlet/Catalog

www.ingramcontent.com/pod-product-compliance
Lightning Source LLC
Chambersburg PA
CBHW051411200326
41520CB00023B/7194